FAITH
AND THE
FUTURE
FORCE

JODY HOUSER | STEPHEN SEGOVIA | BARRY KITSON | DIEGO BERNARD | CARY NORD

CONTENTS

Collection Cover Art: Kano

Assistant Editor: Ben Peterson
Associate Editor: Danny Khazem
Editor: Warren Simons

VALIANT.

Faith® and the Future Force. Published by Valiant Entertainment LLC. Office of Publication: 350
Seventh Avenue, New York, NY 10001. Compilation copyright © 2017 Valiant Entertainment LLC. All
rights reserved. Contains materials originally published in single magazine form as Faith and the
Future Force #1-4. Copyright © 2017 Valiant Entertainment LLC. All rights reserved. All characters,
their distinctive likeness and related indicia featured in this publication are trademarks of Valiant
Entertainment LLC. The stories, characters, and incidents featured in this publication are entirely
fictional. Valiant Entertainment does not read or accept unsolicited submissions of ideas, stories, or
artwork. Printed in the U.S.A. First Printing. ISBN: 9781682152331.

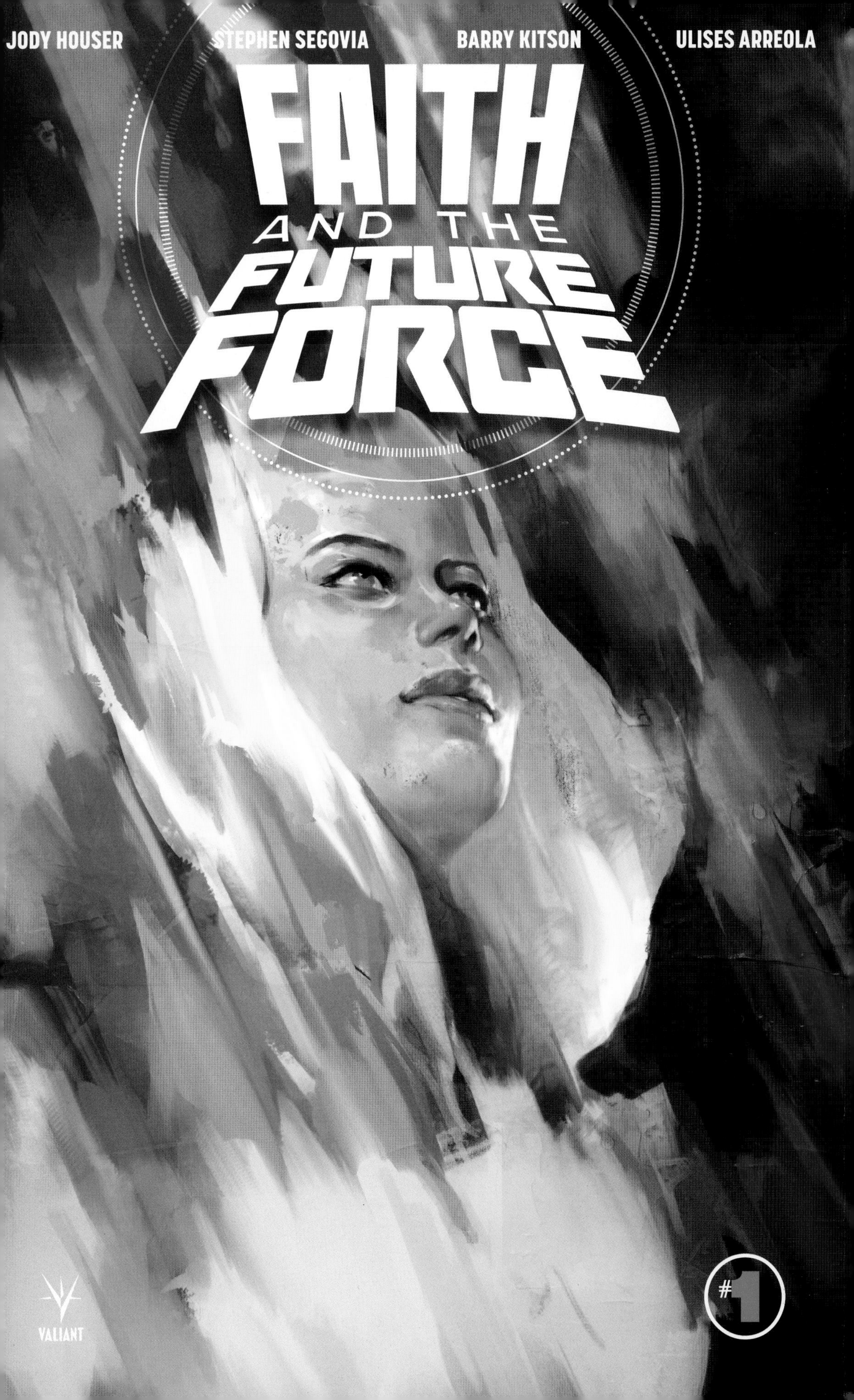
JODY HOUSER
STEPHEN SEGOVIA
BARRY KITSON
ULISES ARREOLA
FAITH AND THE FUTURE FORCE
VALIANT
#1

FAITH AND THE FUTURE FORCE

Brilliant physicist Neela Sethi unlocked the secrets of time travel last year - relatively speaking - and began her epic journey across time. She's since traveled to a time before man, tried to kill history, seen the end of the universe and befriended Ank, a dinosaur-like woman.

Now, Neela, Timewalker along with her partner Ank protect the time stream from anyone or anything that threatens it.

Today, they're in our present to recruit the help of Faith Herbert, celebrity hero and fangirl with the power of flight.

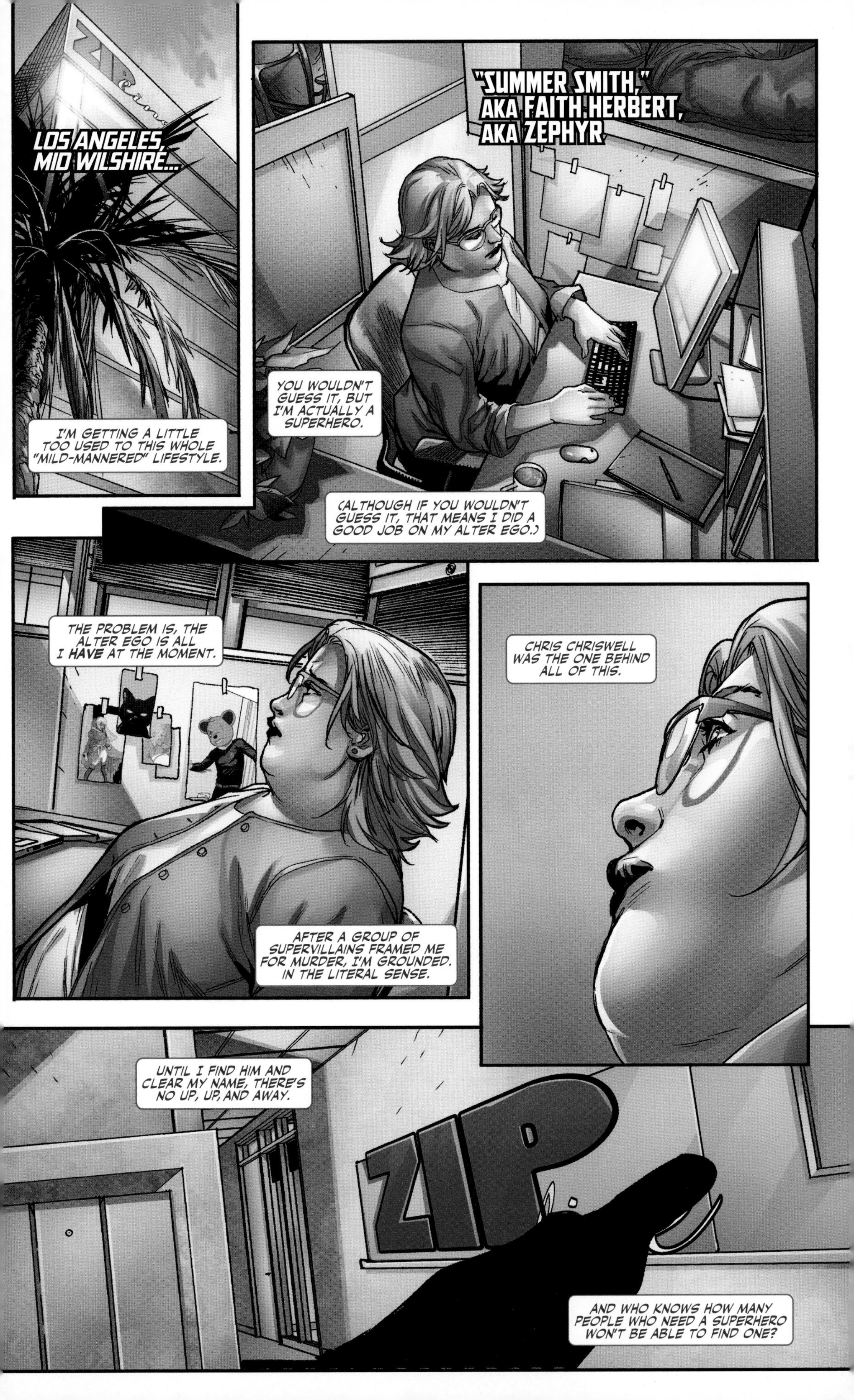
LOS ANGELES, MID WILSHIRE...
I'M GETTING A LITTLE TOO USED TO THIS WHOLE "MILD-MANNERED" LIFESTYLE.
"SUMMER SMITH," AKA FAITH HERBERT, AKA ZEPHYR
YOU WOULDN'T GUESS IT, BUT I'M ACTUALLY A SUPERHERO.
(ALTHOUGH IF YOU WOULDN'T GUESS IT, THAT MEANS I DID A GOOD JOB ON MY ALTER EGO.)
THE PROBLEM IS, THE ALTER EGO IS ALL I HAVE AT THE MOMENT.
AFTER A GROUP OF SUPERVILLAINS FRAMED ME FOR MURDER, I'M GROUNDED. IN THE LITERAL SENSE.
CHRIS CHRISWELL WAS THE ONE BEHIND ALL OF THIS.
UNTIL I FIND HIM AND CLEAR MY NAME, THERE'S NO UP, UP, AND AWAY.
ZIP
AND WHO KNOWS HOW MANY PEOPLE WHO NEED A SUPERHERO WON'T BE ABLE TO FIND ONE?

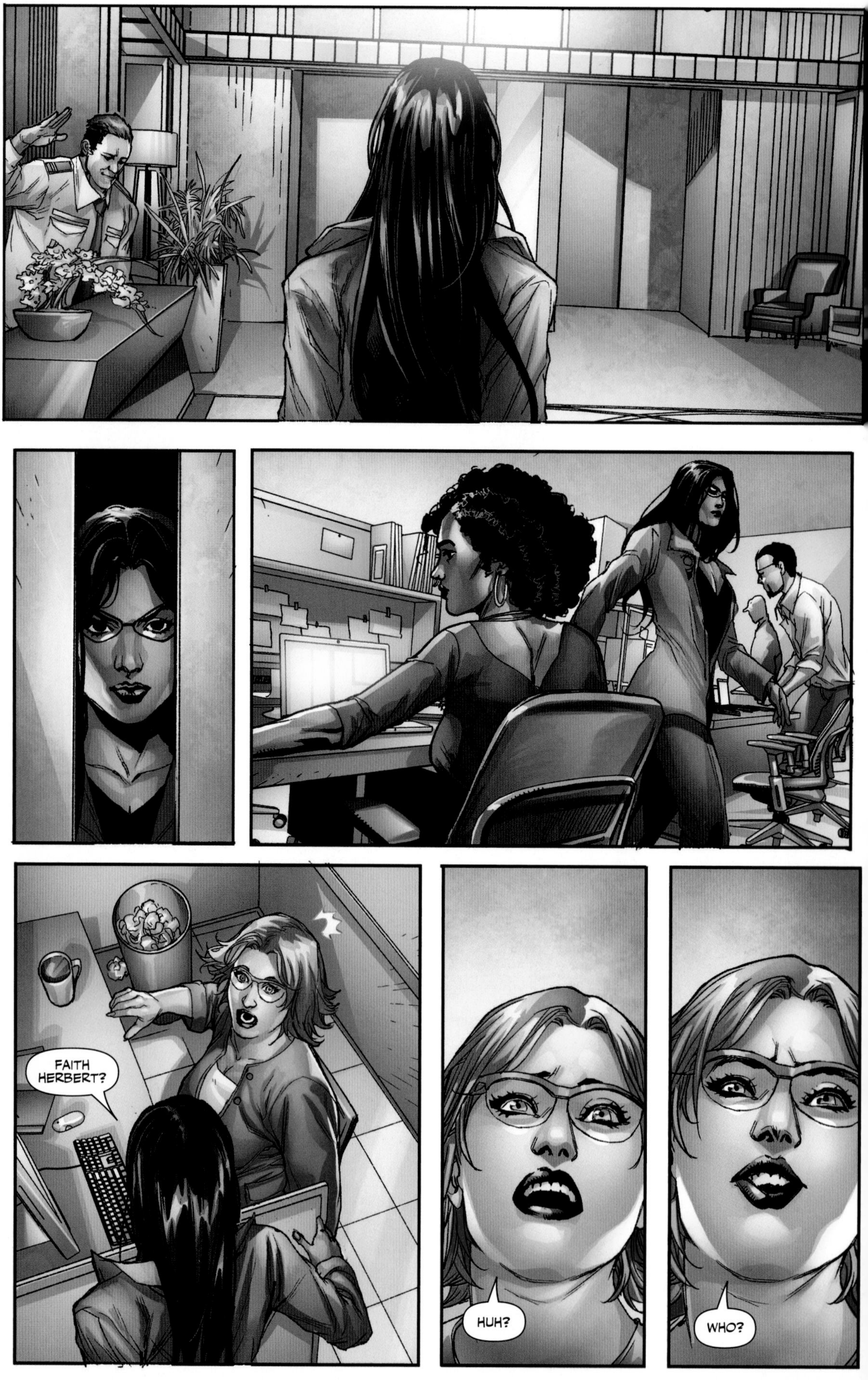
FAITH HERBERT?
HUH?
WHO?

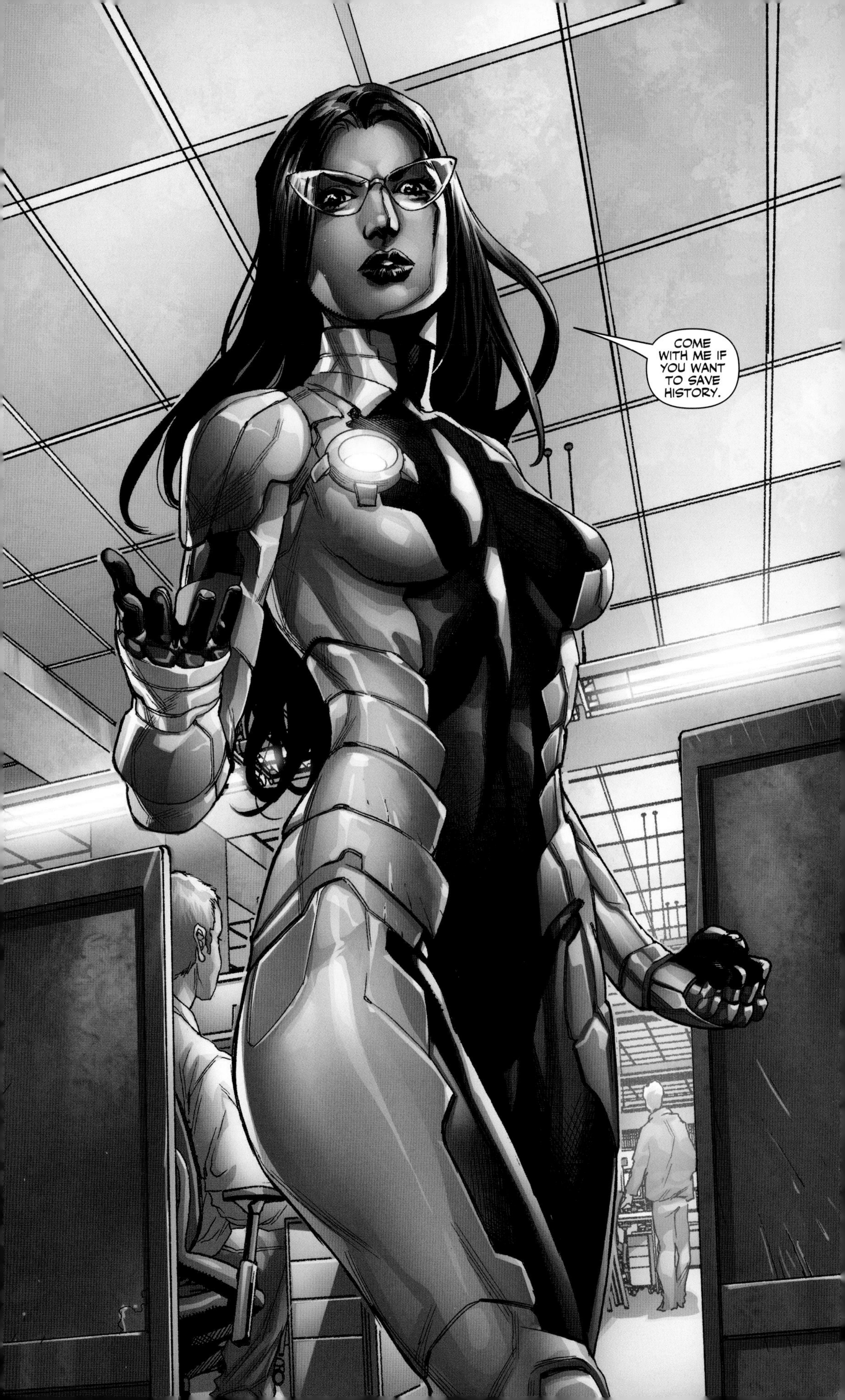
COME WITH ME IF YOU WANT TO SAVE HISTORY.

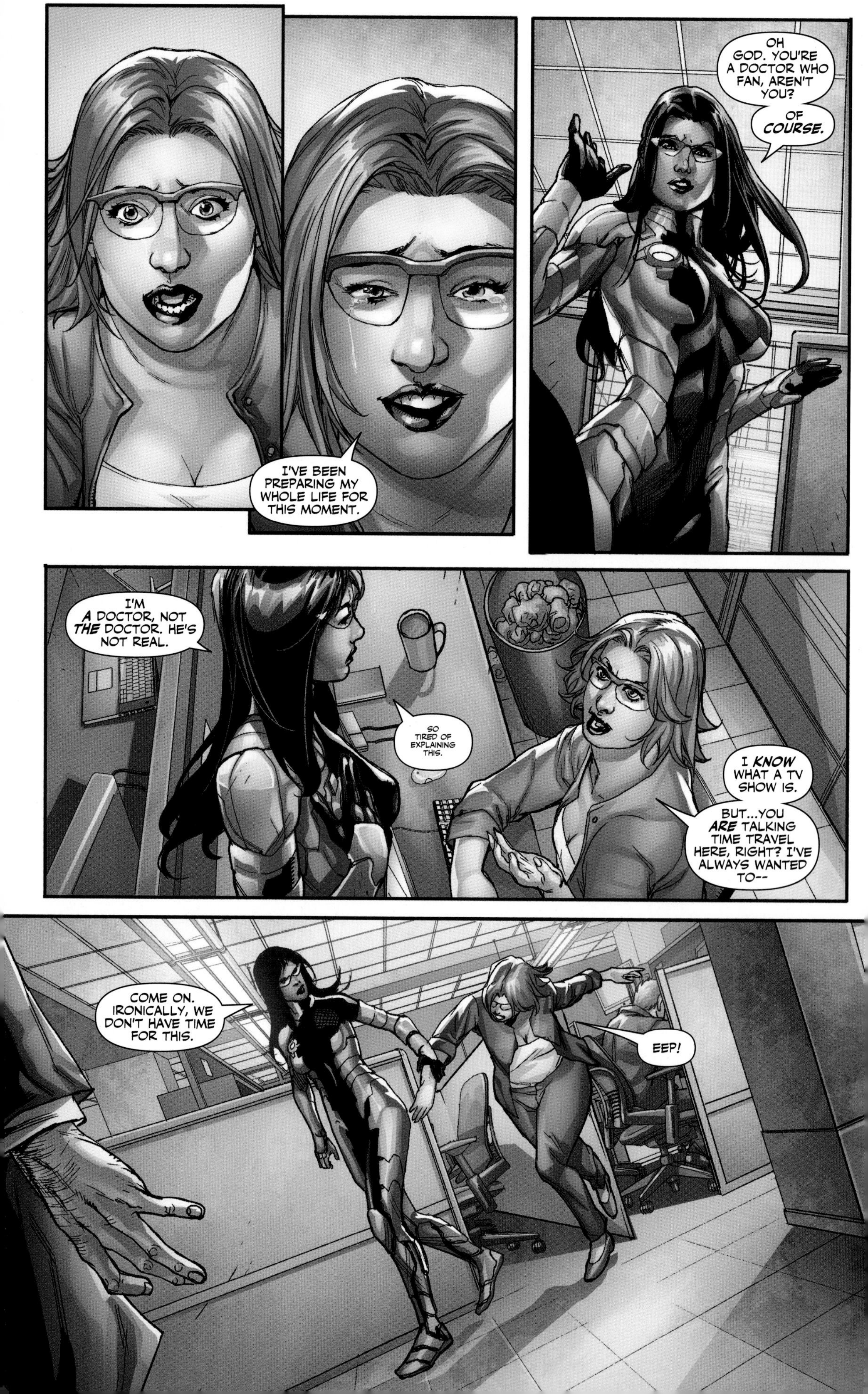
I'VE BEEN PREPARING MY WHOLE LIFE FOR THIS MOMENT.
OH GOD. YOU'RE A DOCTOR WHO FAN, AREN'T YOU?
OF *COURSE.*
I'M *A* DOCTOR, NOT *THE* DOCTOR. HE'S NOT REAL.
SO TIRED OF EXPLAINING THIS.
I *KNOW* WHAT A TV SHOW IS.
BUT...YOU *ARE* TALKING TIME TRAVEL HERE, RIGHT? I'VE ALWAYS WANTED TO--
COME ON. IRONICALLY, WE DON'T HAVE TIME FOR THIS.
EEP!

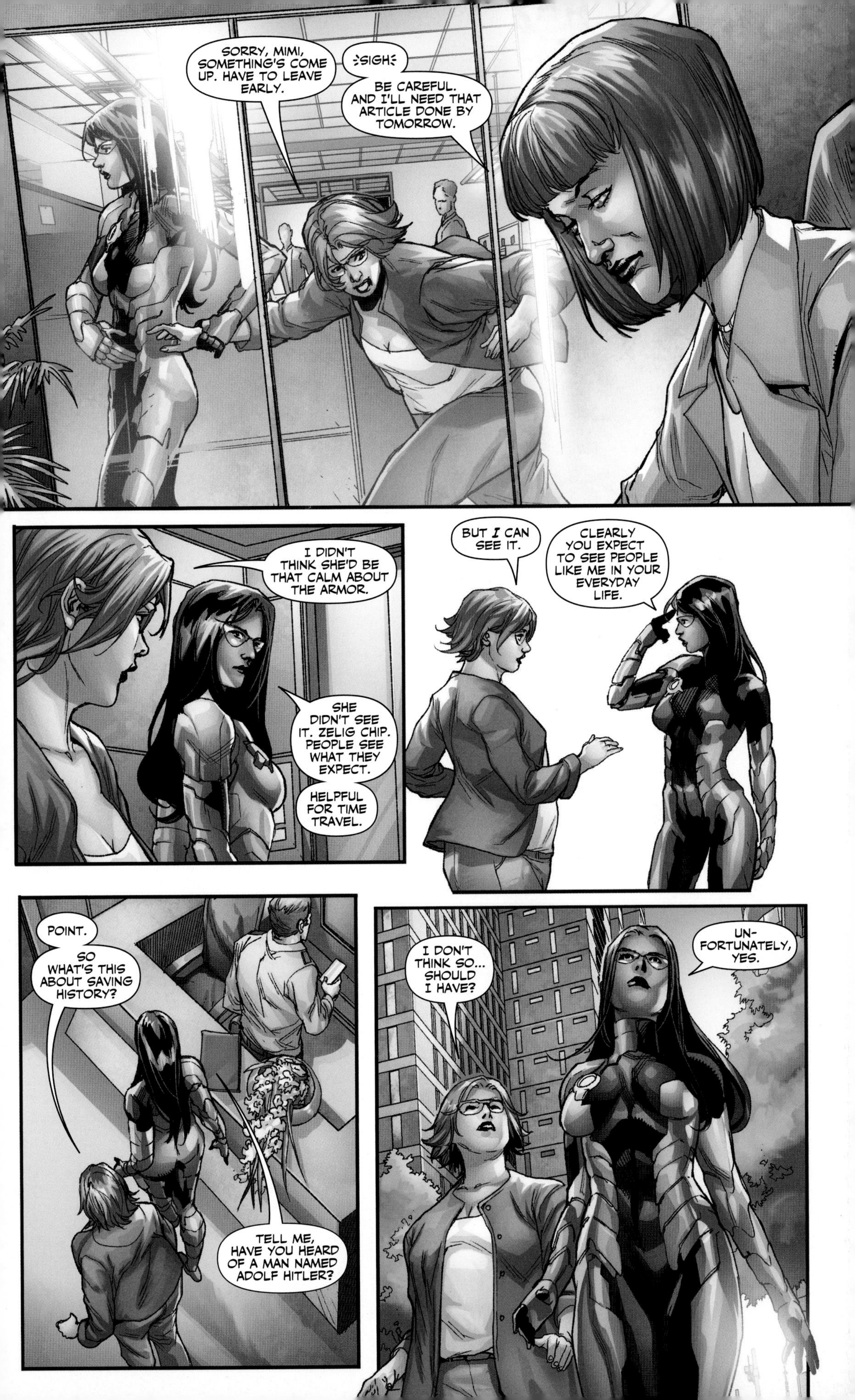
SORRY, MIMI, SOMETHING'S COME UP. HAVE TO LEAVE EARLY.
SIGH
BE CAREFUL. AND I'LL NEED THAT ARTICLE DONE BY TOMORROW.
I DIDN'T THINK SHE'D BE THAT CALM ABOUT THE ARMOR.
SHE DIDN'T SEE IT. ZELIG CHIP. PEOPLE SEE WHAT THEY EXPECT.
HELPFUL FOR TIME TRAVEL.
BUT I CAN SEE IT.
CLEARLY YOU EXPECT TO SEE PEOPLE LIKE ME IN YOUR EVERYDAY LIFE.
POINT.
SO WHAT'S THIS ABOUT SAVING HISTORY?
TELL ME, HAVE YOU HEARD OF A MAN NAMED ADOLF HITLER?
I DON'T THINK SO... SHOULD I HAVE?
UN-FORTUNATELY, YES.

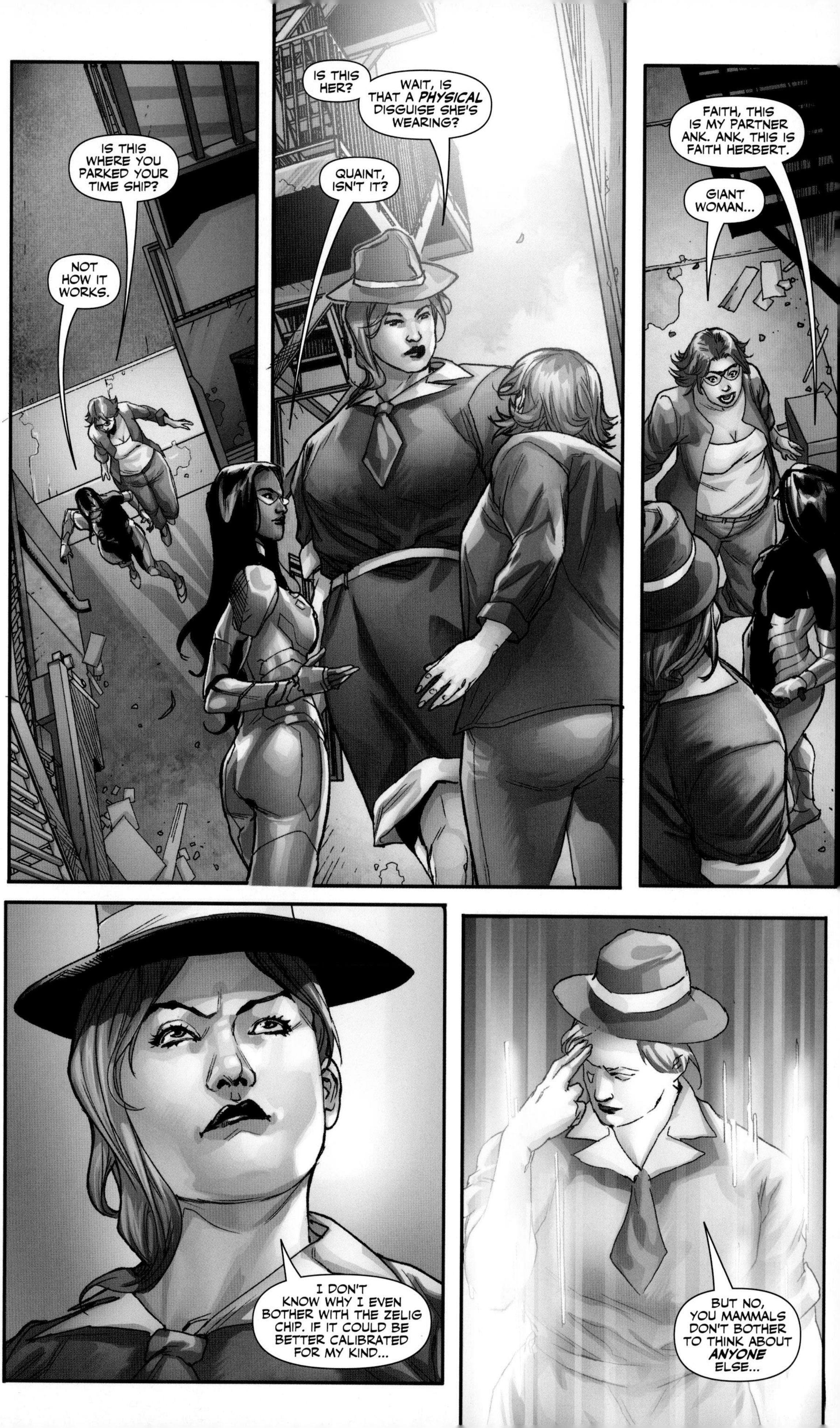
IS THIS WHERE YOU PARKED YOUR TIME SHIP?
NOT HOW IT WORKS.
IS THIS HER?
WAIT, IS THAT A *PHYSICAL* DISGUISE SHE'S WEARING?
QUAINT, ISN'T IT?
FAITH, THIS IS MY PARTNER ANK. ANK, THIS IS FAITH HERBERT.
GIANT WOMAN...
I DON'T KNOW WHY I EVEN BOTHER WITH THE ZELIG CHIP. IF IT COULD BE BETTER CALIBRATED FOR MY KIND...
BUT NO, YOU MAMMALS DON'T BOTHER TO THINK ABOUT *ANYONE* ELSE...

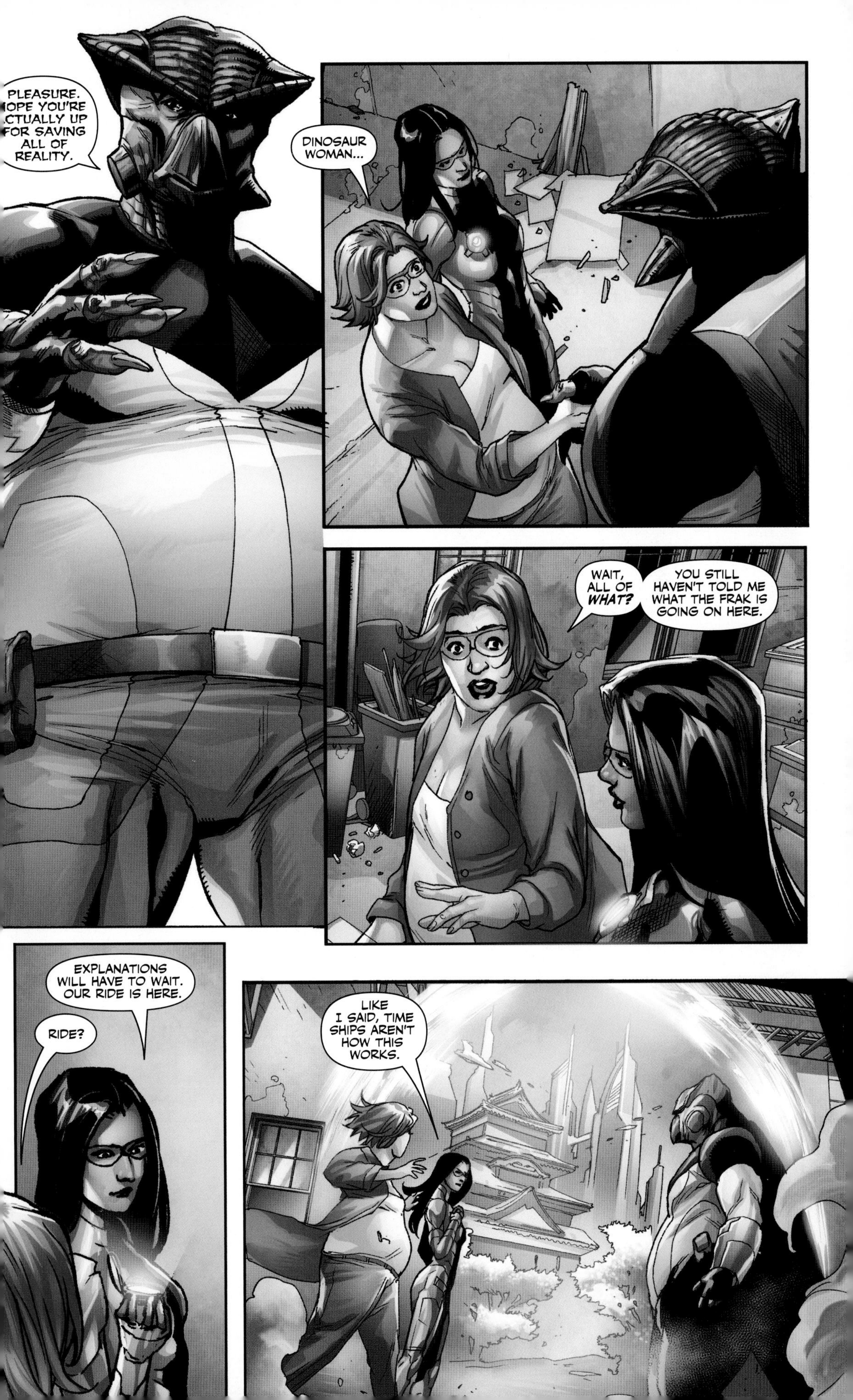
PLEASURE. OPE YOU'RE CTUALLY UP FOR SAVING ALL OF REALITY.
DINOSAUR WOMAN...
WAIT, ALL OF *WHAT?*
YOU STILL HAVEN'T TOLD ME WHAT THE FRAK IS GOING ON HERE.
EXPLANATIONS WILL HAVE TO WAIT. OUR RIDE IS HERE.
RIDE?
LIKE I SAID, TIME SHIPS AREN'T HOW THIS WORKS.

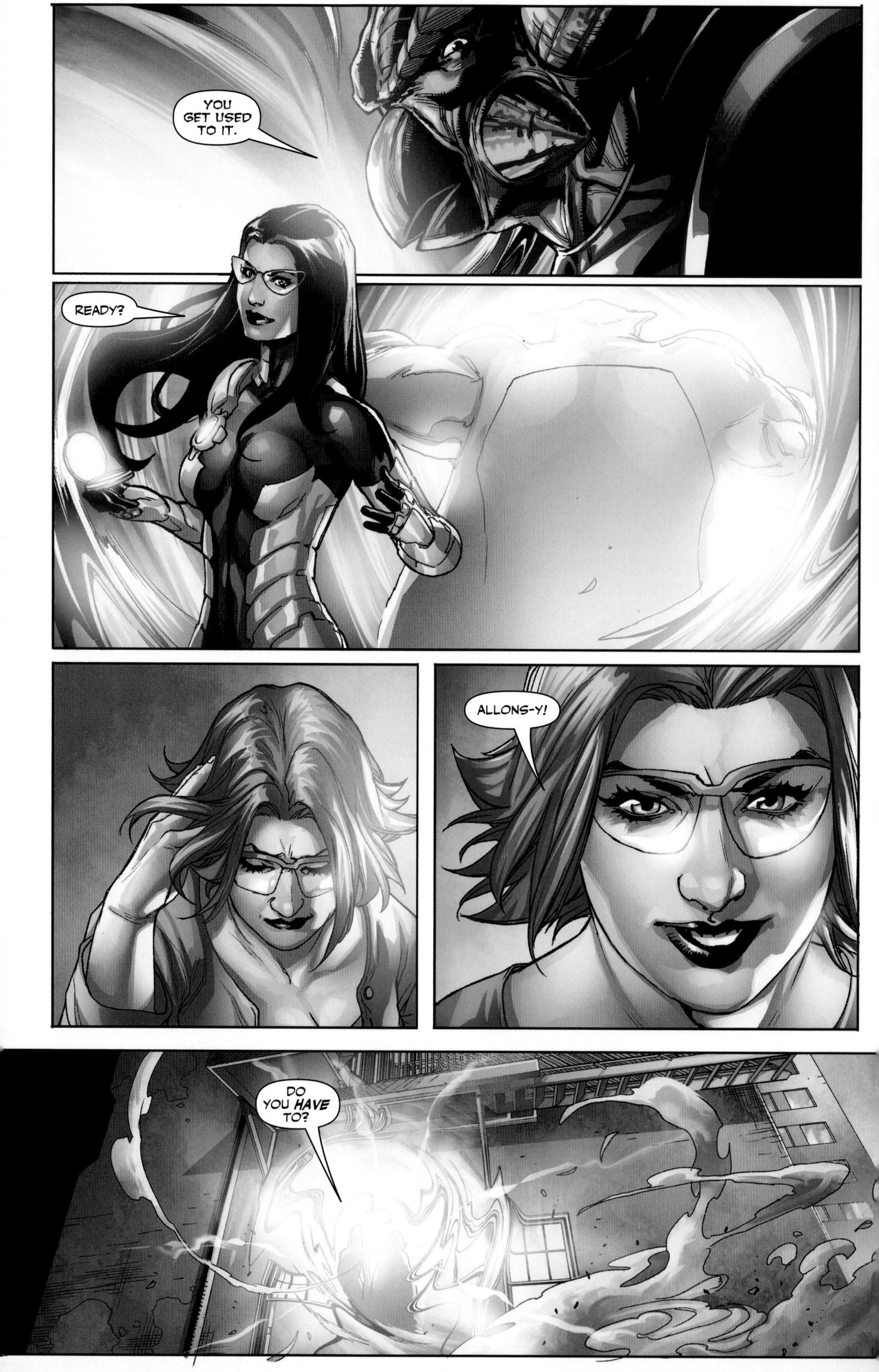
YOU GET USED TO IT.
READY?
ALLONS-Y!
DO YOU *HAVE* TO?

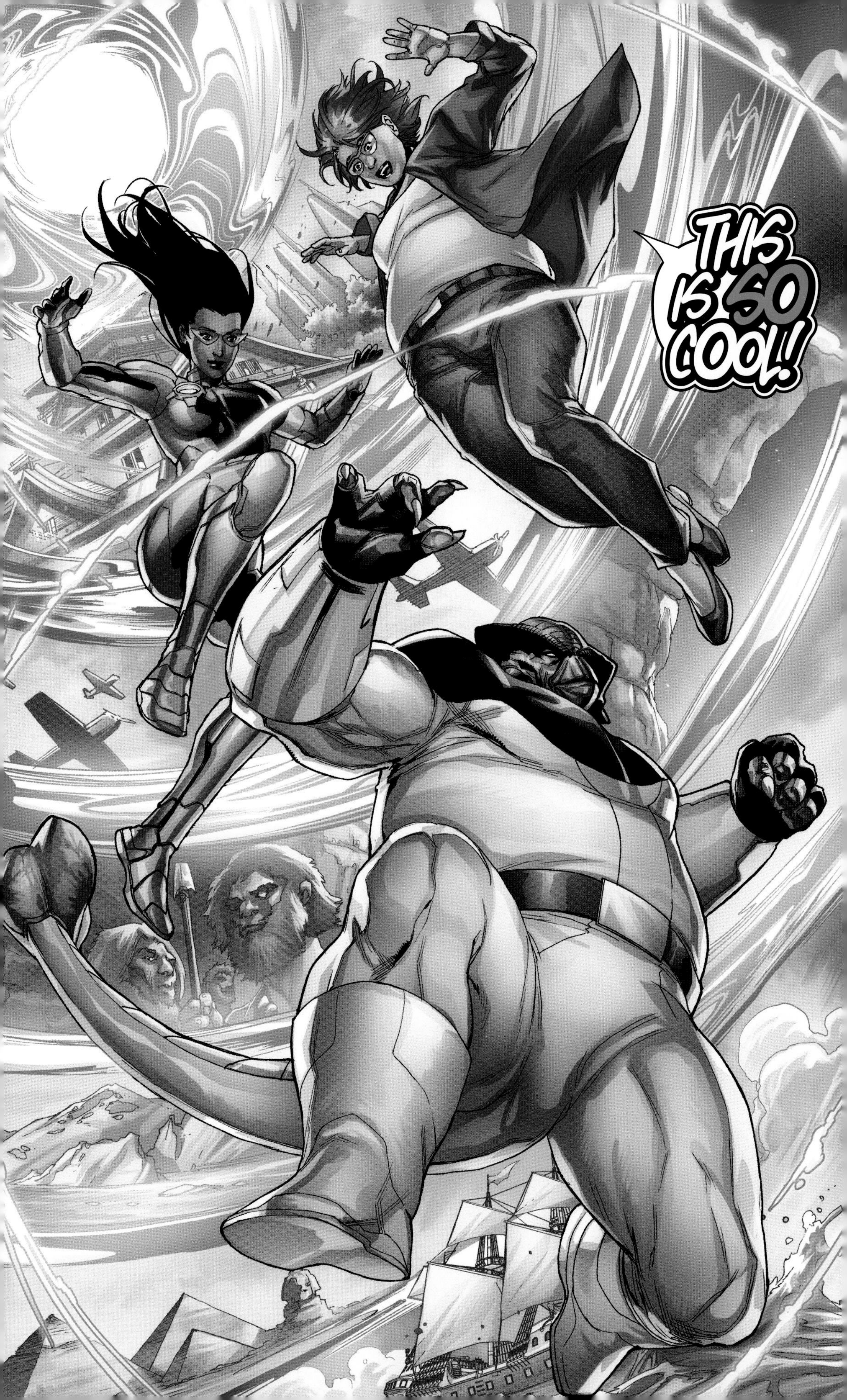
THIS IS SO COOL!

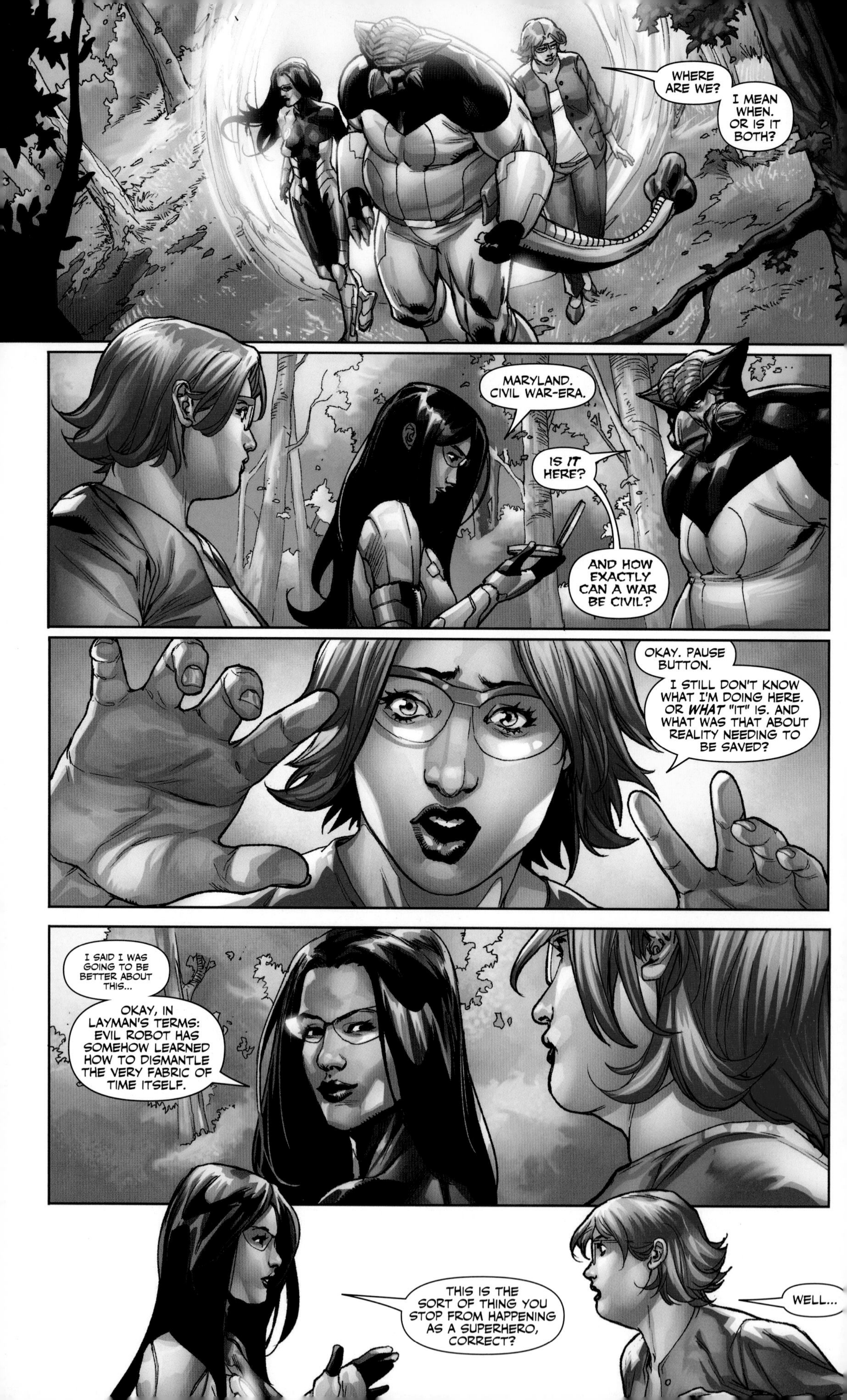
WHERE ARE WE?
I MEAN WHEN. OR IS IT BOTH?
MARYLAND. CIVIL WAR-ERA.
IS *IT* HERE?
AND HOW EXACTLY CAN A WAR BE CIVIL?
OKAY. PAUSE BUTTON.
I STILL DON'T KNOW WHAT I'M DOING HERE. OR *WHAT* "IT" IS. AND WHAT WAS THAT ABOUT REALITY NEEDING TO BE SAVED?
I SAID I WAS GOING TO BE BETTER ABOUT THIS...
OKAY, IN LAYMAN'S TERMS: EVIL ROBOT HAS SOMEHOW LEARNED HOW TO DISMANTLE THE VERY FABRIC OF TIME ITSELF.
THIS IS THE SORT OF THING YOU STOP FROM HAPPENING AS A SUPERHERO, CORRECT?
WELL...

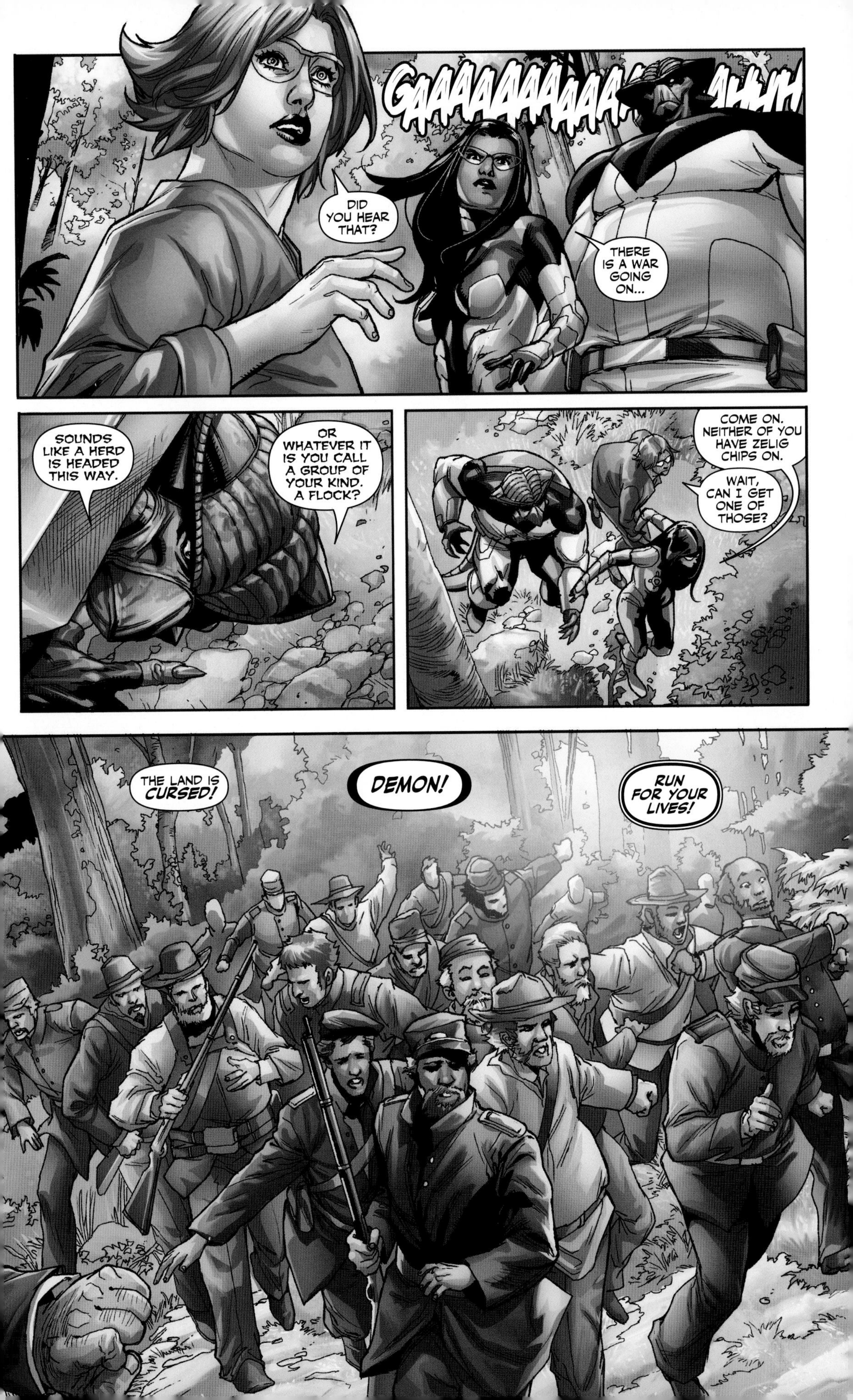
GAAAAAAAAAAAAHHHH
DID YOU HEAR THAT?
THERE IS A WAR GOING ON...
SOUNDS LIKE A HERD IS HEADED THIS WAY.
OR WHATEVER IT IS YOU CALL A GROUP OF YOUR KIND. A FLOCK?
COME ON. NEITHER OF YOU HAVE ZELIG CHIPS ON.
WAIT, CAN I GET ONE OF THOSE?
THE LAND IS CURSED!
DEMON!
RUN FOR YOUR LIVES!

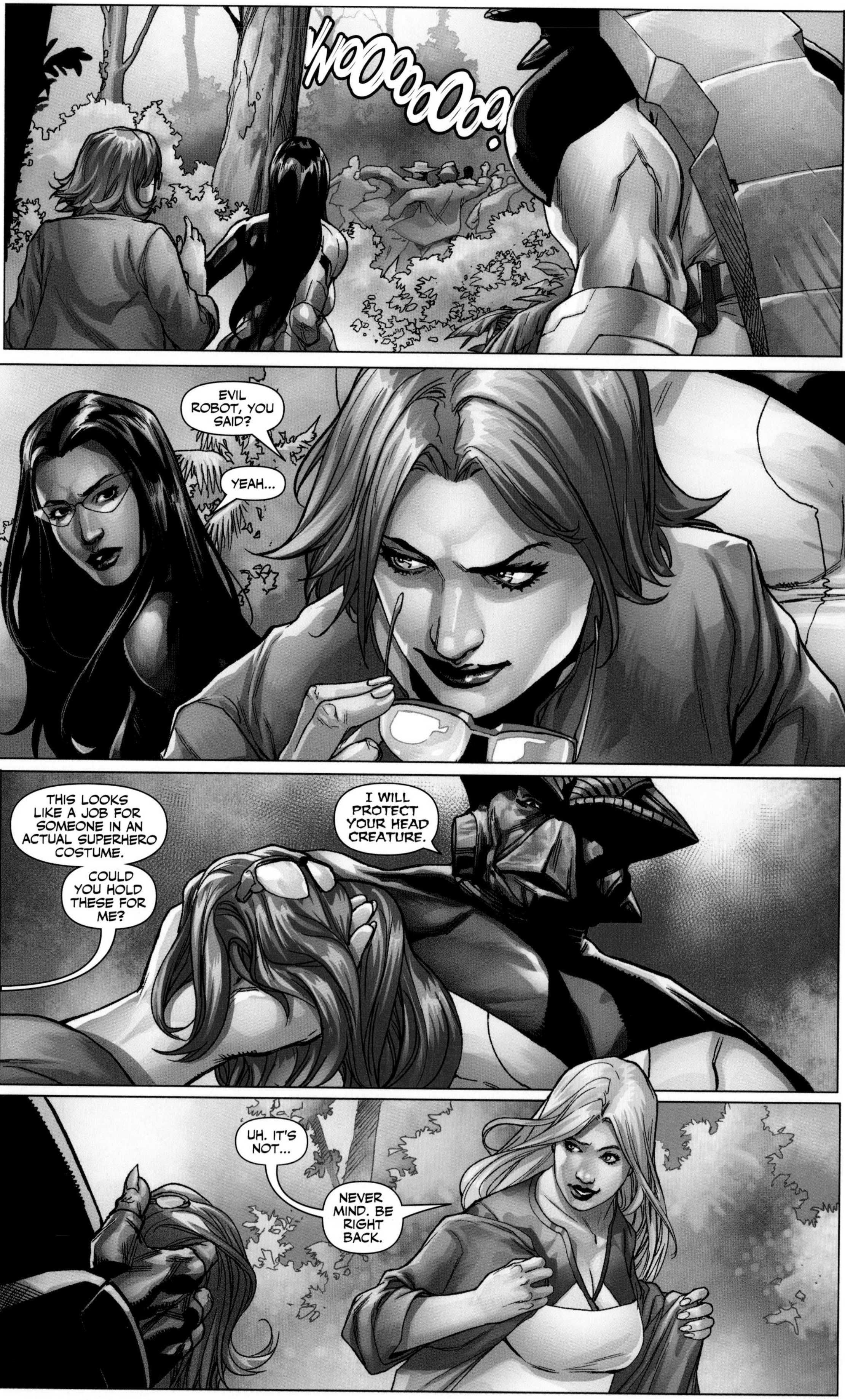

NOOOOOOOO!
EVIL ROBOT, YOU SAID?
YEAH...
THIS LOOKS LIKE A JOB FOR SOMEONE IN AN ACTUAL SUPERHERO COSTUME.
COULD YOU HOLD THESE FOR ME?
I WILL PROTECT YOUR HEAD CREATURE.
UH. IT'S NOT...
NEVER MIND. BE RIGHT BACK.

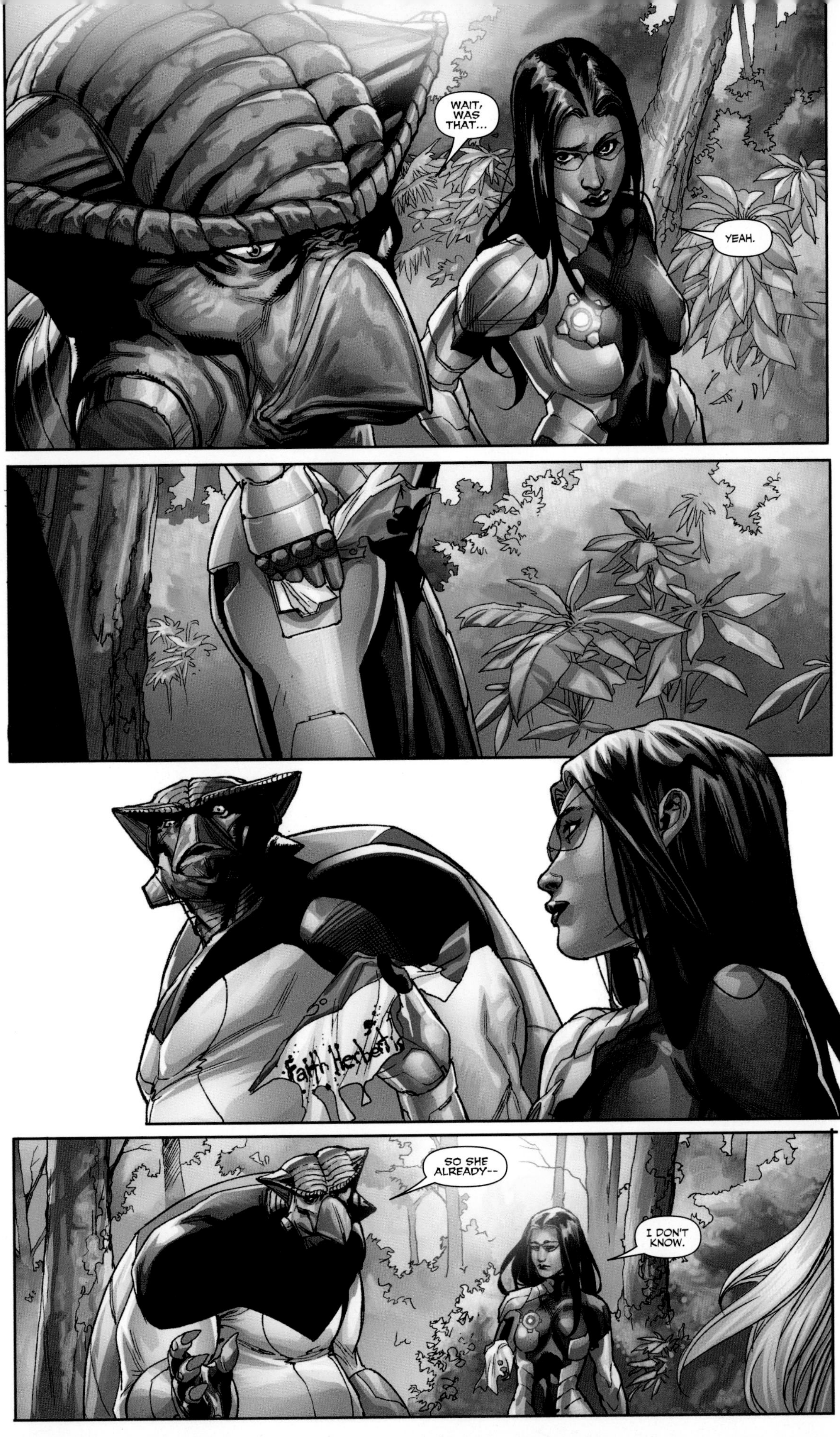
WAIT, WAS THAT...
YEAH.
Faith Herbert
SO SHE ALREADY--
I DON'T KNOW.

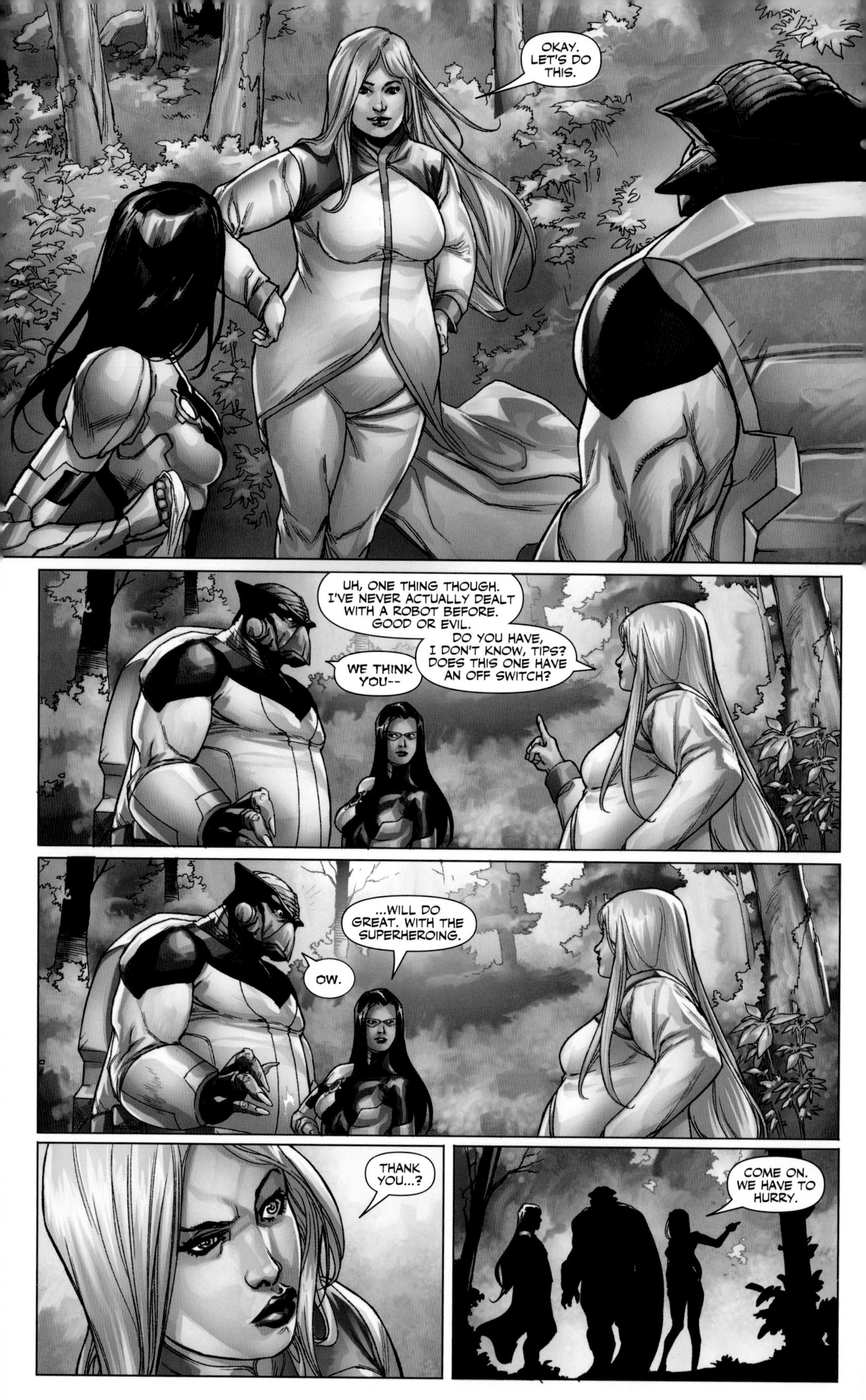
OKAY. LET'S DO THIS.
UH, ONE THING THOUGH. I'VE NEVER ACTUALLY DEALT WITH A ROBOT BEFORE. GOOD OR EVIL.
DO YOU HAVE, I DON'T KNOW, TIPS? DOES THIS ONE HAVE AN OFF SWITCH?
WE THINK YOU--
...WILL DO GREAT. WITH THE SUPERHEROING.
OW.
THANK YOU...?
COME ON. WE HAVE TO HURRY.

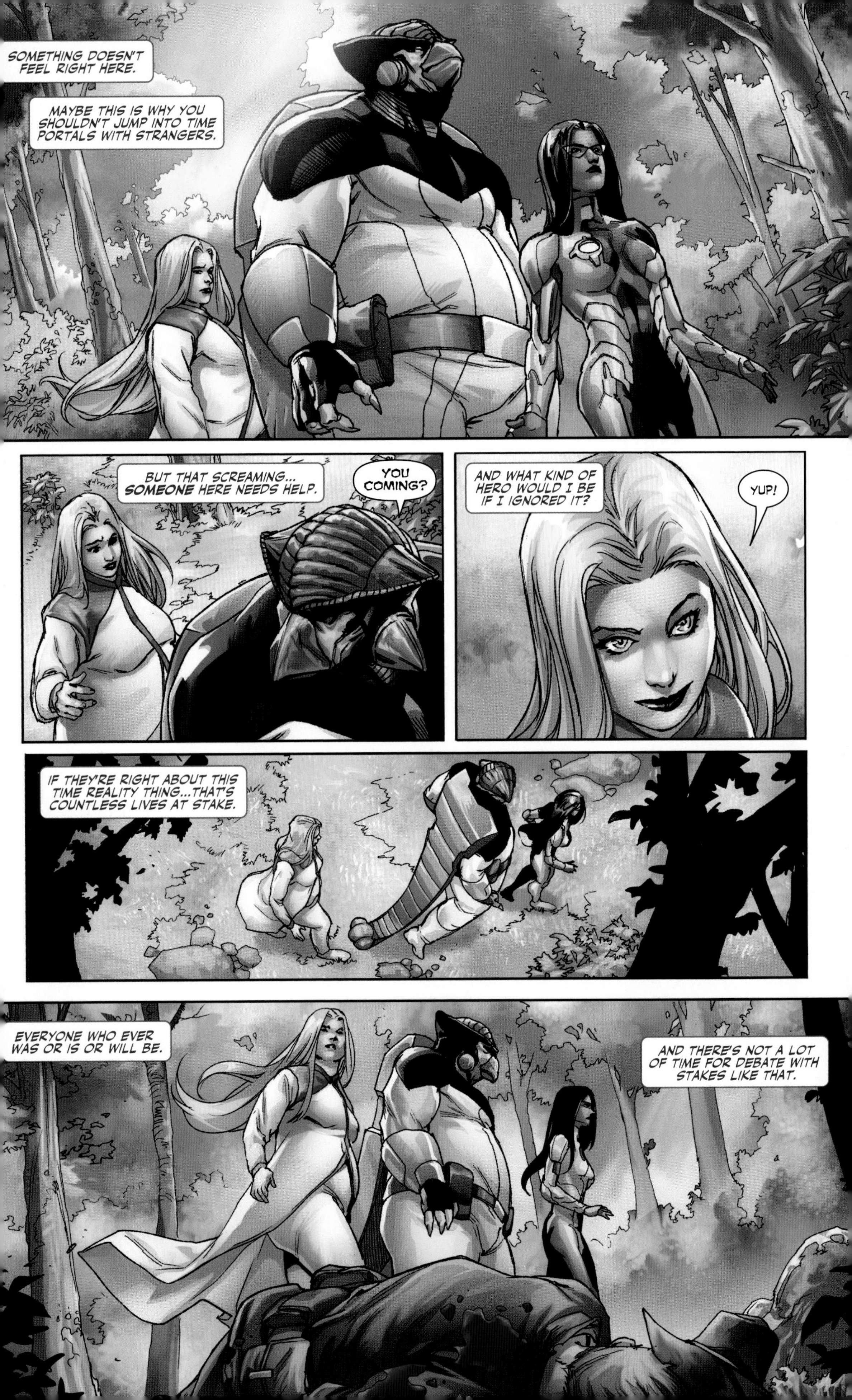
SOMETHING DOESN'T FEEL RIGHT HERE.
MAYBE THIS IS WHY YOU SHOULDN'T JUMP INTO TIME PORTALS WITH STRANGERS.
BUT THAT SCREAMING... SOMEONE HERE NEEDS HELP.
YOU COMING?
AND WHAT KIND OF HERO WOULD I BE IF I IGNORED IT?
YUP!
IF THEY'RE RIGHT ABOUT THIS TIME REALITY THING...THAT'S COUNTLESS LIVES AT STAKE.
EVERYONE WHO EVER WAS OR IS OR WILL BE.
AND THERE'S NOT A LOT OF TIME FOR DEBATE WITH STAKES LIKE THAT.

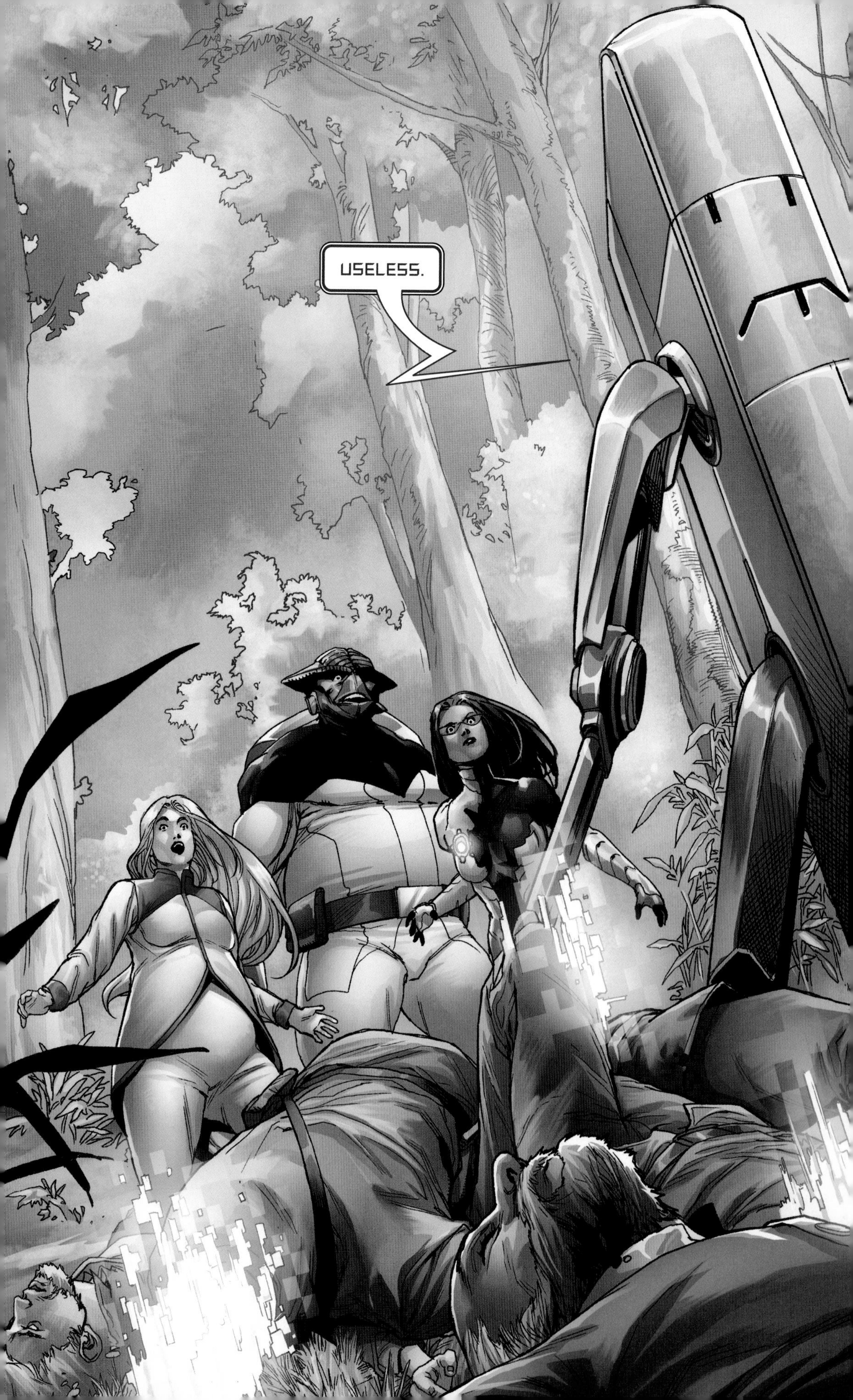
USELESS.

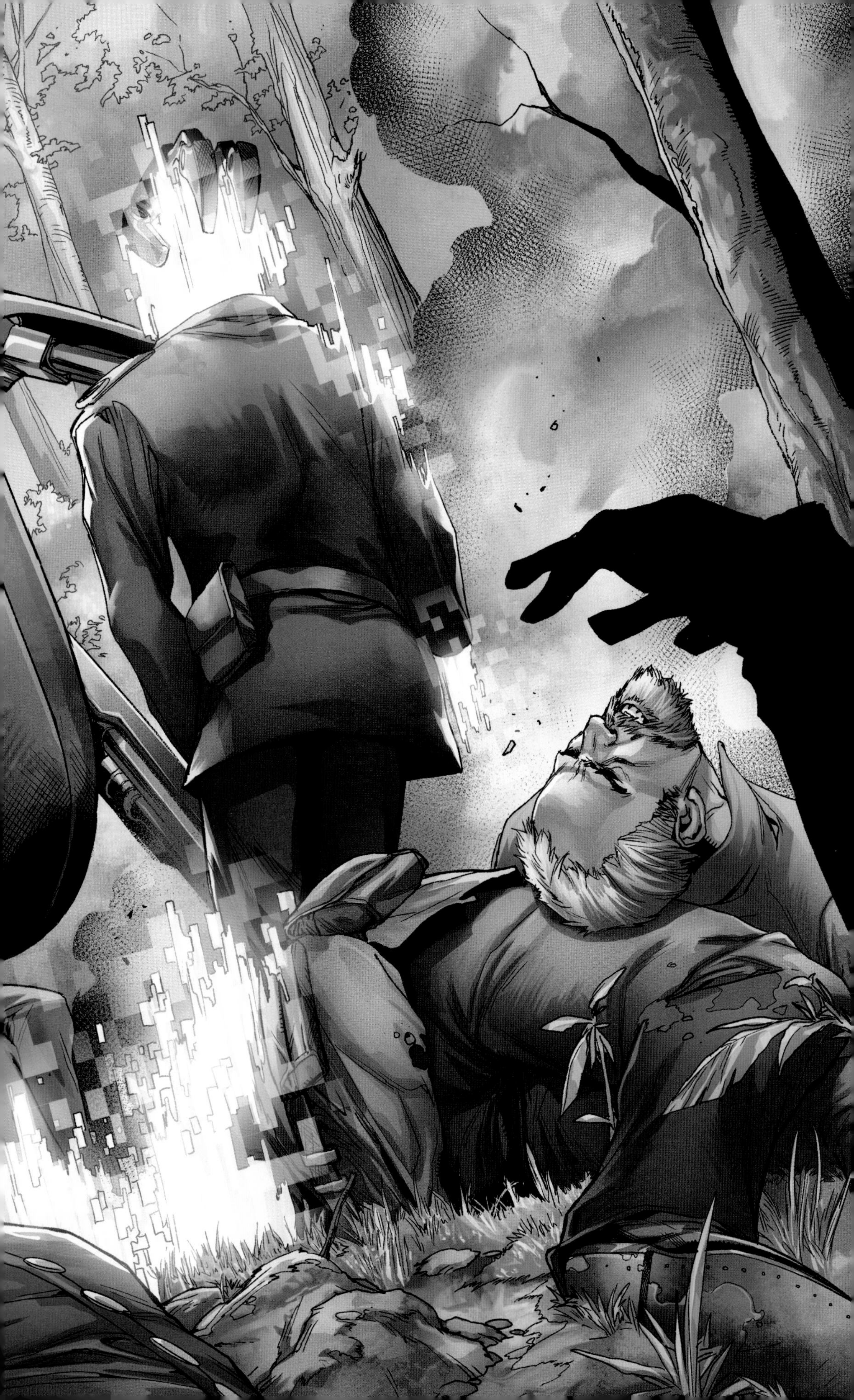

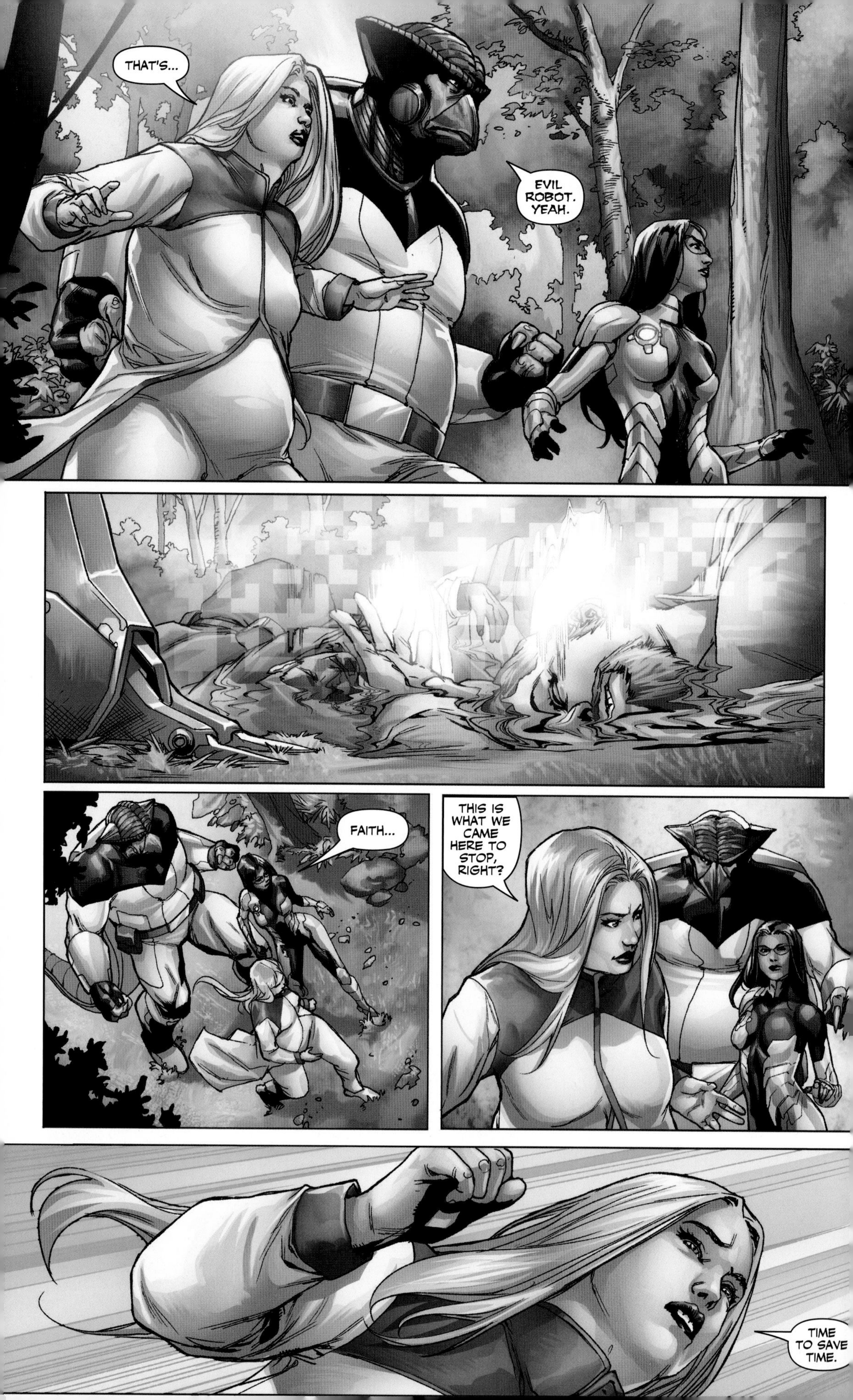
THAT'S...
EVIL ROBOT. YEAH.
FAITH...
THIS IS WHAT WE CAME HERE TO STOP, RIGHT?
TIME TO SAVE TIME.

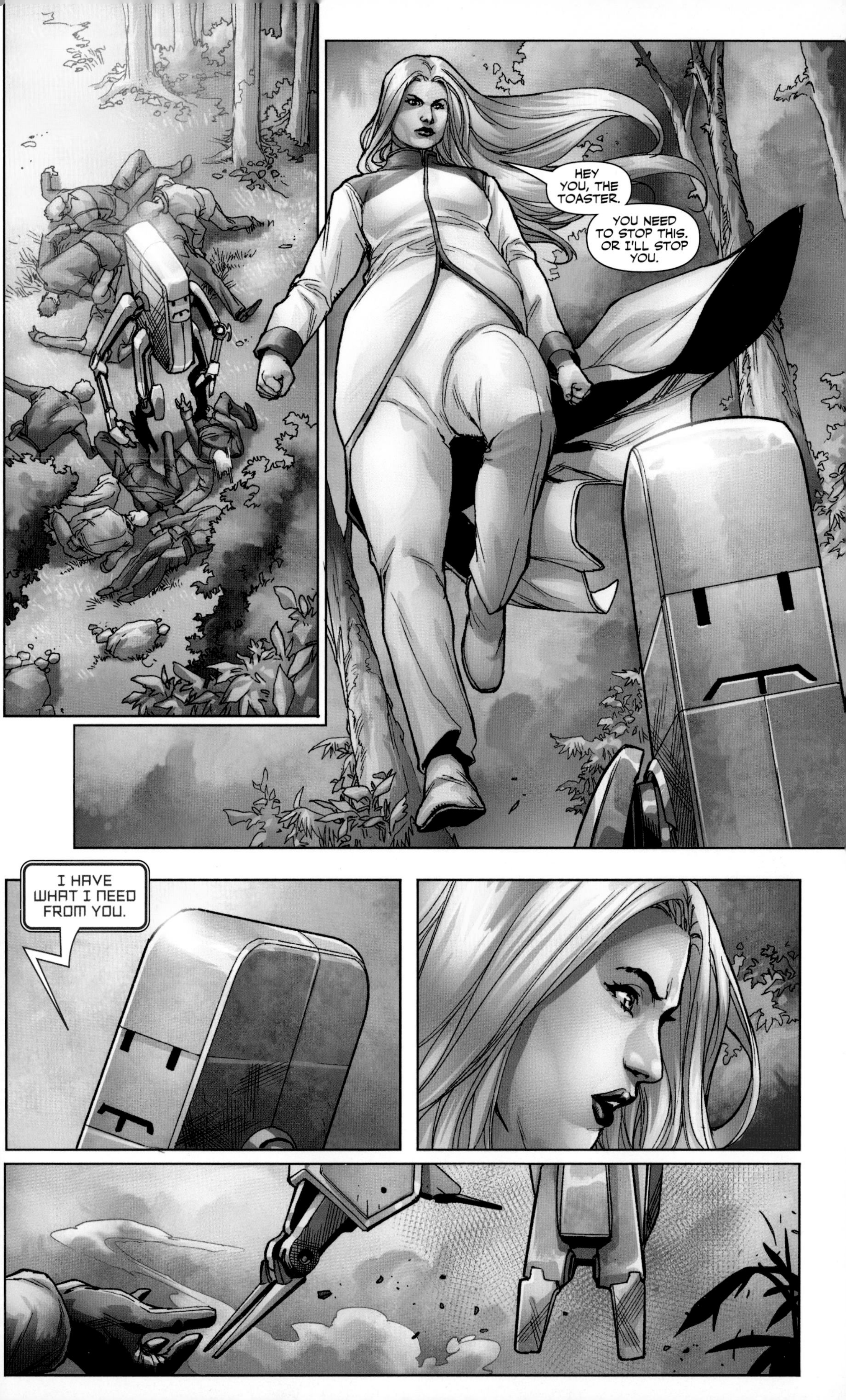
HEY YOU, THE TOASTER.
YOU NEED TO STOP THIS. OR I'LL STOP YOU.
I HAVE WHAT I NEED FROM YOU.

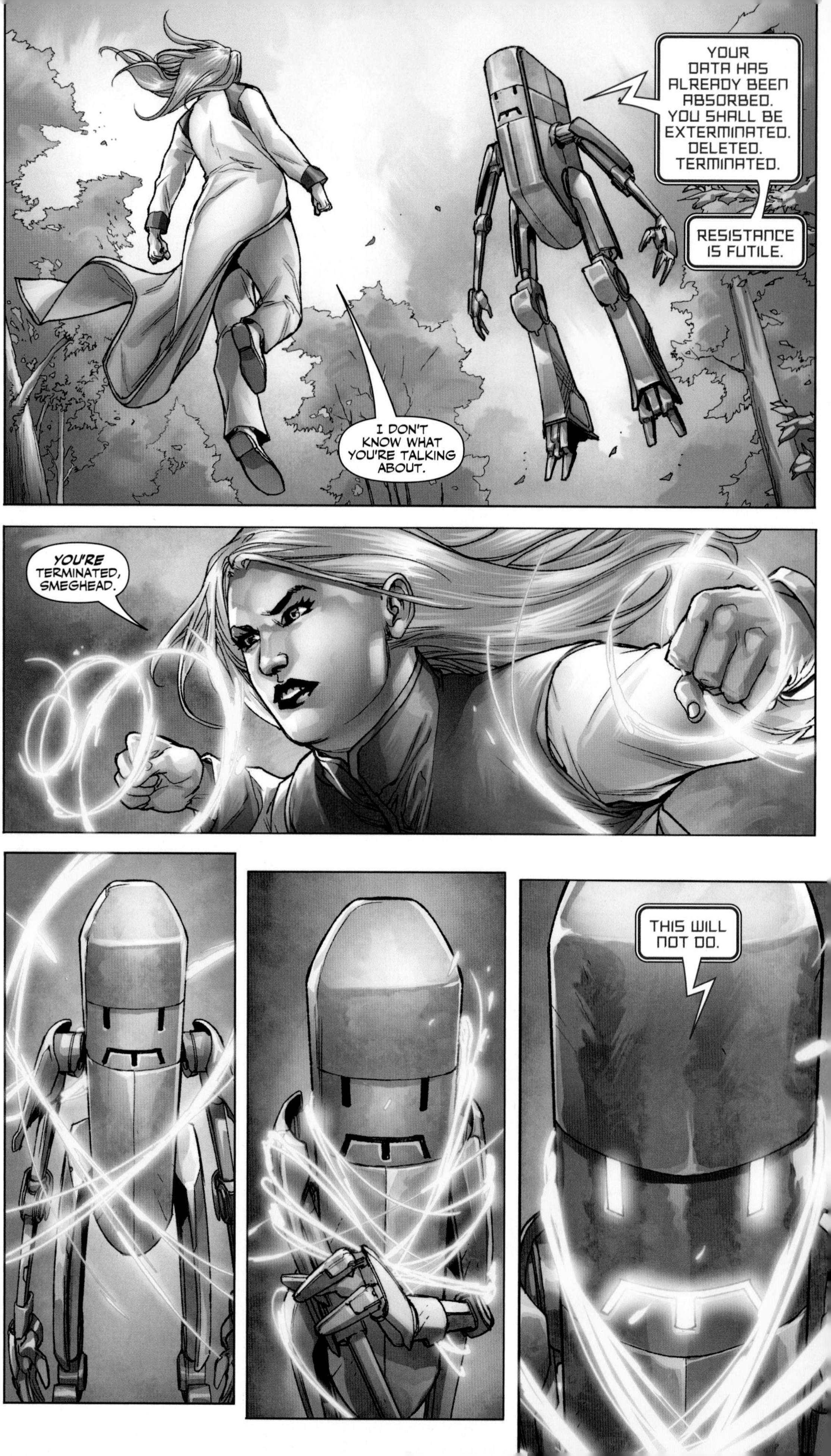
YOUR DATA HAS ALREADY BEEN ABSORBED. YOU SHALL BE EXTERMINATED. DELETED. TERMINATED.
RESISTANCE IS FUTILE.
I DON'T KNOW WHAT YOU'RE TALKING ABOUT.
YOU'RE TERMINATED, SMEGHEAD.
THIS WILL NOT DO.

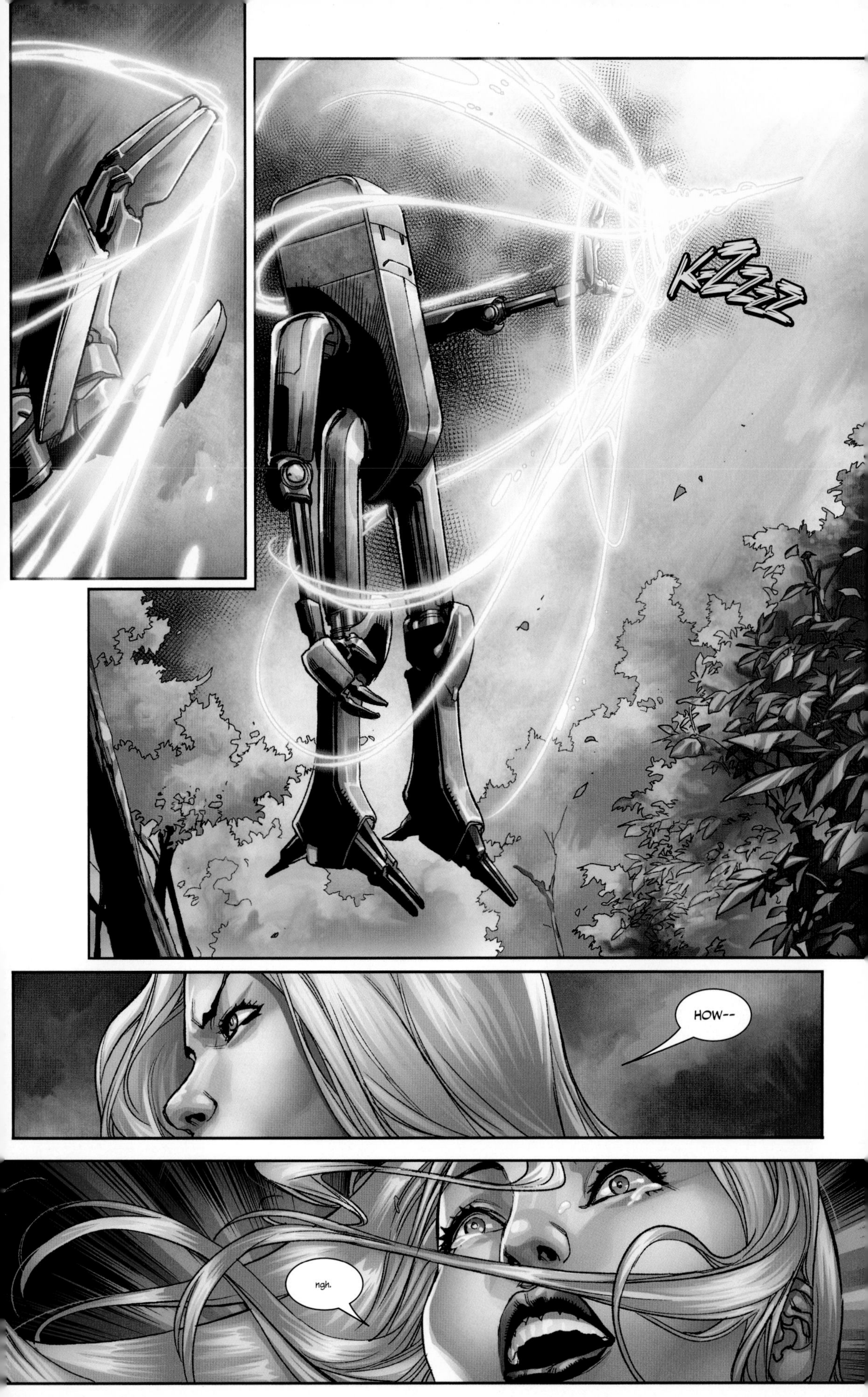
KZZZZ
HOW--
ngh.

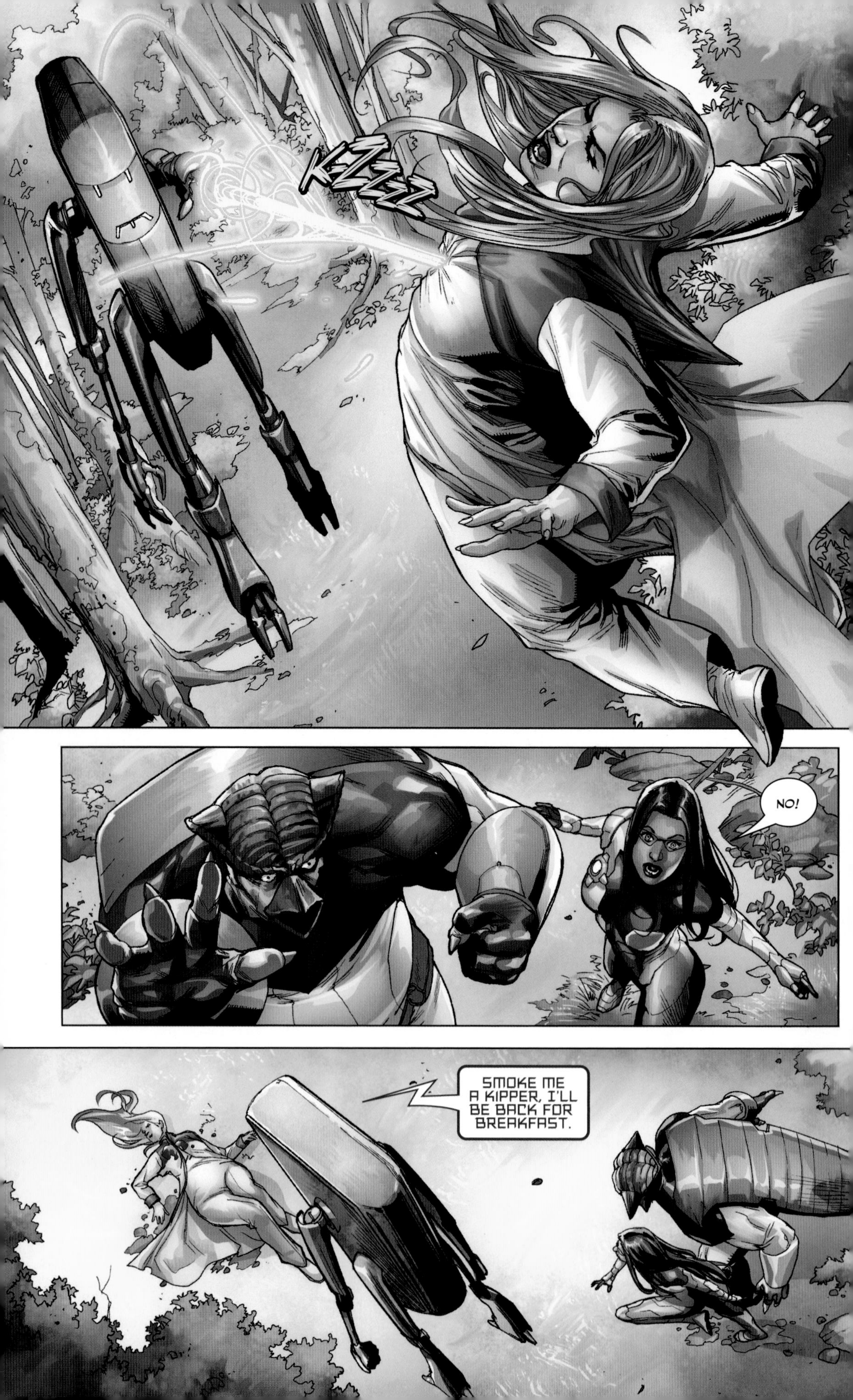
K-ZZZZ
NO!
SMOKE ME A KIPPER, I'LL BE BACK FOR BREAKFAST.

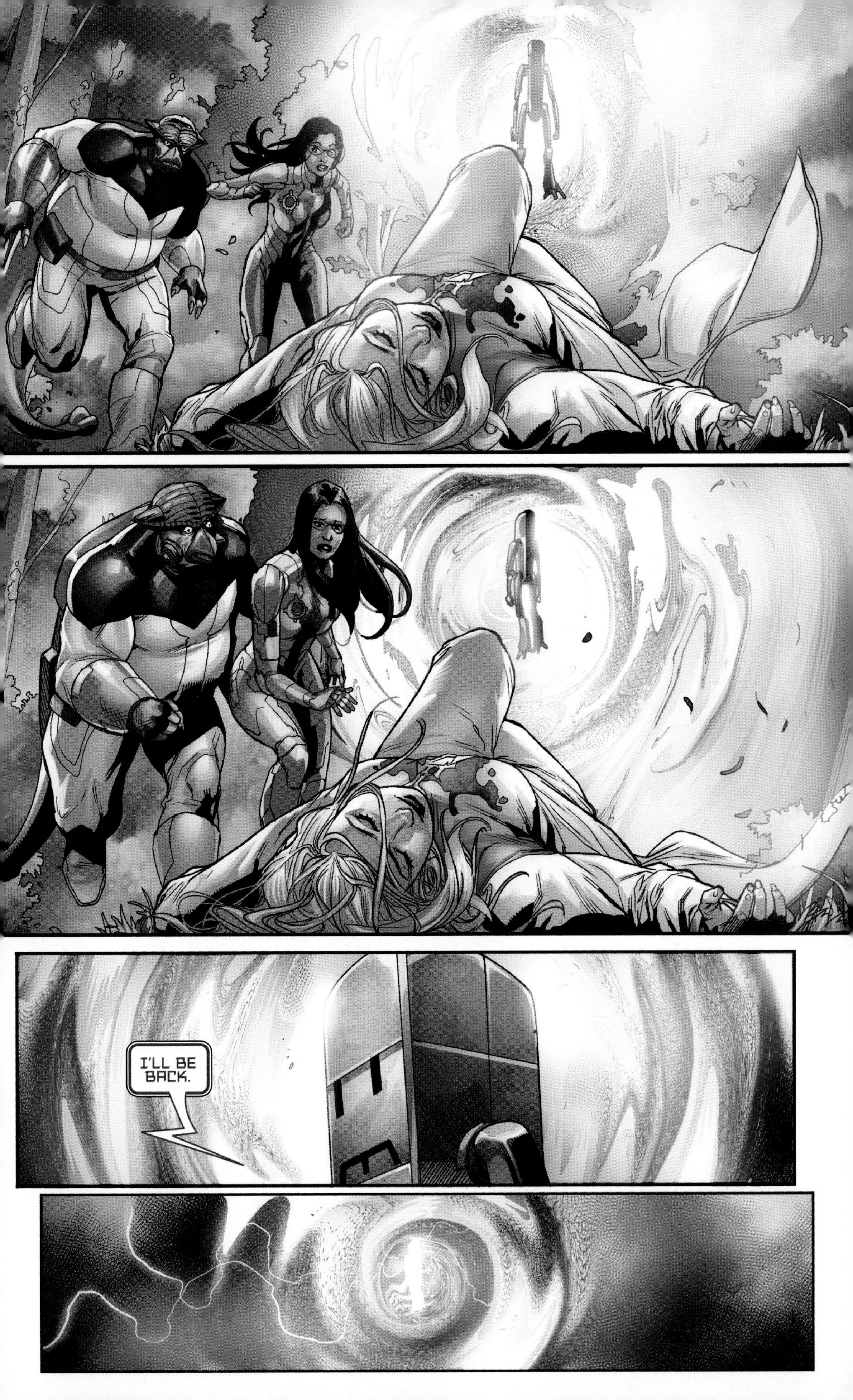
I'LL BE BACK.

SHE...SHE'S
GONE.

WHAT...
WHAT CAN
WE DO?

I THOUGHT
SHE WAS SUPPOSED
TO STOP THIS.

IF
X23>Y72*X7
%P37<Q42=
X76-4/10

SPEAK REAL
WORDS.

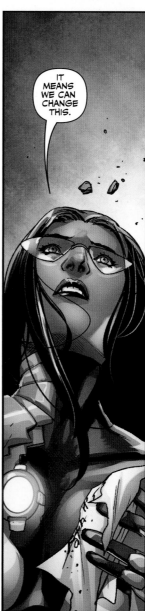

IT
MEANS
WE CAN
CHANGE
THIS.

YOU'D
BETTER HURRY.
I DON'T THINK
WE HAVE--

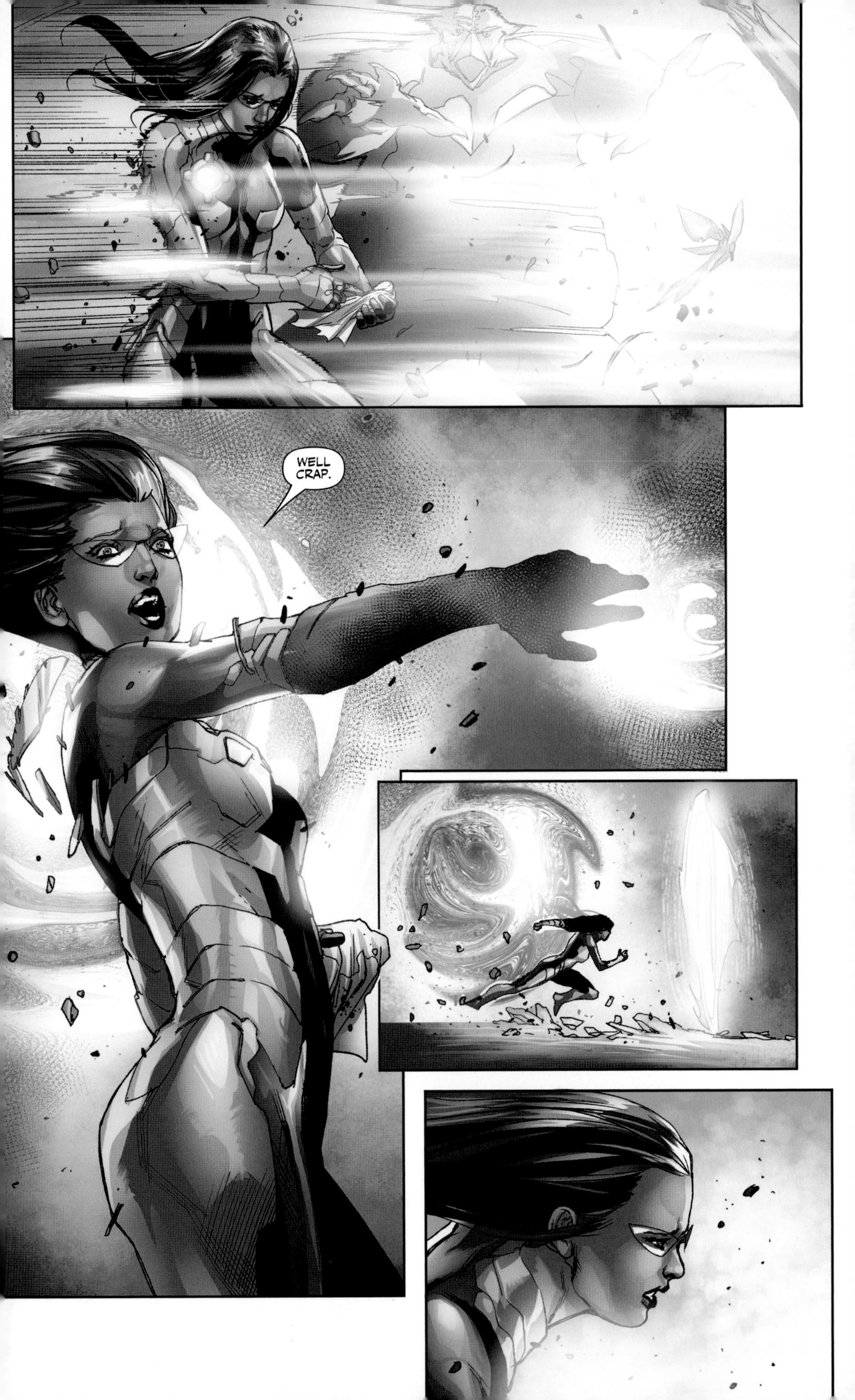
WELL CRAP.

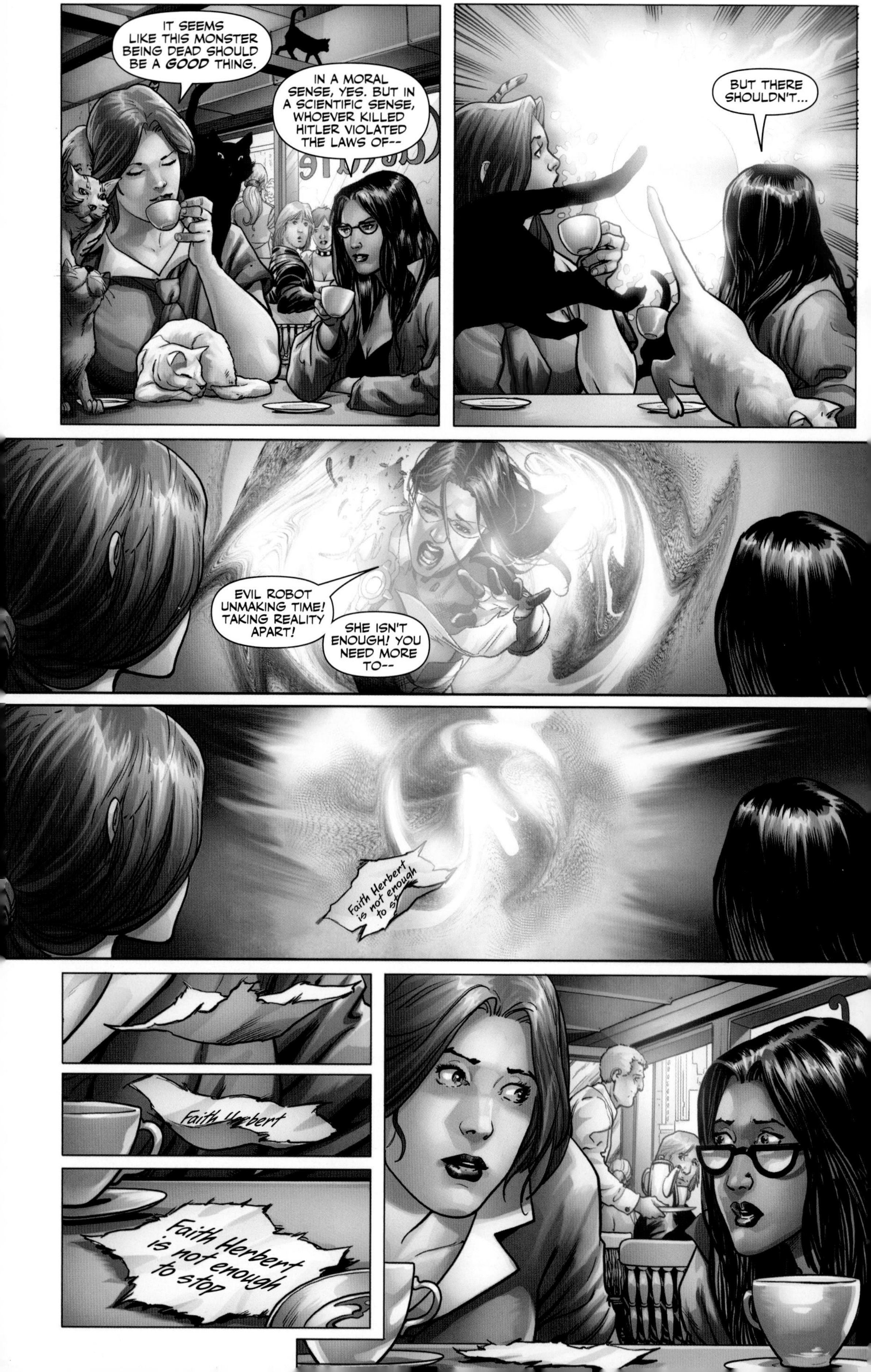
IT SEEMS LIKE THIS MONSTER BEING DEAD SHOULD BE A GOOD THING.
IN A MORAL SENSE, YES. BUT IN A SCIENTIFIC SENSE, WHOEVER KILLED HITLER VIOLATED THE LAWS OF--
BUT THERE SHOULDN'T...
EVIL ROBOT UNMAKING TIME! TAKING REALITY APART!
SHE ISN'T ENOUGH! YOU NEED MORE TO--
Faith Herbert is not enough to st
Faith Herbert
Faith Herbert is not enough to stop

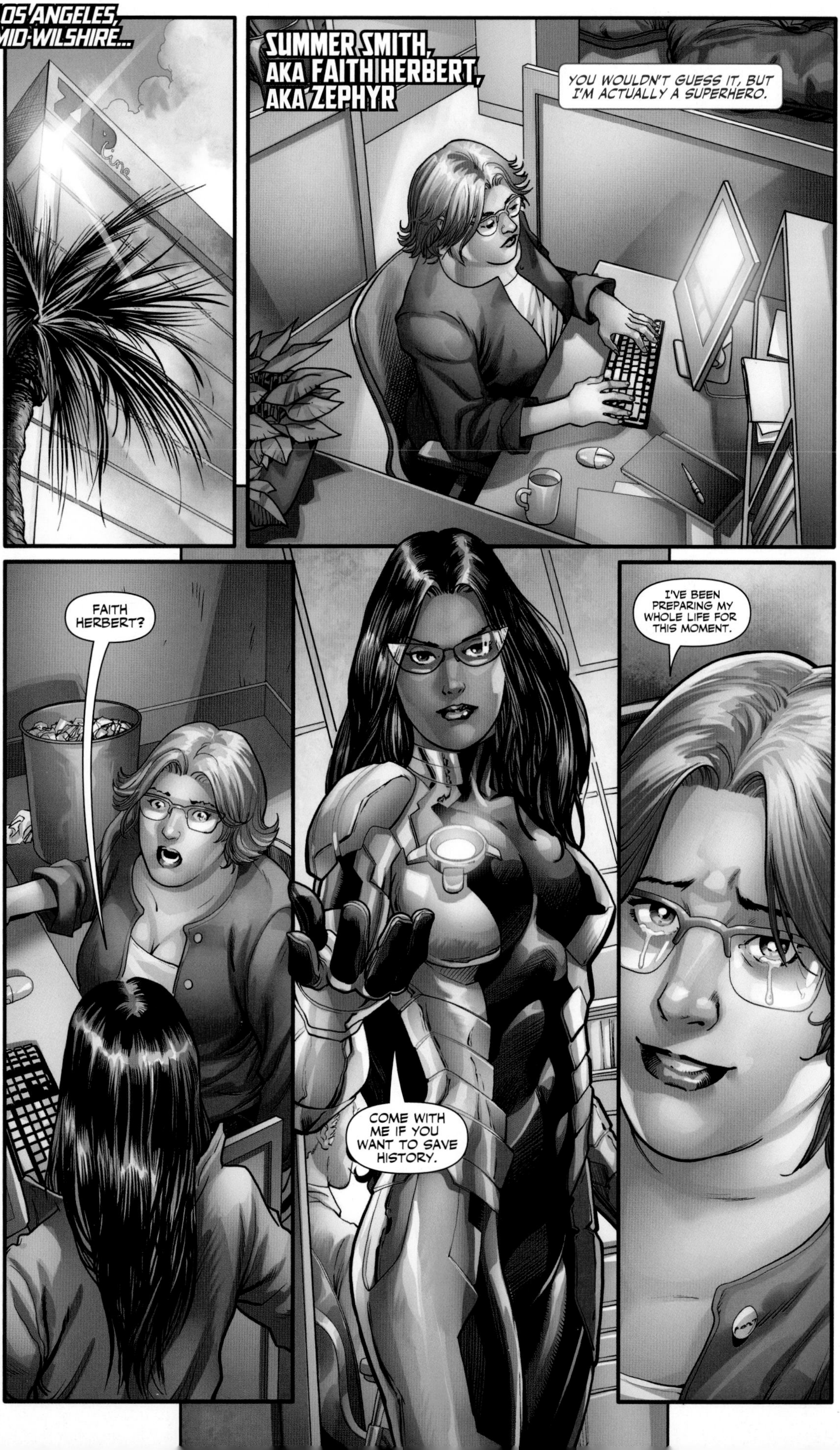
LOS ANGELES, MID-WILSHIRE...
SUMMER SMITH, AKA FAITH HERBERT, AKA ZEPHYR
YOU WOULDN'T GUESS IT, BUT I'M ACTUALLY A SUPERHERO.
FAITH HERBERT?
COME WITH ME IF YOU WANT TO SAVE HISTORY.
I'VE BEEN PREPARING MY WHOLE LIFE FOR THIS MOMENT.

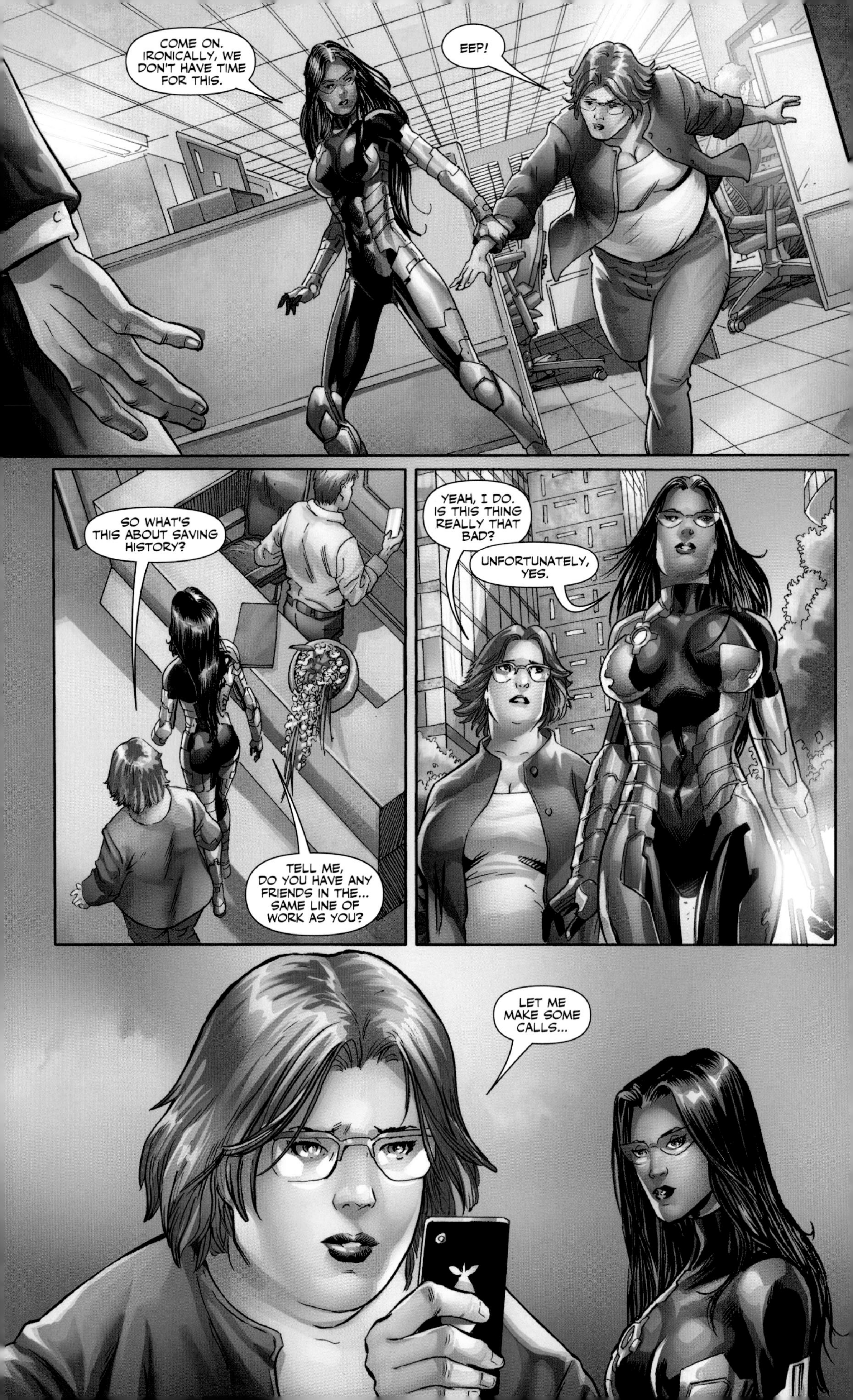
COME ON. IRONICALLY, WE DON'T HAVE TIME FOR THIS.
EEP!
SO WHAT'S THIS ABOUT SAVING HISTORY?
TELL ME, DO YOU HAVE ANY FRIENDS IN THE... SAME LINE OF WORK AS YOU?
YEAH, I DO. IS THIS THING REALLY THAT BAD?
UNFORTUNATELY, YES.
LET ME MAKE SOME CALLS...

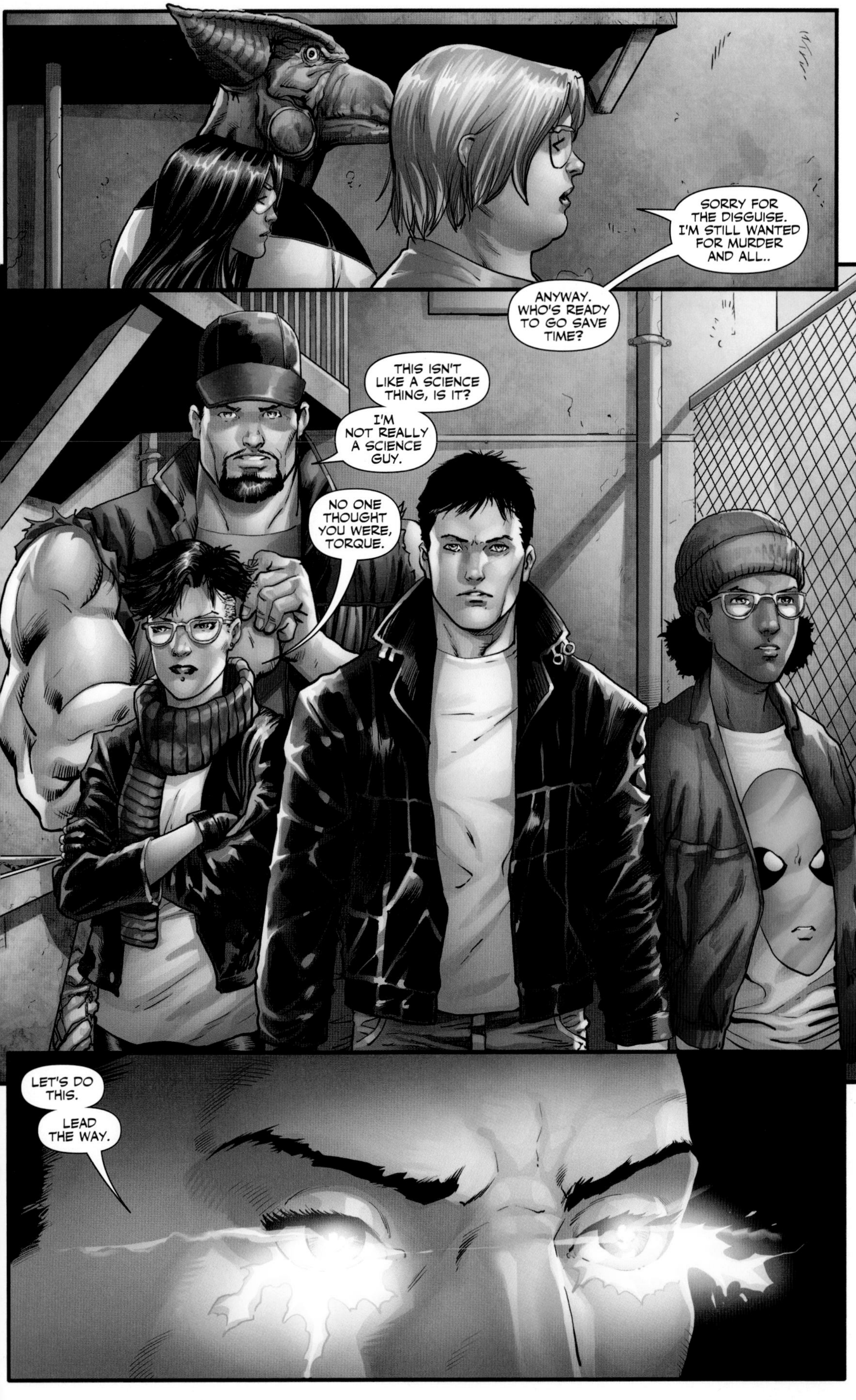

SORRY FOR THE DISGUISE. I'M STILL WANTED FOR MURDER AND ALL..
ANYWAY. WHO'S READY TO GO SAVE TIME?
THIS ISN'T LIKE A SCIENCE THING, IS IT?
I'M NOT REALLY A SCIENCE GUY.
NO ONE THOUGHT YOU WERE, TORQUE.
LET'S DO THIS.
LEAD THE WAY.

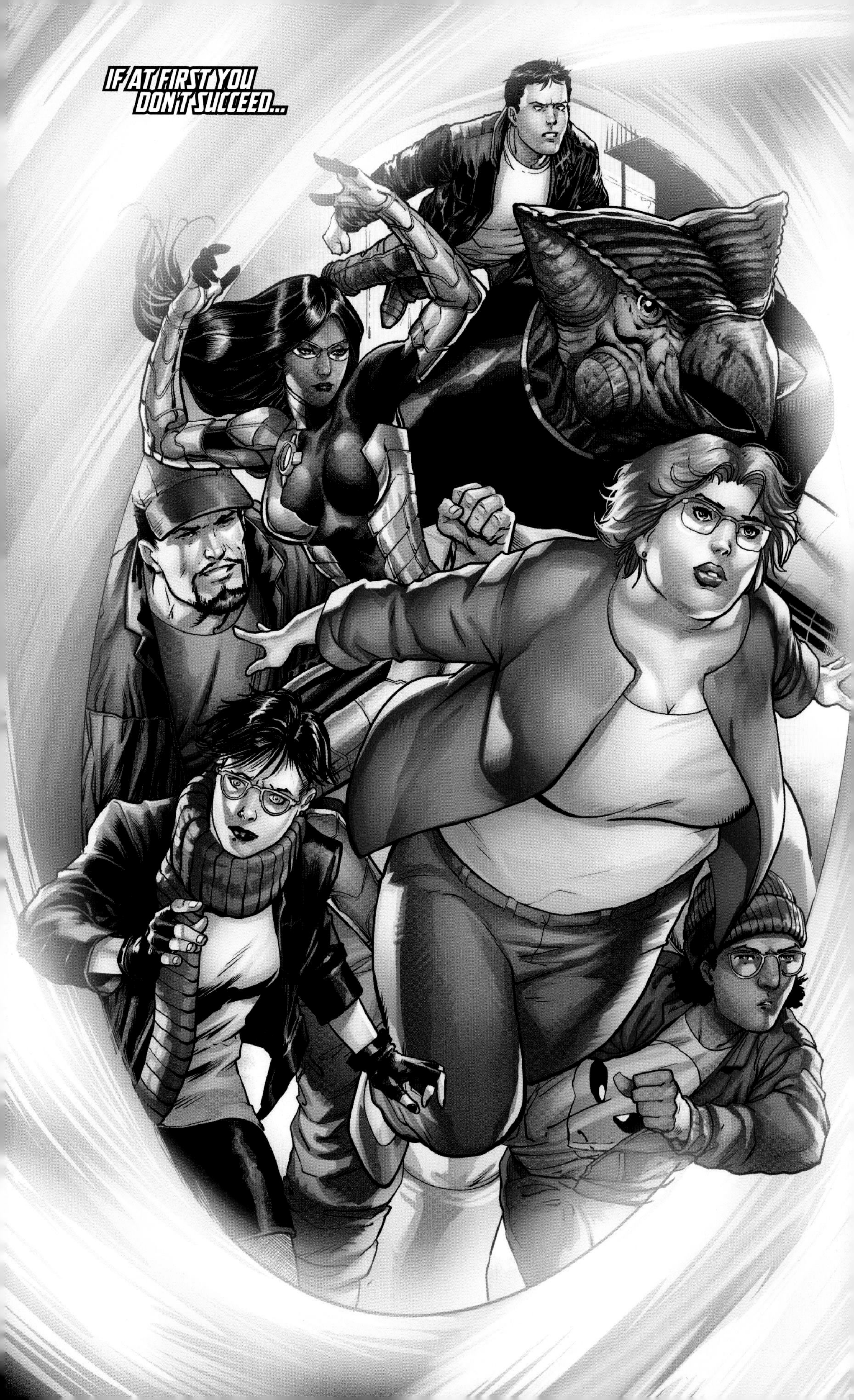
IF AT FIRST YOU DON'T SUCCEED...

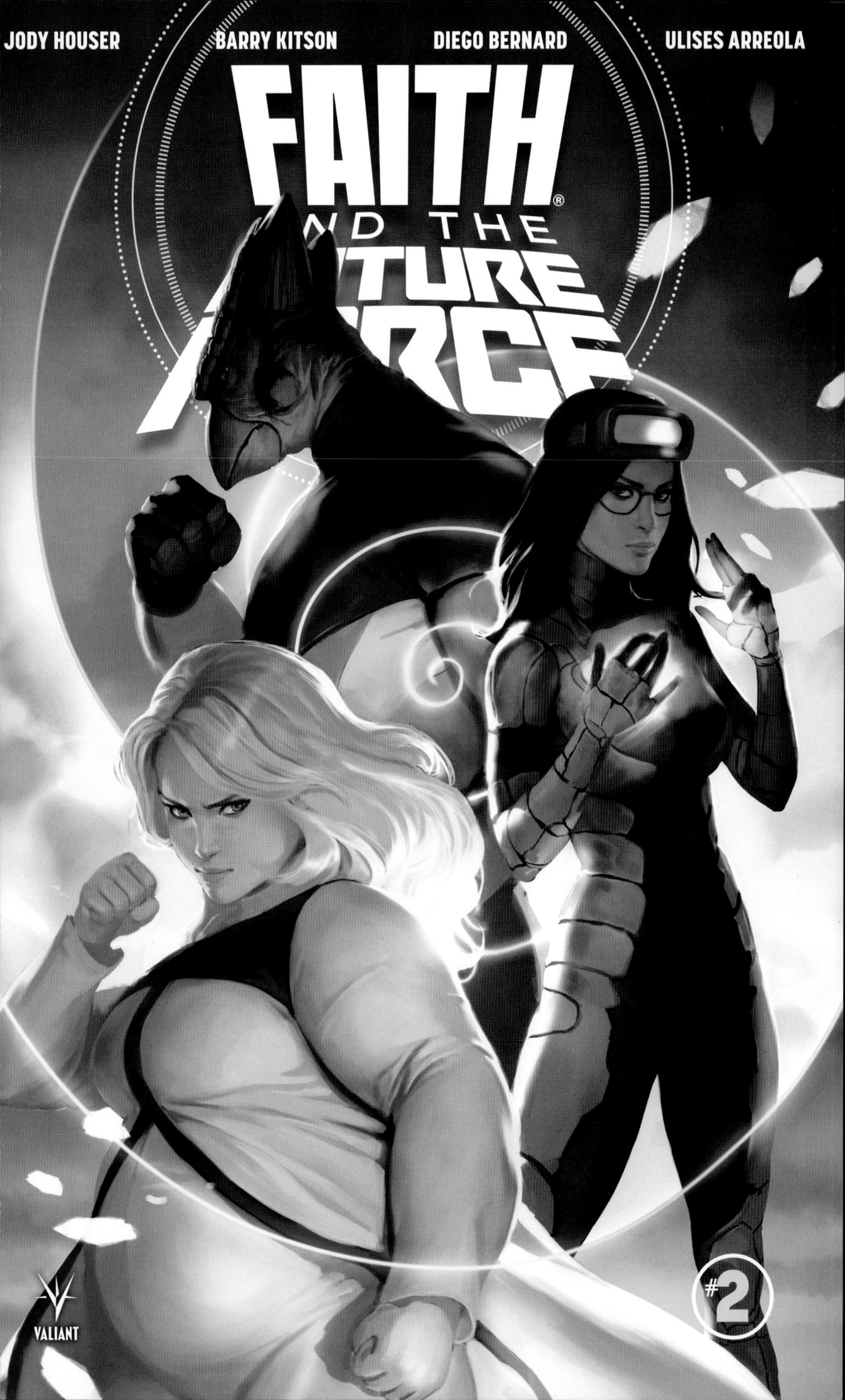
JODY HOUSER
BARRY KITSON
DIEGO BERNARD
ULISES ARREOLA
FAITH
#2
VALIANT

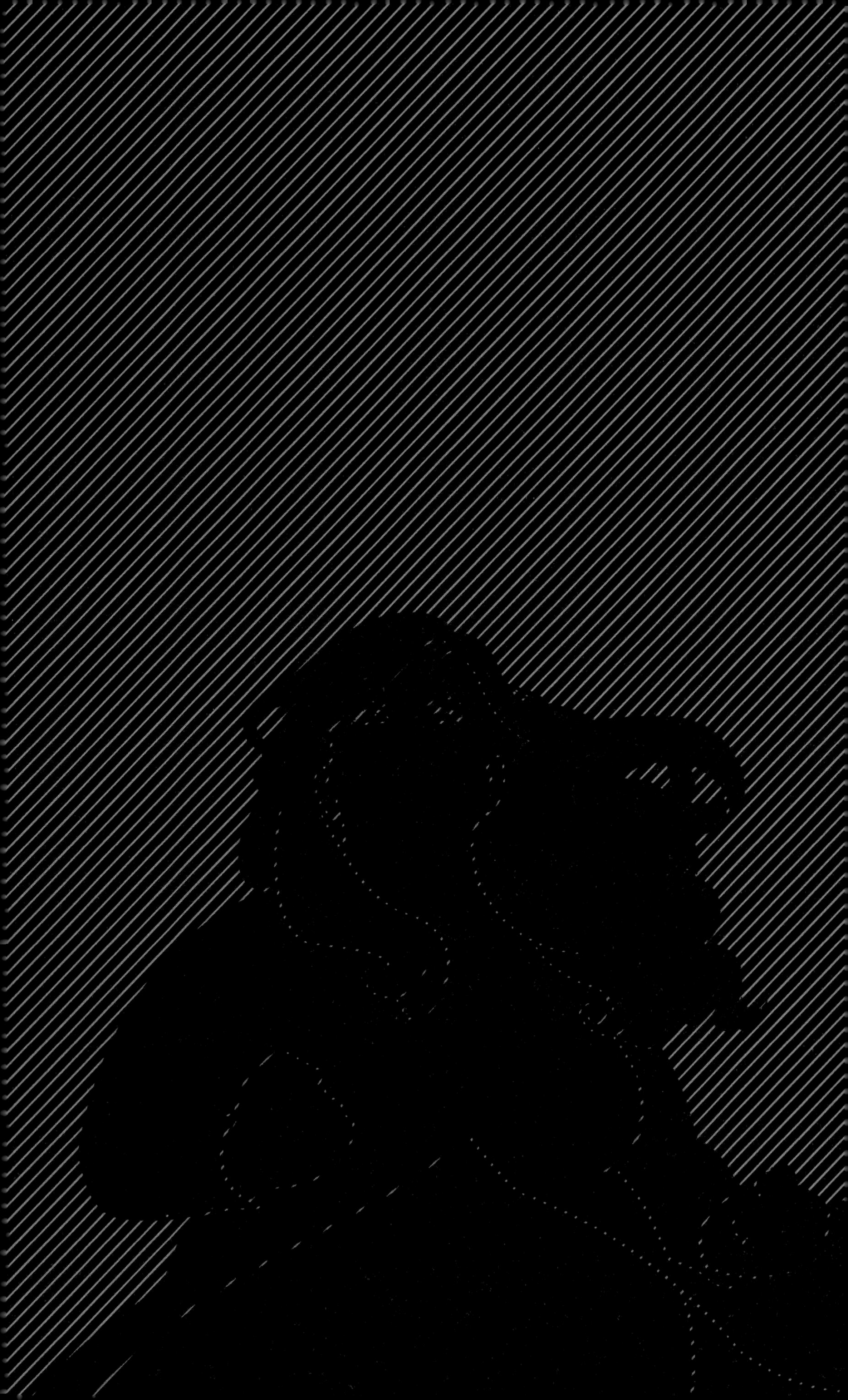

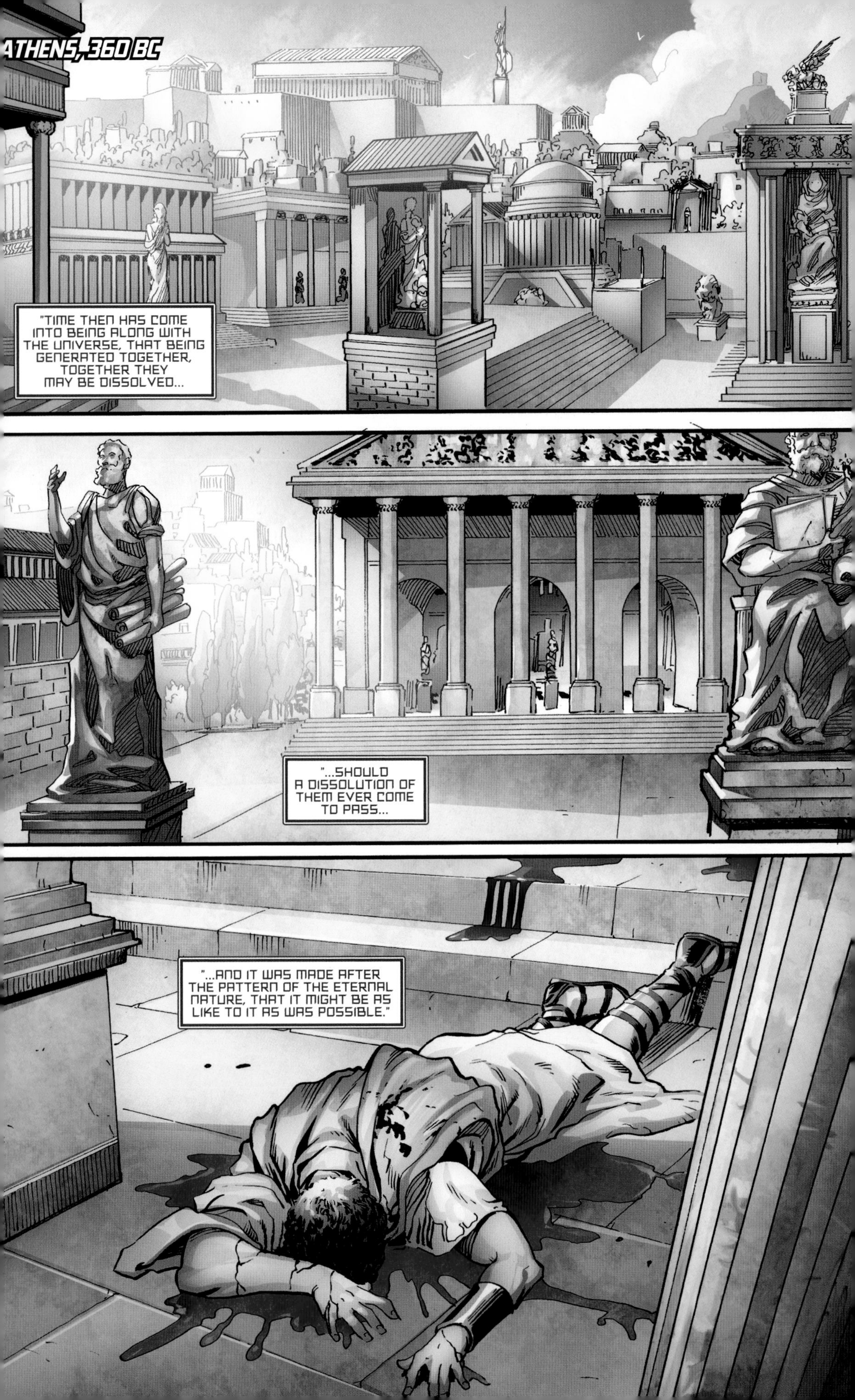
ATHENS, 360 BC
"TIME THEN HAS COME INTO BEING ALONG WITH THE UNIVERSE, THAT BEING GENERATED TOGETHER, TOGETHER THEY MAY BE DISSOLVED...
"...SHOULD A DISSOLUTION OF THEM EVER COME TO PASS...
"...AND IT WAS MADE AFTER THE PATTERN OF THE ETERNAL NATURE, THAT IT MIGHT BE AS LIKE TO IT AS WAS POSSIBLE."

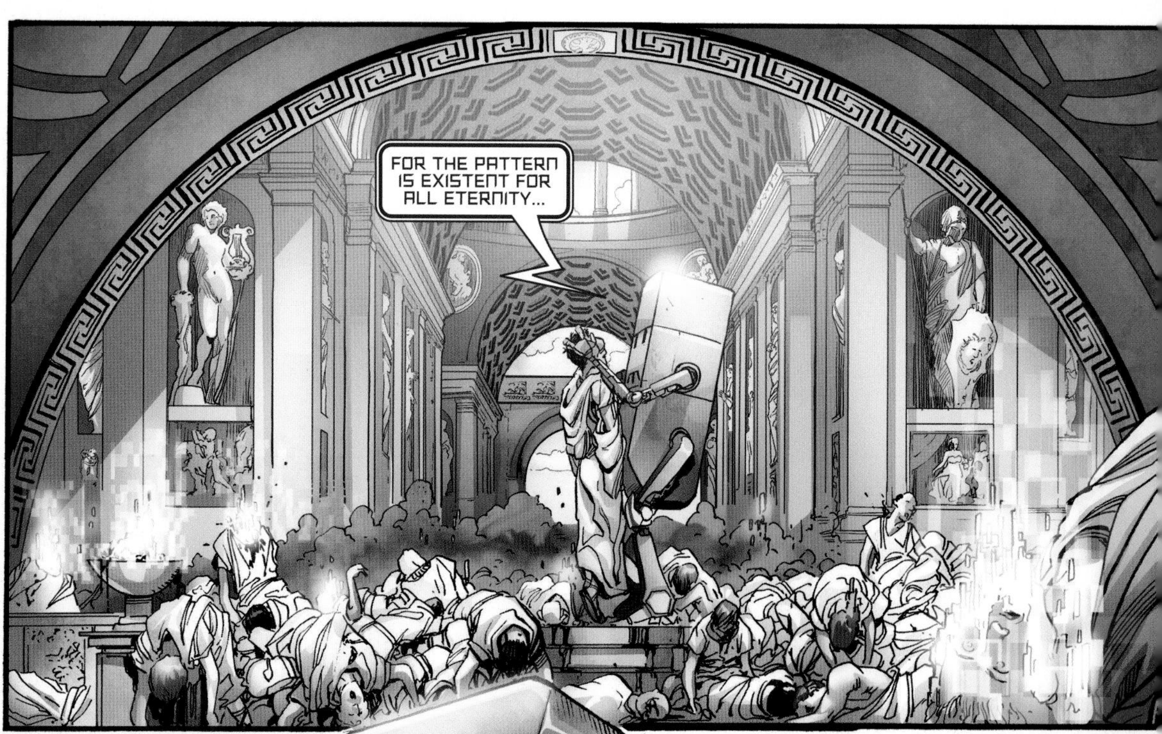
FOR THE PATTERN IS EXISTENT FOR ALL ETERNITY...

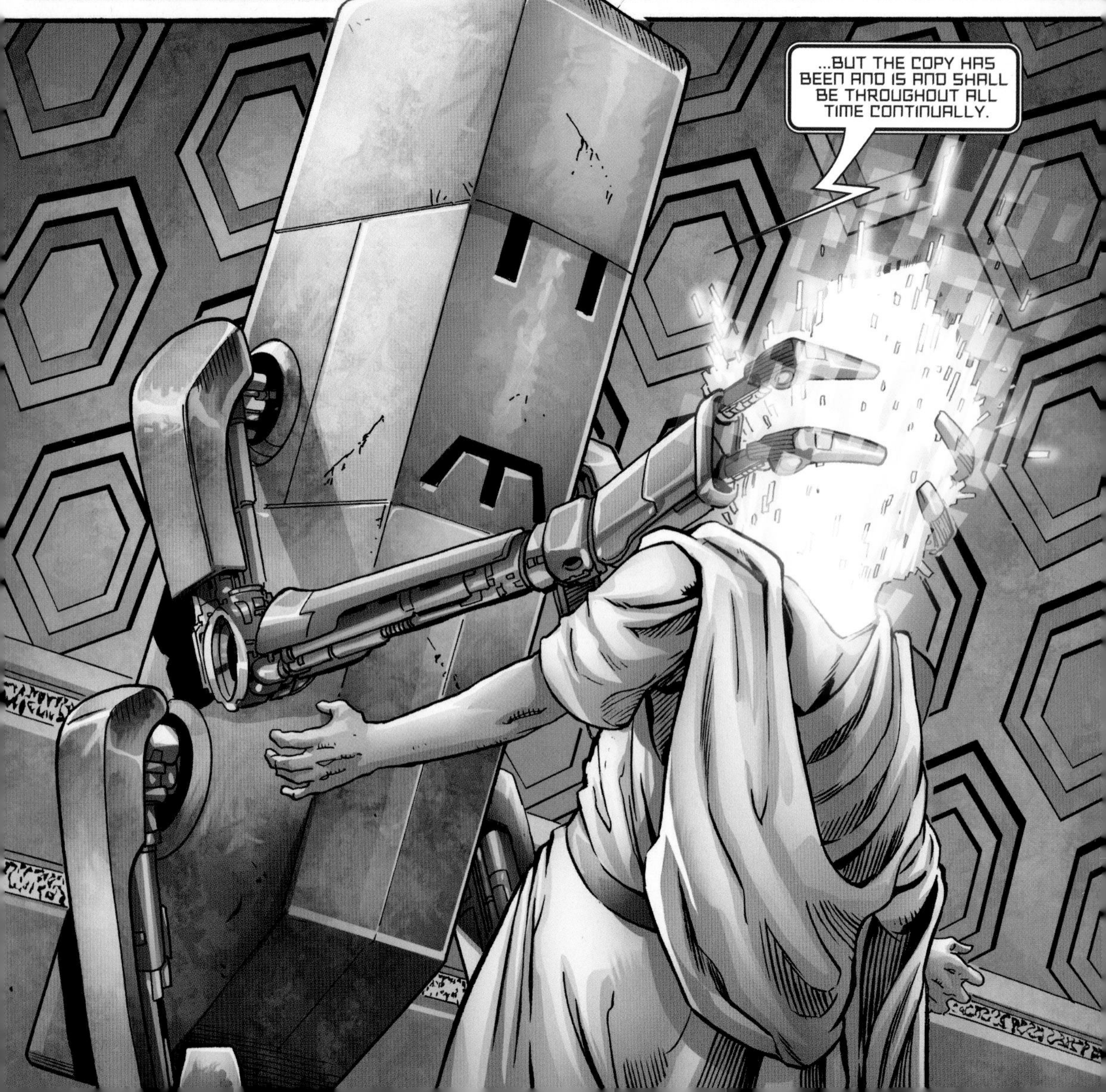
...BUT THE COPY HAS BEEN AND IS AND SHALL BE THROUGHOUT ALL TIME CONTINUALLY.

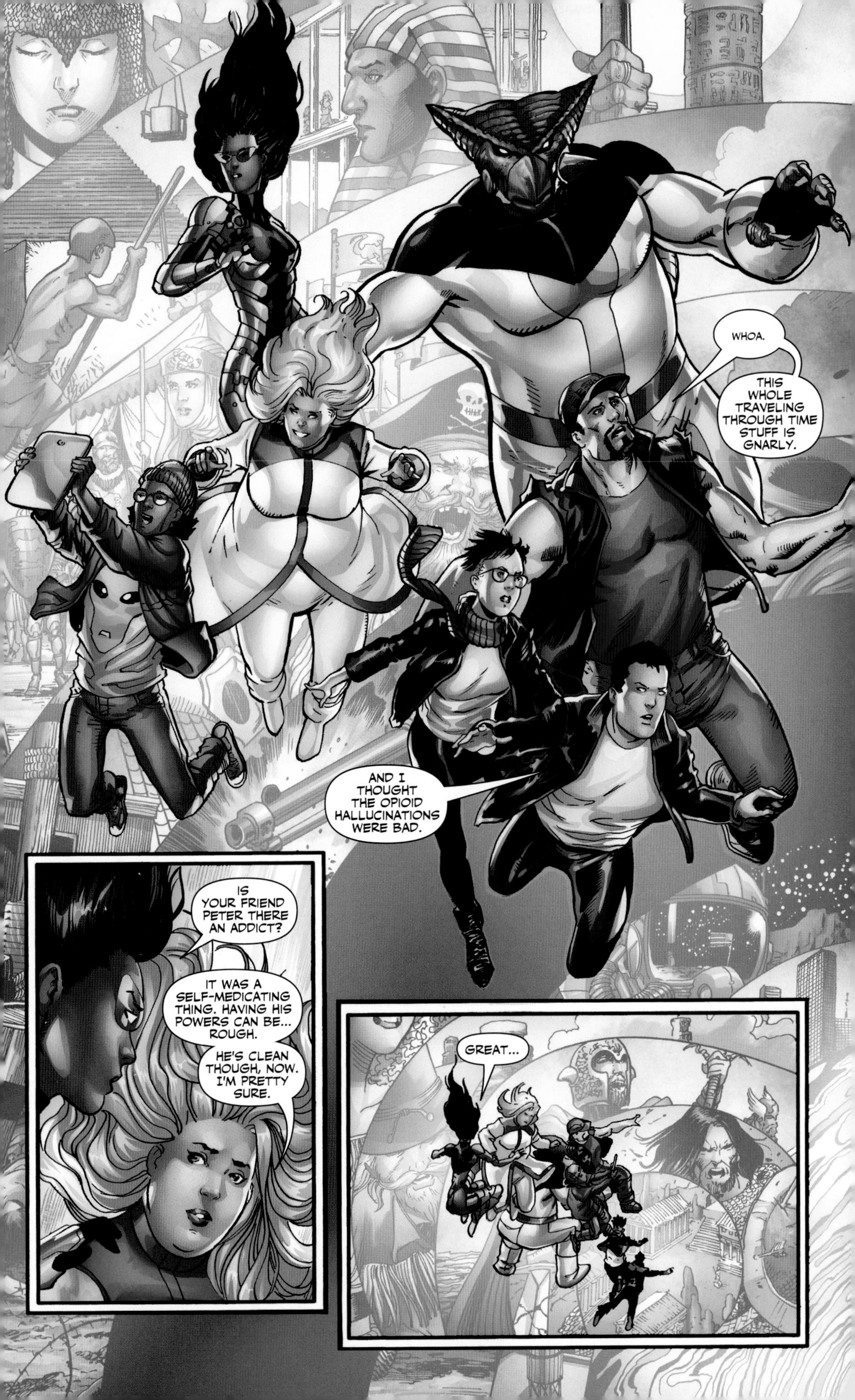
WHOA.
THIS WHOLE TRAVELING THROUGH TIME STUFF IS GNARLY.
AND I THOUGHT THE OPIOID HALLUCINATIONS WERE BAD.
IS YOUR FRIEND PETER THERE AN ADDICT?
IT WAS A SELF-MEDICATING THING. HAVING HIS POWERS CAN BE... ROUGH.
HE'S CLEAN THOUGH, NOW. I'M PRETTY SURE.
GREAT...

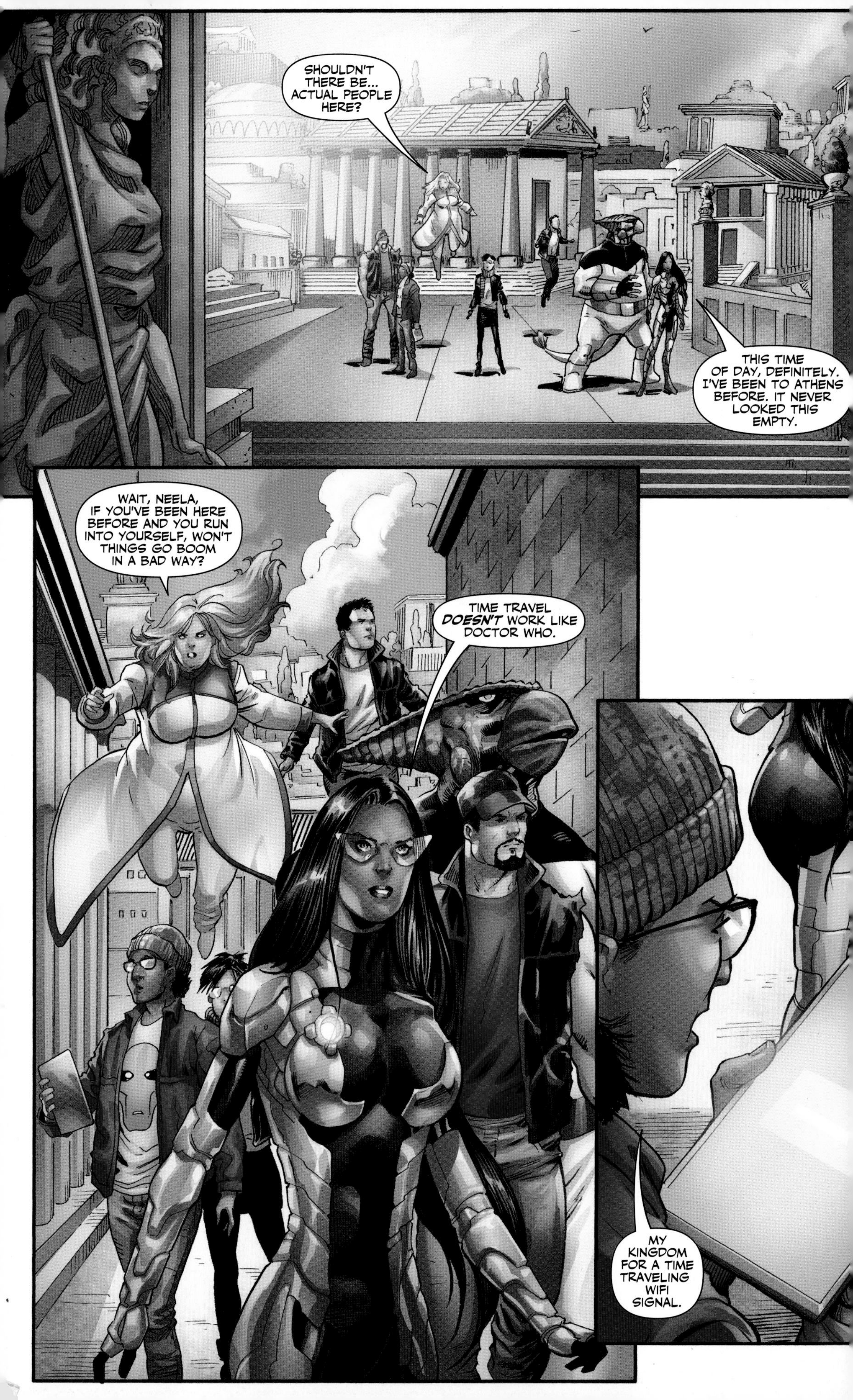
SHOULDN'T THERE BE... ACTUAL PEOPLE HERE?
THIS TIME OF DAY, DEFINITELY. I'VE BEEN TO ATHENS BEFORE. IT NEVER LOOKED THIS EMPTY.
WAIT, NEELA, IF YOU'VE BEEN HERE BEFORE AND YOU RUN INTO YOURSELF, WON'T THINGS GO BOOM IN A BAD WAY?
TIME TRAVEL DOESN'T WORK LIKE DOCTOR WHO.
MY KINGDOM FOR A TIME TRAVELING WIFI SIGNAL.

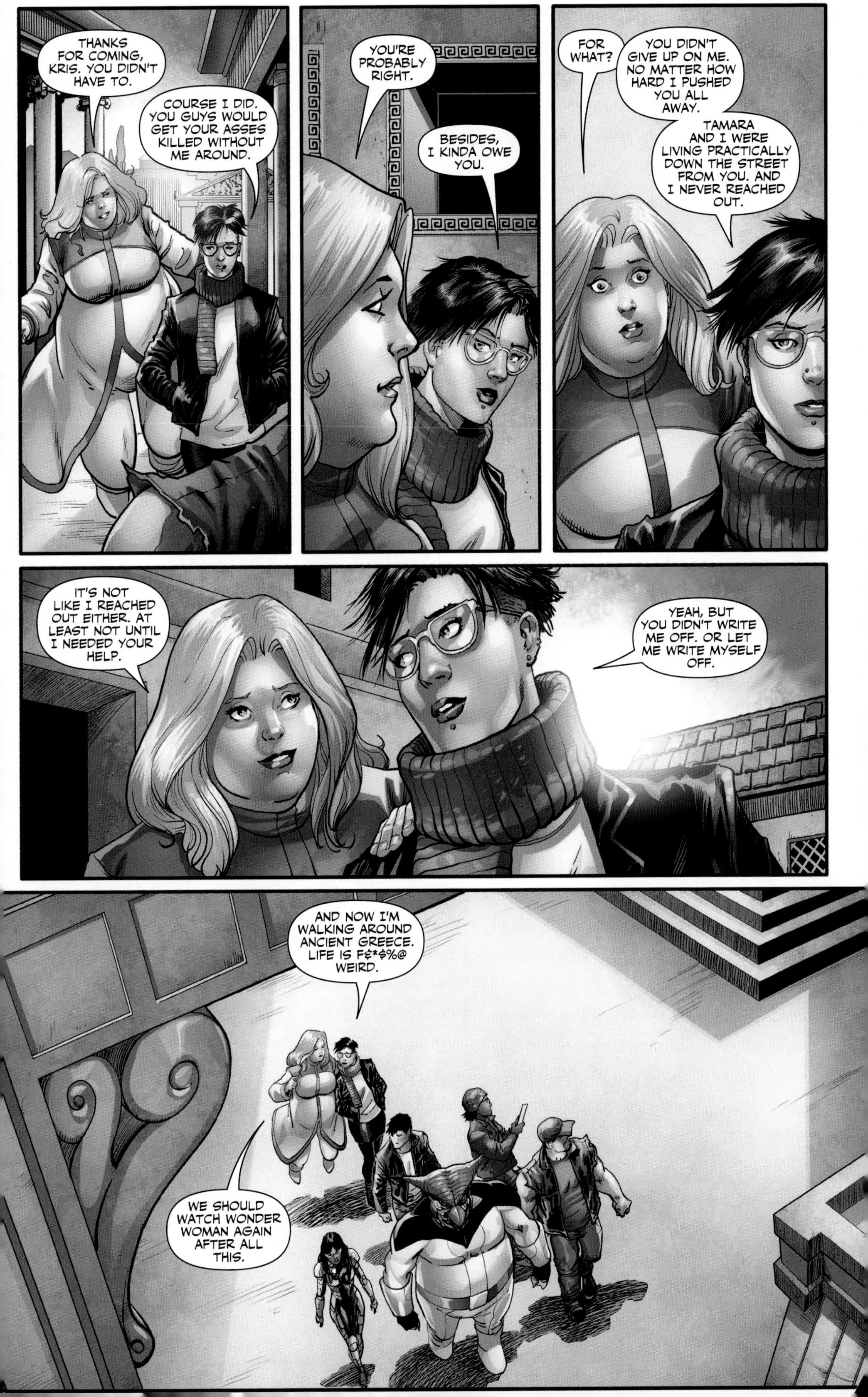
THANKS FOR COMING, KRIS. YOU DIDN'T HAVE TO.
COURSE I DID. YOU GUYS WOULD GET YOUR ASSES KILLED WITHOUT ME AROUND.
YOU'RE PROBABLY RIGHT.
BESIDES, I KINDA OWE YOU.
FOR WHAT?
YOU DIDN'T GIVE UP ON ME. NO MATTER HOW HARD I PUSHED YOU ALL AWAY.
TAMARA AND I WERE LIVING PRACTICALLY DOWN THE STREET FROM YOU. AND I NEVER REACHED OUT.
IT'S NOT LIKE I REACHED OUT EITHER. AT LEAST NOT UNTIL I NEEDED YOUR HELP.
YEAH, BUT YOU DIDN'T WRITE ME OFF. OR LET ME WRITE MYSELF OFF.
AND NOW I'M WALKING AROUND ANCIENT GREECE. LIFE IS F&*$%@ WEIRD.
WE SHOULD WATCH WONDER WOMAN AGAIN AFTER ALL THIS.

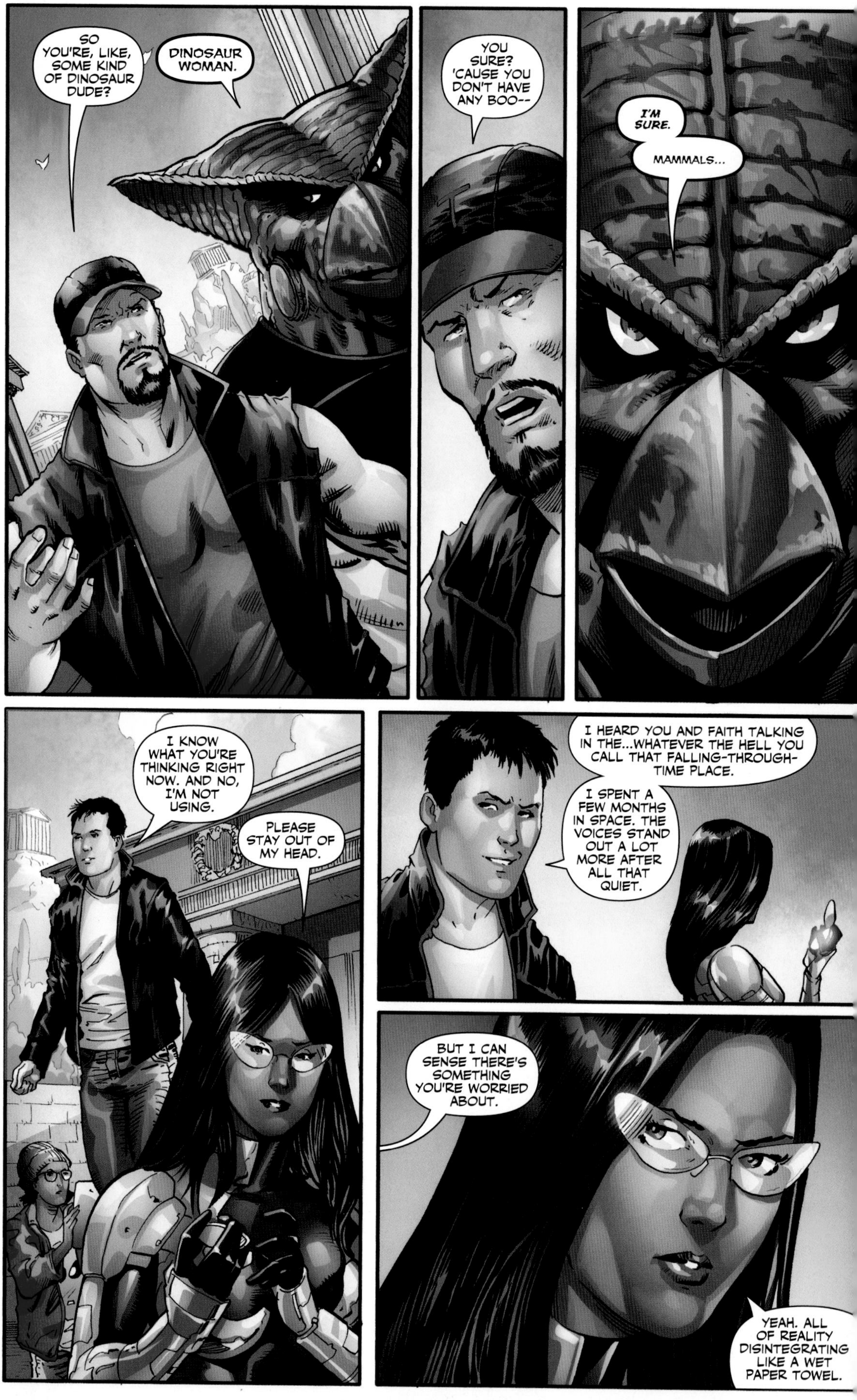
SO YOU'RE, LIKE, SOME KIND OF DINOSAUR DUDE?
DINOSAUR WOMAN.
YOU SURE? 'CAUSE YOU DON'T HAVE ANY BOO--
I'M SURE.
MAMMALS...
I KNOW WHAT YOU'RE THINKING RIGHT NOW. AND NO, I'M NOT USING.
PLEASE STAY OUT OF MY HEAD.
I HEARD YOU AND FAITH TALKING IN THE...WHATEVER THE HELL YOU CALL THAT FALLING-THROUGH-TIME PLACE.
I SPENT A FEW MONTHS IN SPACE. THE VOICES STAND OUT A LOT MORE AFTER ALL THAT QUIET.
BUT I CAN SENSE THERE'S SOMETHING YOU'RE WORRIED ABOUT.
YEAH. ALL OF REALITY DISINTEGRATING LIKE A WET PAPER TOWEL.

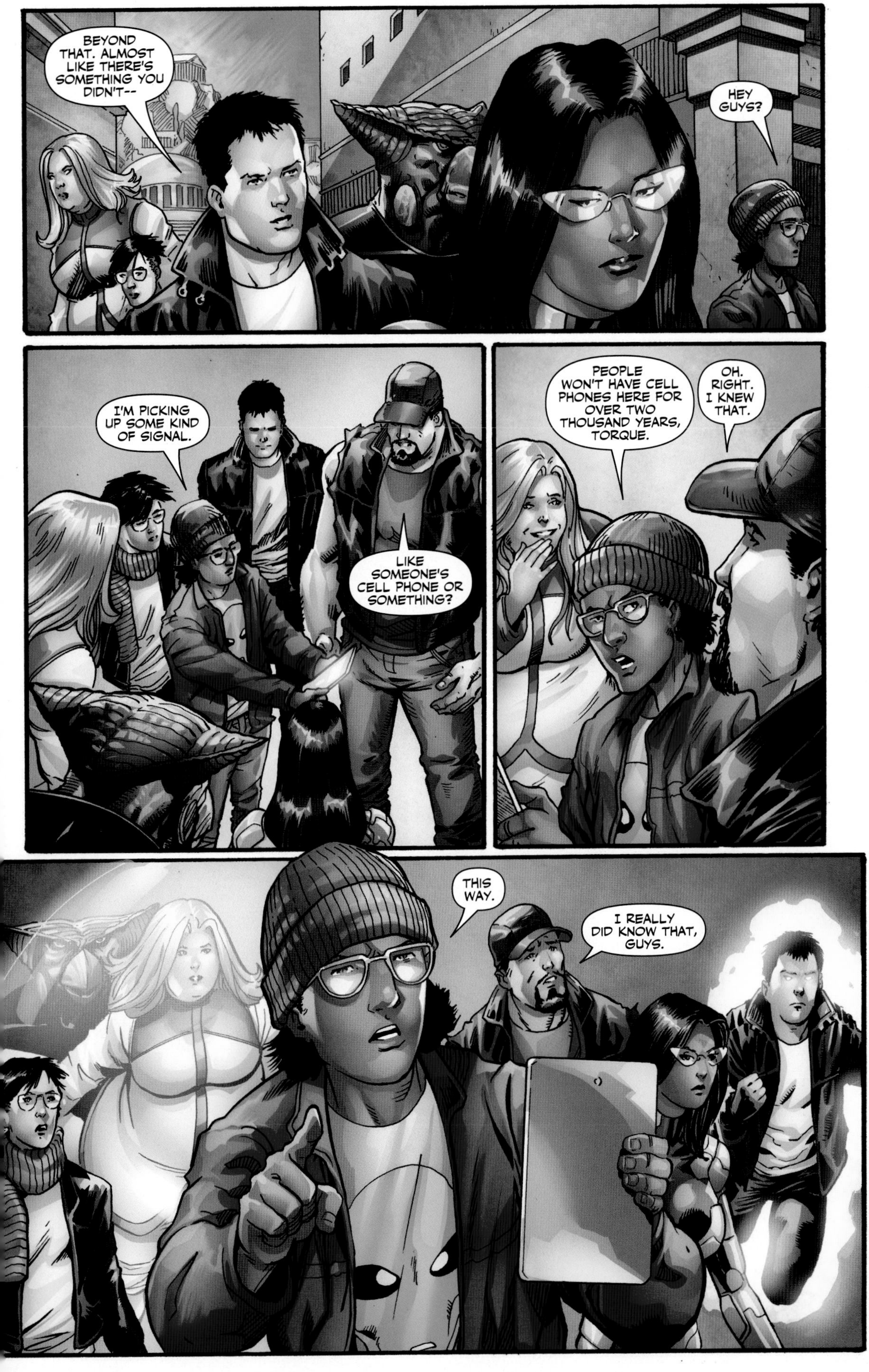
BEYOND THAT. ALMOST LIKE THERE'S SOMETHING YOU DIDN'T--
HEY GUYS?
I'M PICKING UP SOME KIND OF SIGNAL.
LIKE SOMEONE'S CELL PHONE OR SOMETHING?
PEOPLE WON'T HAVE CELL PHONES HERE FOR OVER TWO THOUSAND YEARS, TORQUE.
OH. RIGHT. I KNEW THAT.
THIS WAY.
I REALLY DID KNOW THAT, GUYS.

WE'RE GETTING CLOSE.

IT'S QUIET. I'M NOT HEARING ANYONE BESIDES US.

I'LL TAKE A LOOK. YOU GUYS WAIT HERE.

UH, I'M KIND OF INVULNERABLE AND STUFF. MAYBE I SHOULD BE FIRST TO--

NO, TORQUE. I'M THE ONE WHO BROUGHT YOU ALL HERE.

BUT IT WASN'T SO YOU COULD TAKE ALL THE RISK. IT'S SO TOGETHER WE CAN--

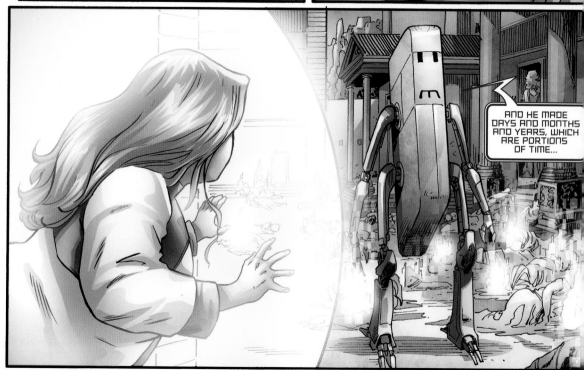

AND HE MADE DAYS AND MONTHS AND YEARS, WHICH ARE PORTIONS OF TIME...

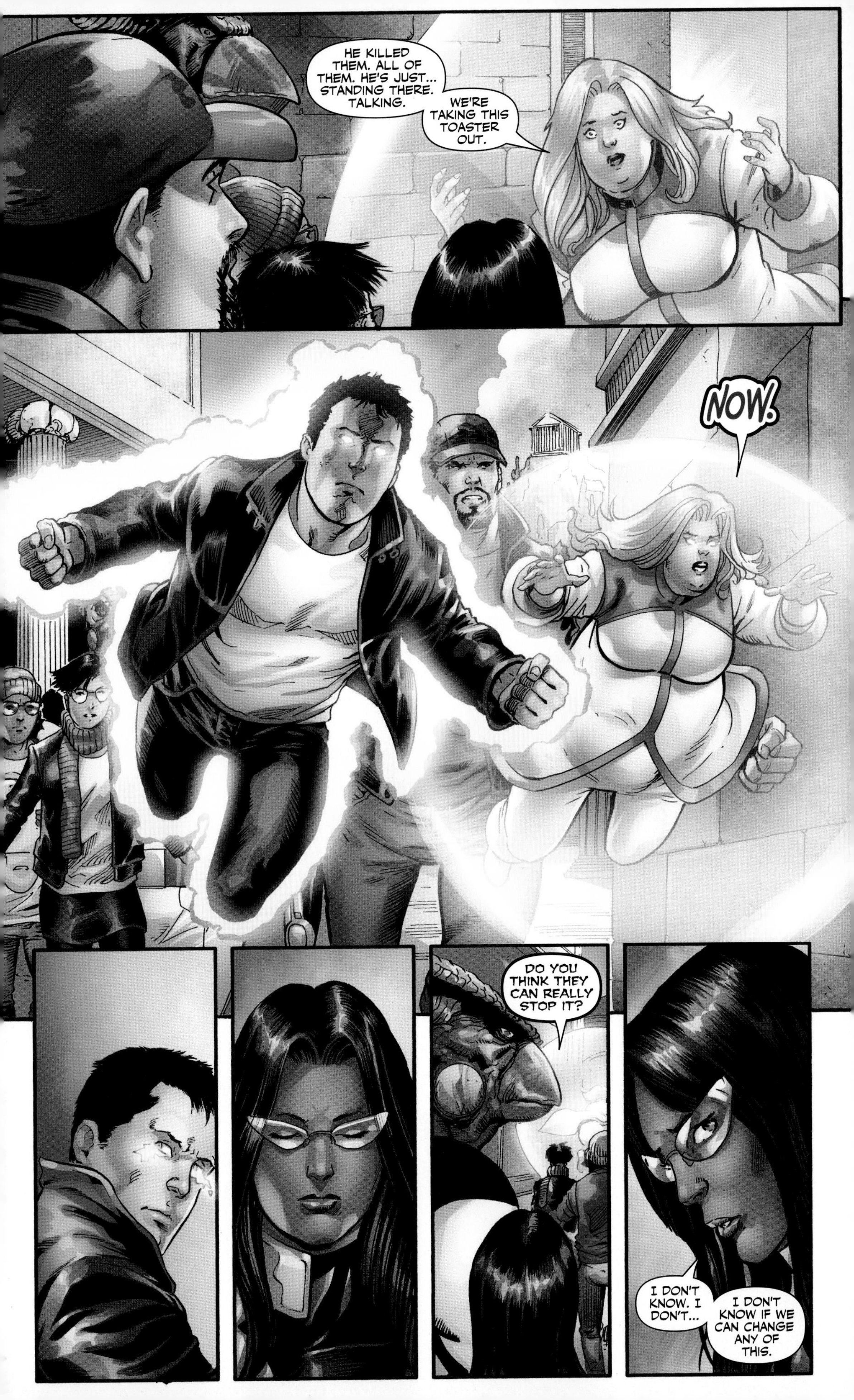
HE KILLED THEM. ALL OF THEM. HE'S JUST... STANDING THERE. TALKING.
WE'RE TAKING THIS TOASTER OUT.
NOW.
DO YOU THINK THEY CAN REALLY STOP IT?
I DON'T KNOW. I DON'T...
I DON'T KNOW IF WE CAN CHANGE ANY OF THIS.

"BECAUSE I DON'T KNOW HOW THAT *THING* IS CHANGING ALL OF THIS."

THIS ENDS RIGHT NOW.

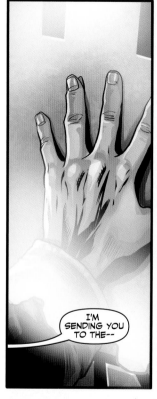

I'M SENDING YOU TO THE--

GAAAAAAAAAAAAAH!

...AND PAST AND FUTURE ARE FORMS OF TIME, THOUGH WE WRONGLY ATTRIBUTE THEM ALSO TO ETERNITY.

UUGH! UUGH! UUGH! UUGH!

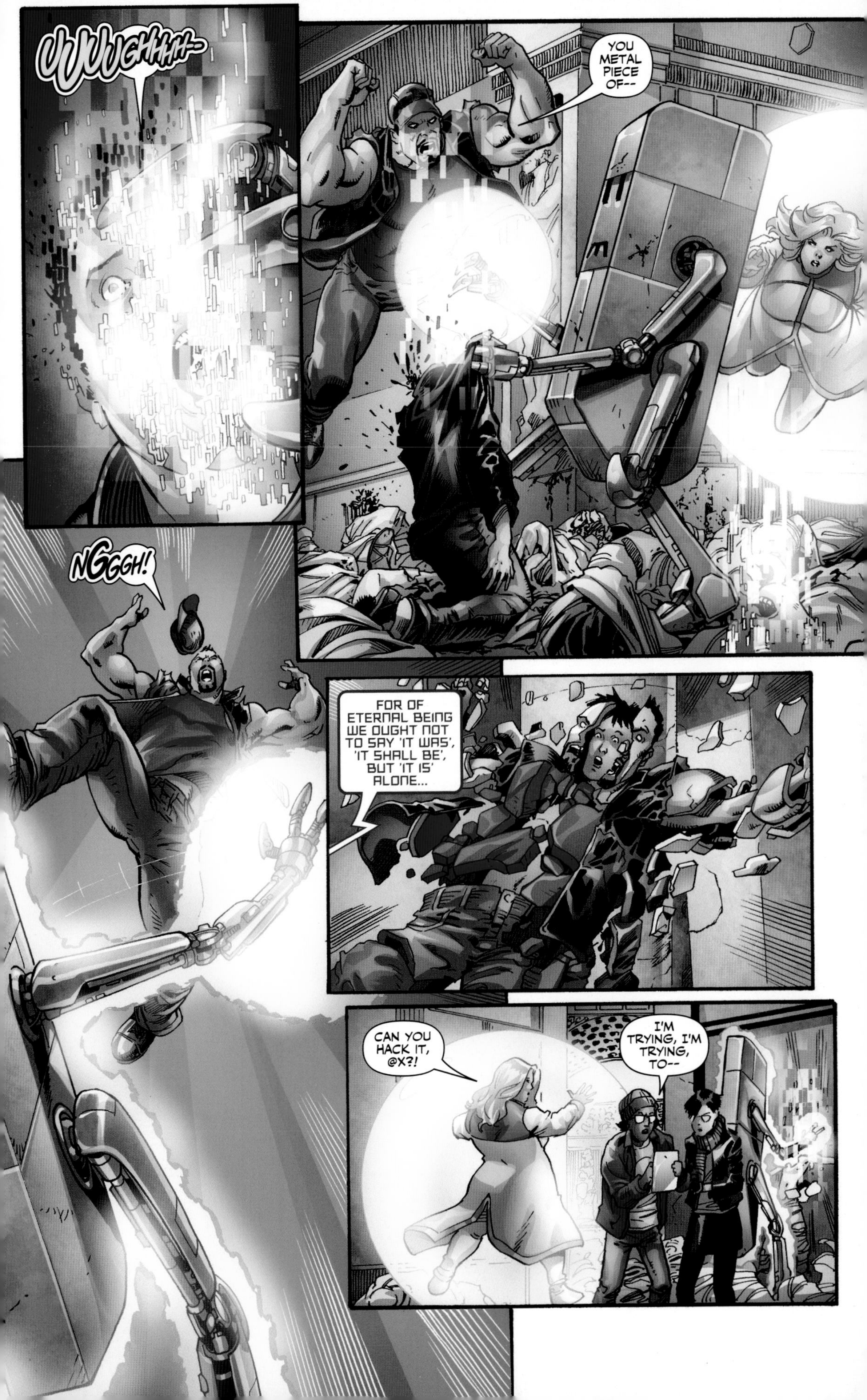
UUUUGHHHH-
YOU METAL PIECE OF--
NGGGH!
FOR OF ETERNAL BEING WE OUGHT NOT TO SAY 'IT WAS', 'IT SHALL BE', BUT 'IT IS' ALONE...
CAN YOU HACK IT, @X?!
I'M TRYING, I'M TRYING, TO--

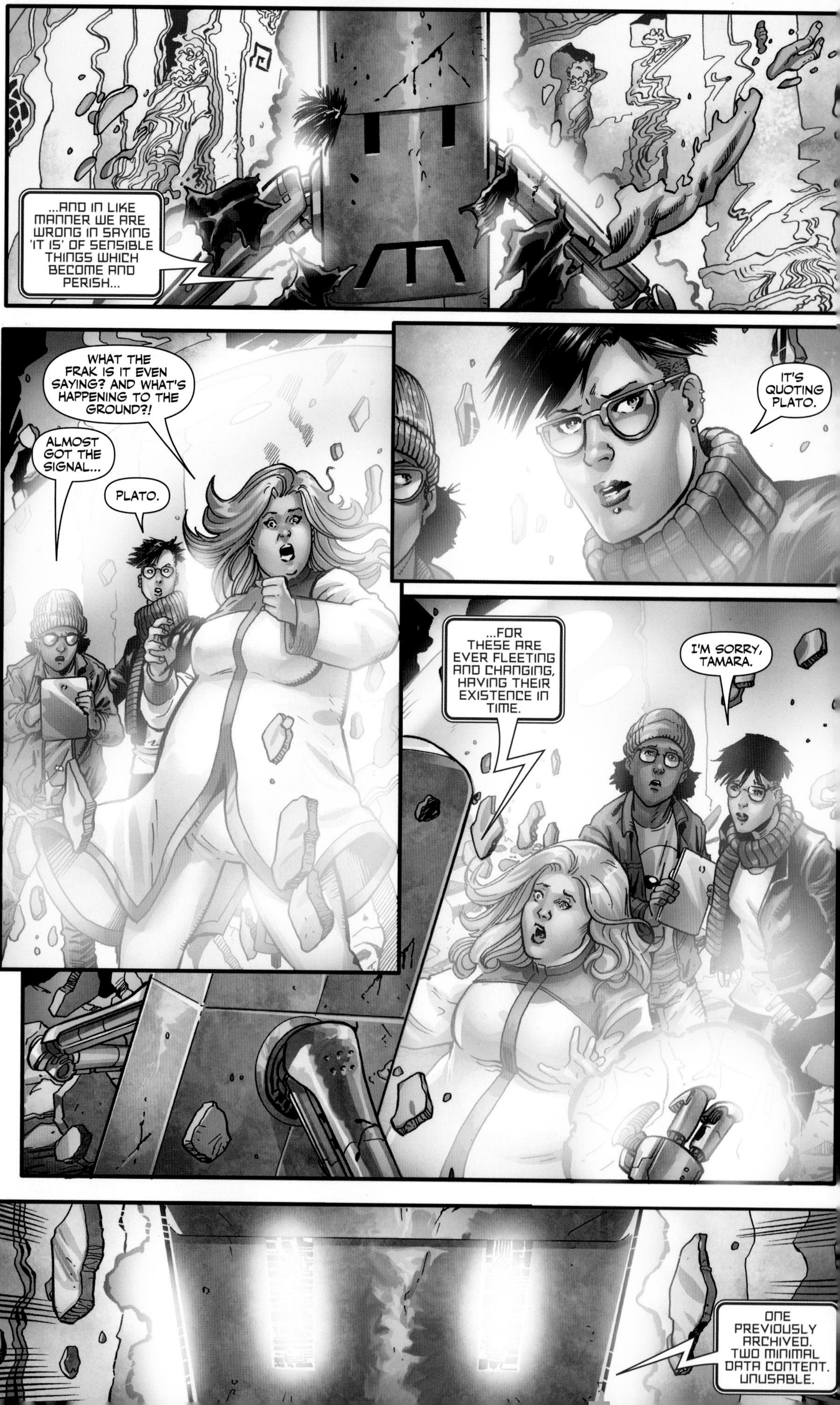
...AND IN LIKE MANNER WE ARE WRONG IN SAYING 'IT IS' OF SENSIBLE THINGS WHICH BECOME AND PERISH...
WHAT THE FRAK IS IT EVEN SAYING? AND WHAT'S HAPPENING TO THE GROUND?!
ALMOST GOT THE SIGNAL...
PLATO.
IT'S QUOTING PLATO.
...FOR THESE ARE EVER FLEETING AND CHANGING, HAVING THEIR EXISTENCE IN TIME.
I'M SORRY, TAMARA.
ONE PREVIOUSLY ARCHIVED. TWO MINIMAL DATA CONTENT. UNUSABLE.

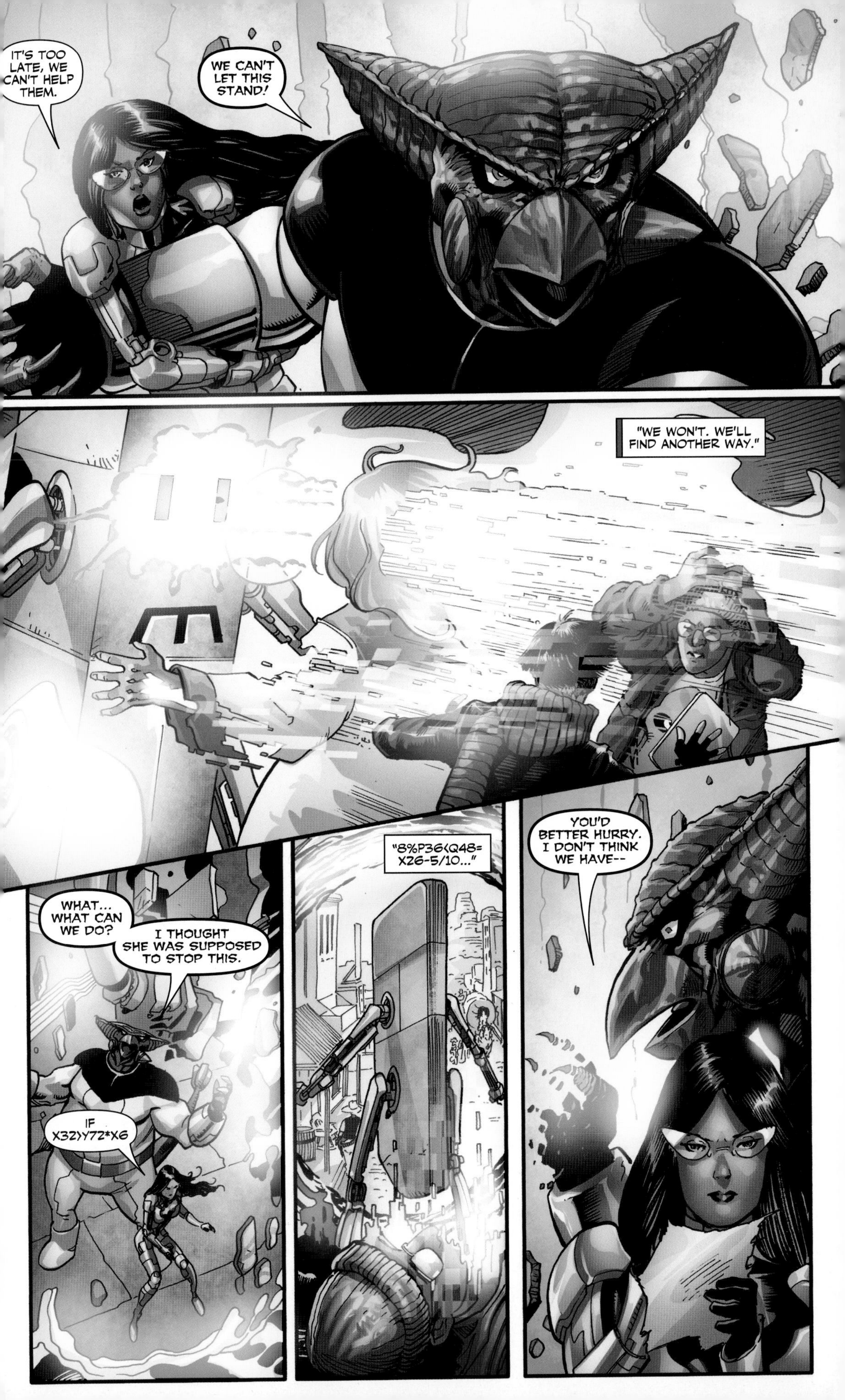
IT'S TOO LATE, WE CAN'T HELP THEM.
WE CAN'T LET THIS STAND!
"WE WON'T. WE'LL FIND ANOTHER WAY."
WHAT... WHAT CAN WE DO?
I THOUGHT SHE WAS SUPPOSED TO STOP THIS.
IF X32>Y72*X6
"8%P36<Q48= X26-5/10..."
YOU'D BETTER HURRY. I DON'T THINK WE HAVE--

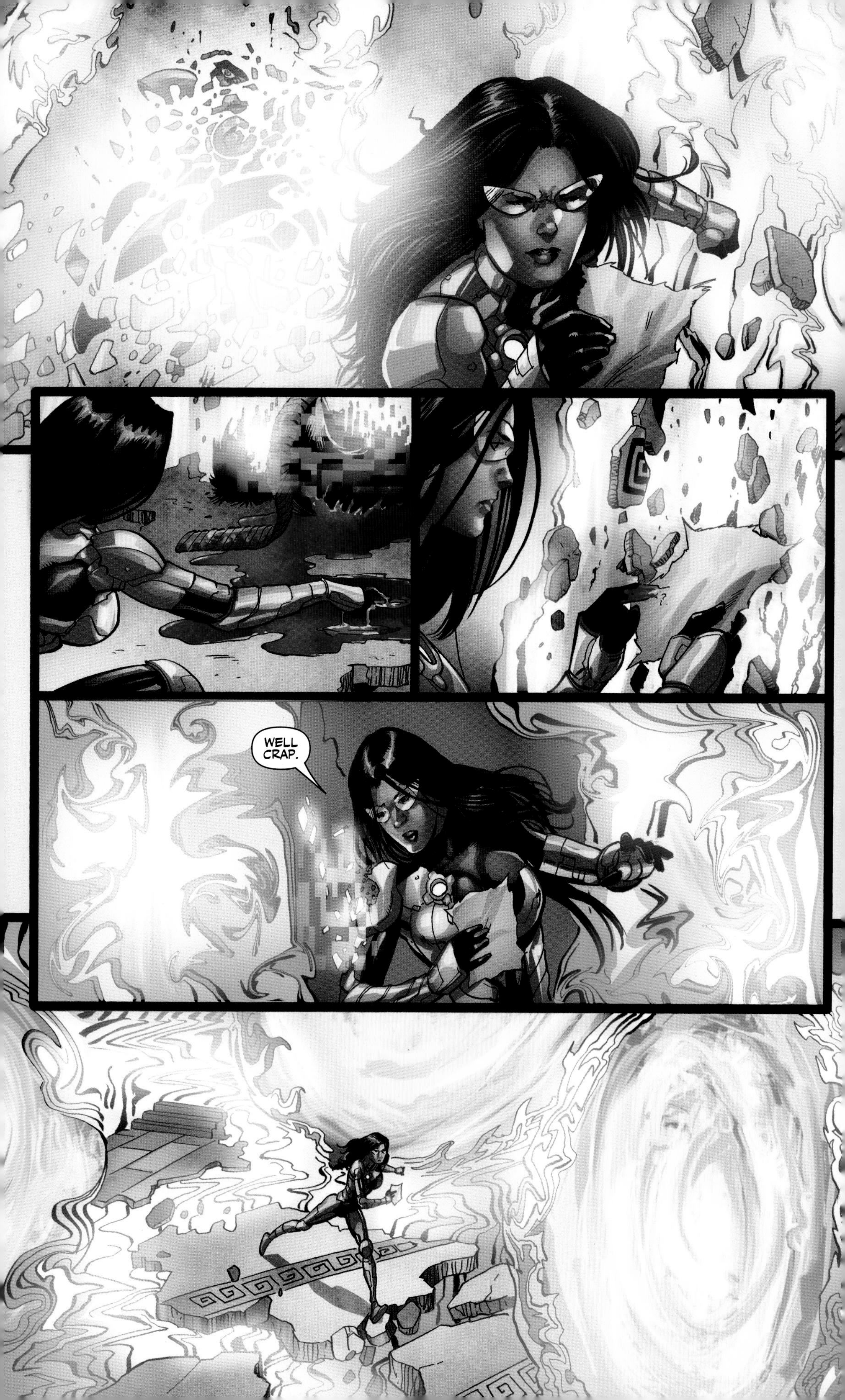
WELL CRAP.

IN A SCIENTIFIC SENSE, WHOEVER DISRUPTED THE AMERICAN CIVIL WAR VIOLATED THE LAWS OF--

BUT THERE SHOULDN'T...

EVIL ROBOT UNMAKING TIME! TAKING REALITY APART!

THE RENEGADES AREN'T ENOUGH! YOU NEED MORE TO--

Faith Herbert is not enough

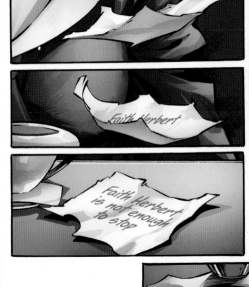

Faith Herbert

Faith Herbert is not enough to stop

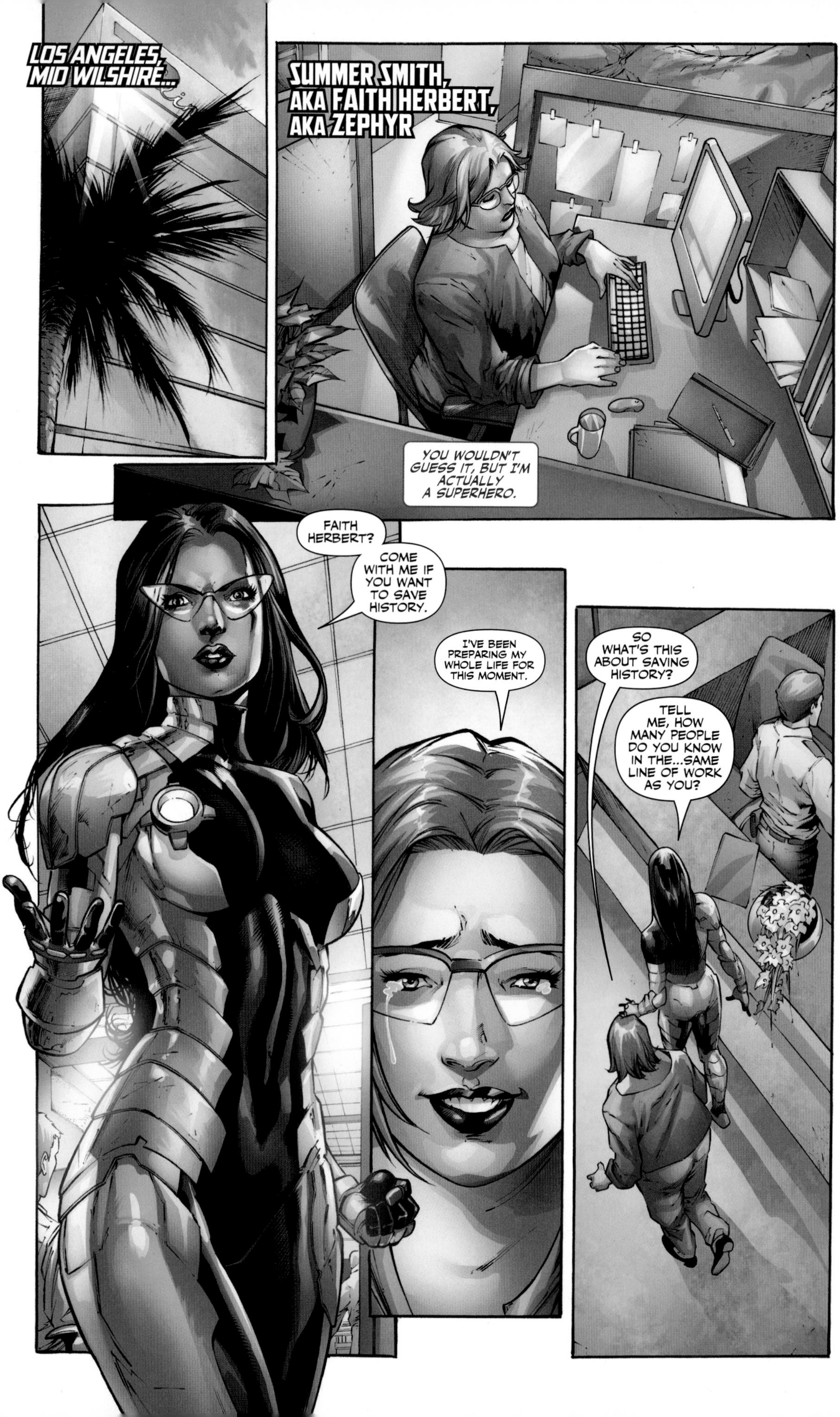
LOS ANGELES, MID WILSHIRE...
SUMMER SMITH, AKA FAITH HERBERT, AKA ZEPHYR
YOU WOULDN'T GUESS IT, BUT I'M ACTUALLY A SUPERHERO.
FAITH HERBERT?
COME WITH ME IF YOU WANT TO SAVE HISTORY.
I'VE BEEN PREPARING MY WHOLE LIFE FOR THIS MOMENT.
SO WHAT'S THIS ABOUT SAVING HISTORY?
TELL ME, HOW MANY PEOPLE DO YOU KNOW IN THE...SAME LINE OF WORK AS YOU?

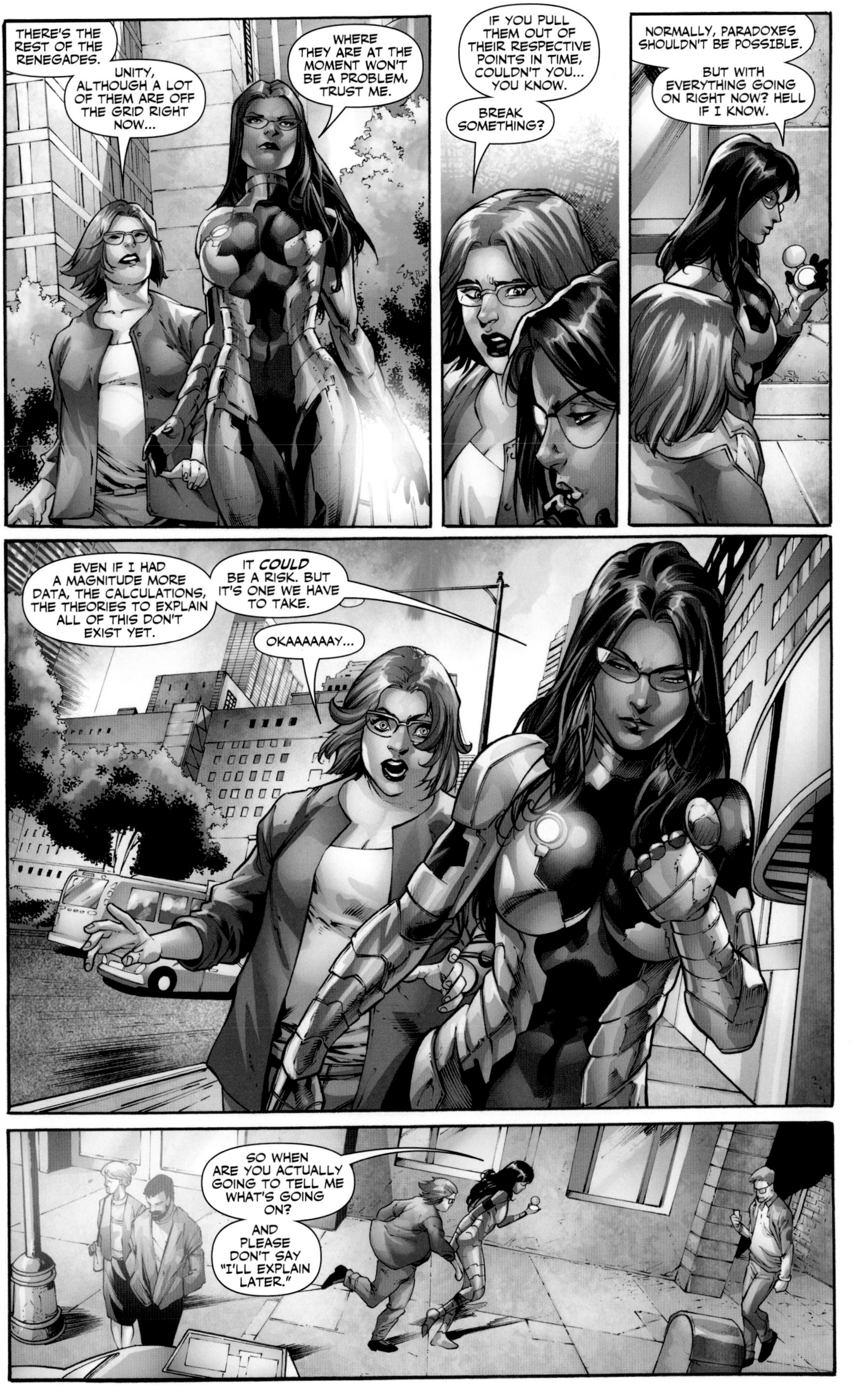
THERE'S THE REST OF THE RENEGADES.
UNITY, ALTHOUGH A LOT OF THEM ARE OFF THE GRID RIGHT NOW...
WHERE THEY ARE AT THE MOMENT WON'T BE A PROBLEM, TRUST ME.
IF YOU PULL THEM OUT OF THEIR RESPECTIVE POINTS IN TIME, COULDN'T YOU... YOU KNOW.
BREAK SOMETHING?
NORMALLY, PARADOXES SHOULDN'T BE POSSIBLE.
BUT WITH EVERYTHING GOING ON RIGHT NOW? HELL IF I KNOW.
EVEN IF I HAD A MAGNITUDE MORE DATA, THE CALCULATIONS, THE THEORIES TO EXPLAIN ALL OF THIS DON'T EXIST YET.
IT *COULD* BE A RISK. BUT IT'S ONE WE HAVE TO TAKE.
OKAAAAAAY...
SO WHEN ARE YOU ACTUALLY GOING TO TELL ME WHAT'S GOING ON?
AND PLEASE DON'T SAY "I'LL EXPLAIN LATER."

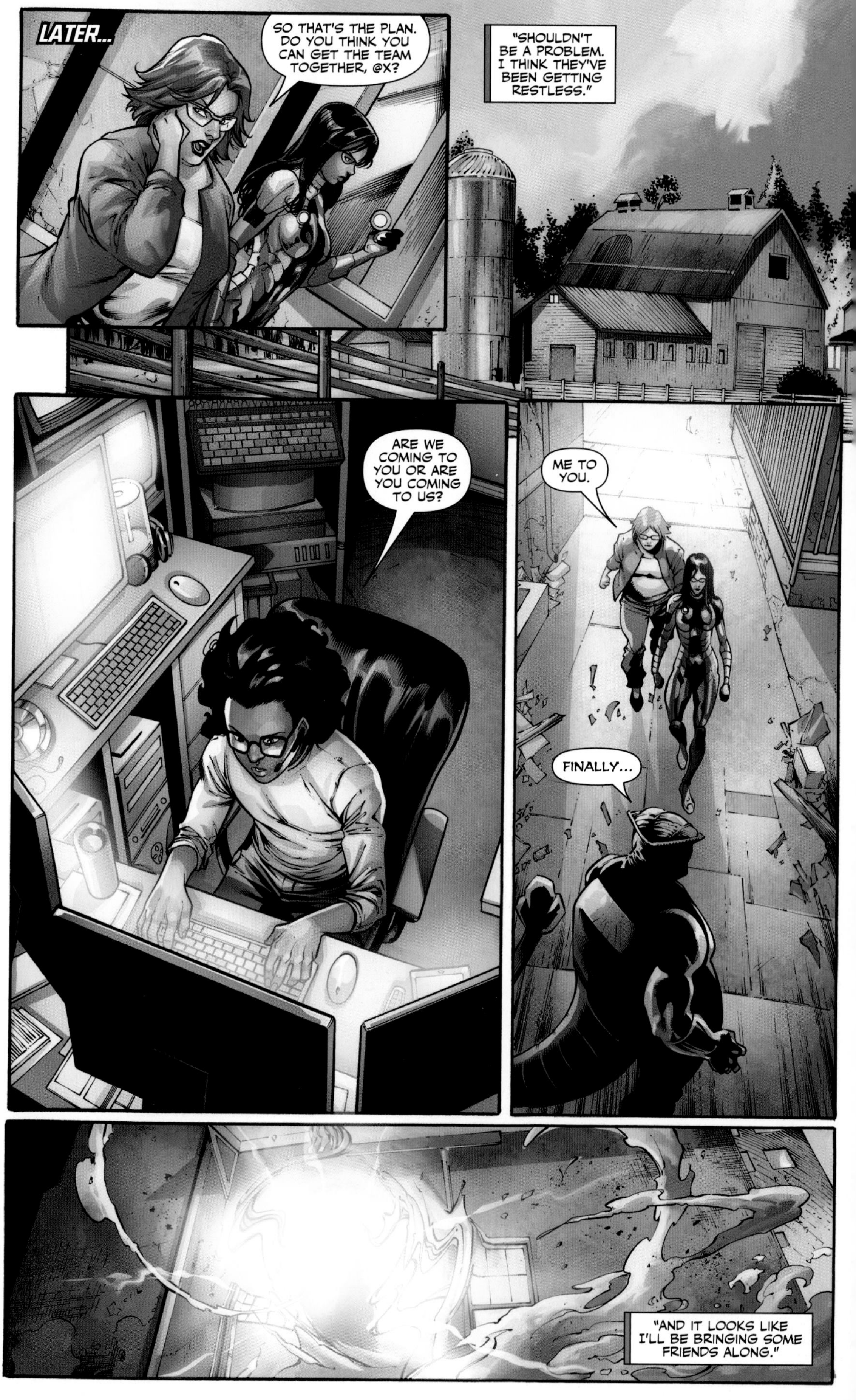
LATER...
SO THAT'S THE PLAN. DO YOU THINK YOU CAN GET THE TEAM TOGETHER, @X?
"SHOULDN'T BE A PROBLEM. I THINK THEY'VE BEEN GETTING RESTLESS."
ARE WE COMING TO YOU OR ARE YOU COMING TO US?
ME TO YOU.
FINALLY...
"AND IT LOOKS LIKE I'LL BE BRINGING SOME FRIENDS ALONG."

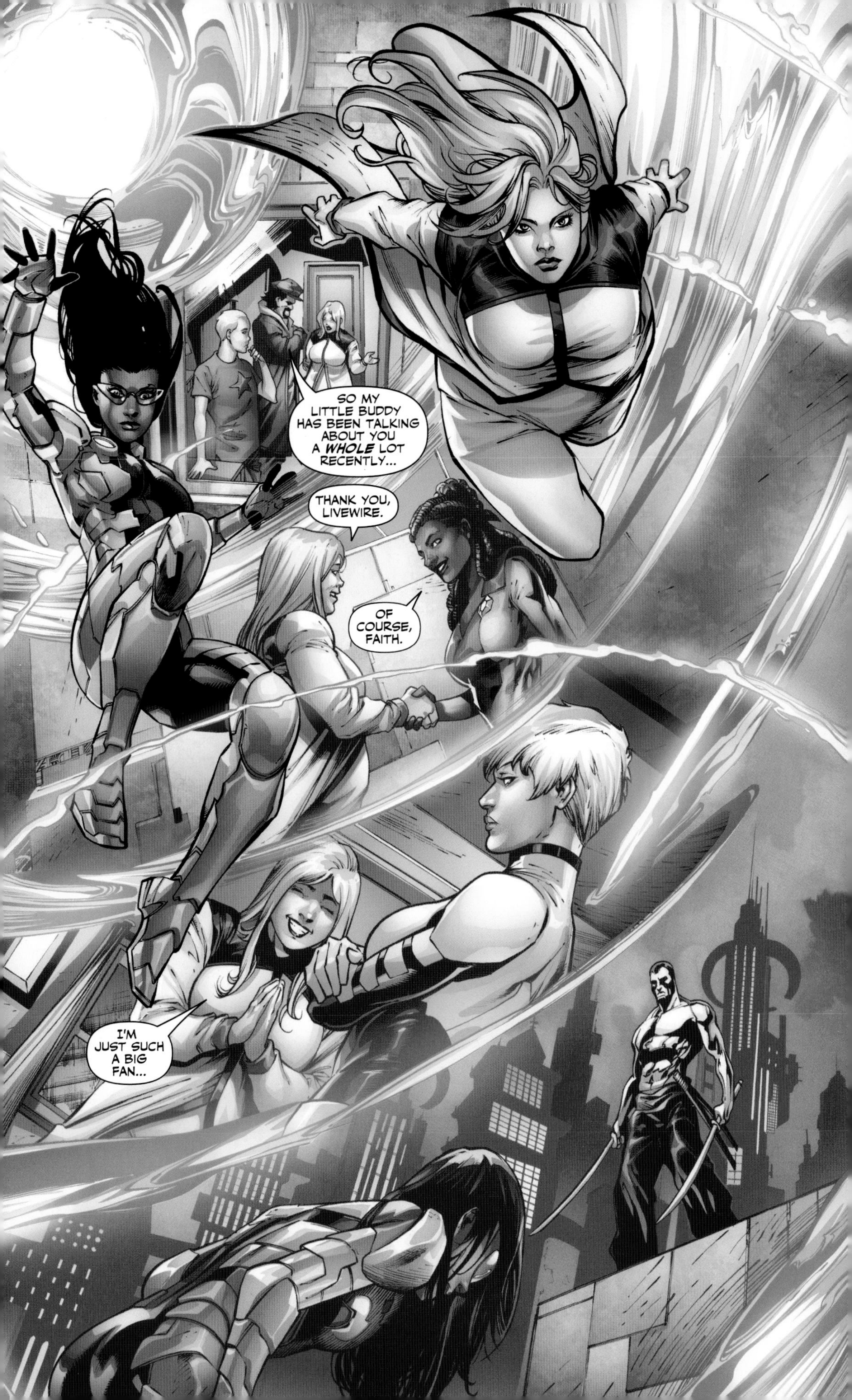
SO MY LITTLE BUDDY HAS BEEN TALKING ABOUT YOU A *WHOLE* LOT RECENTLY...
THANK YOU, LIVEWIRE.
OF COURSE, FAITH.
I'M JUST SUCH A BIG FAN...

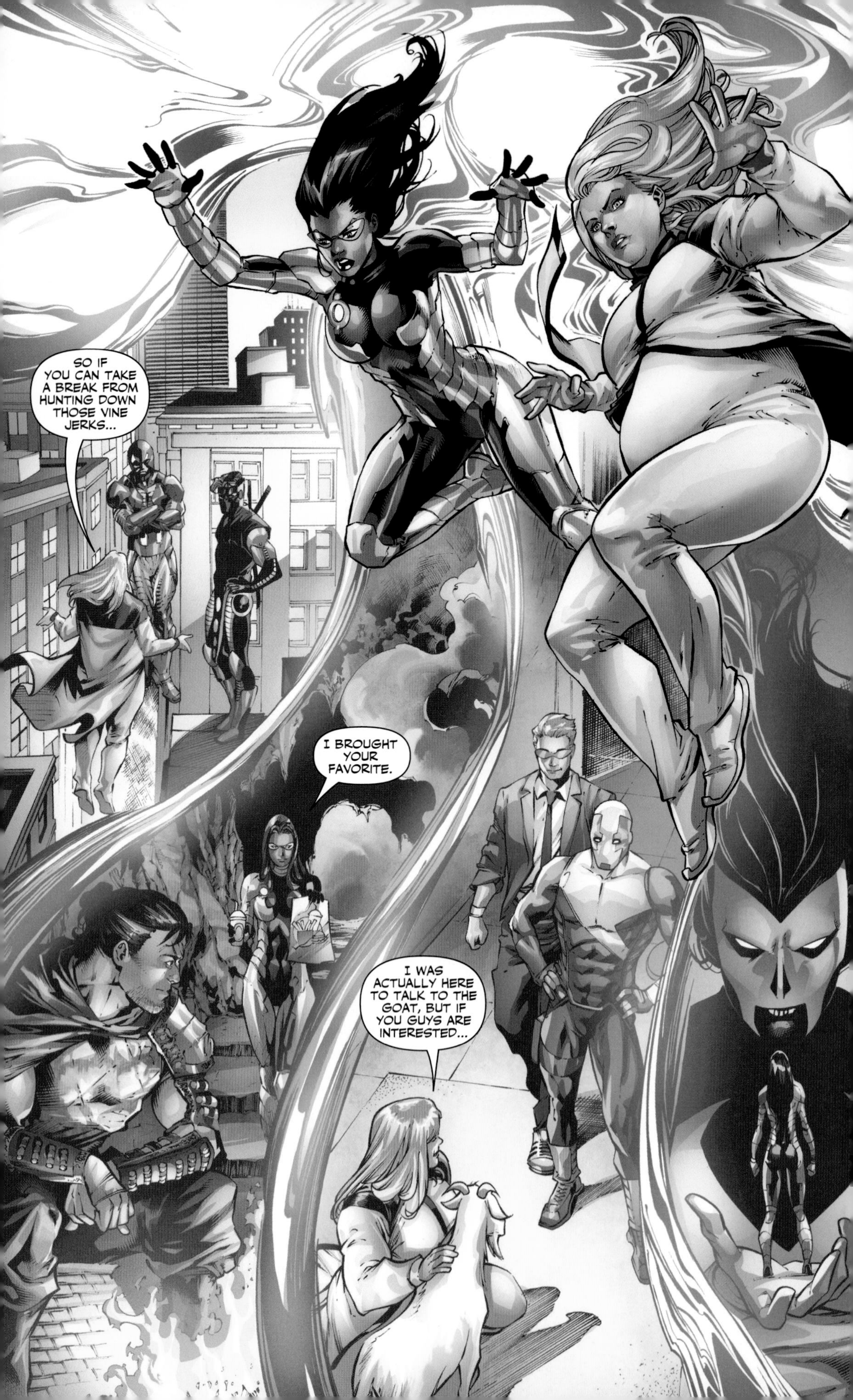
SO IF YOU CAN TAKE A BREAK FROM HUNTING DOWN THOSE VINE JERKS...
I BROUGHT YOUR FAVORITE.
I WAS ACTUALLY HERE TO TALK TO THE GOAT, BUT IF YOU GUYS ARE INTERESTED...

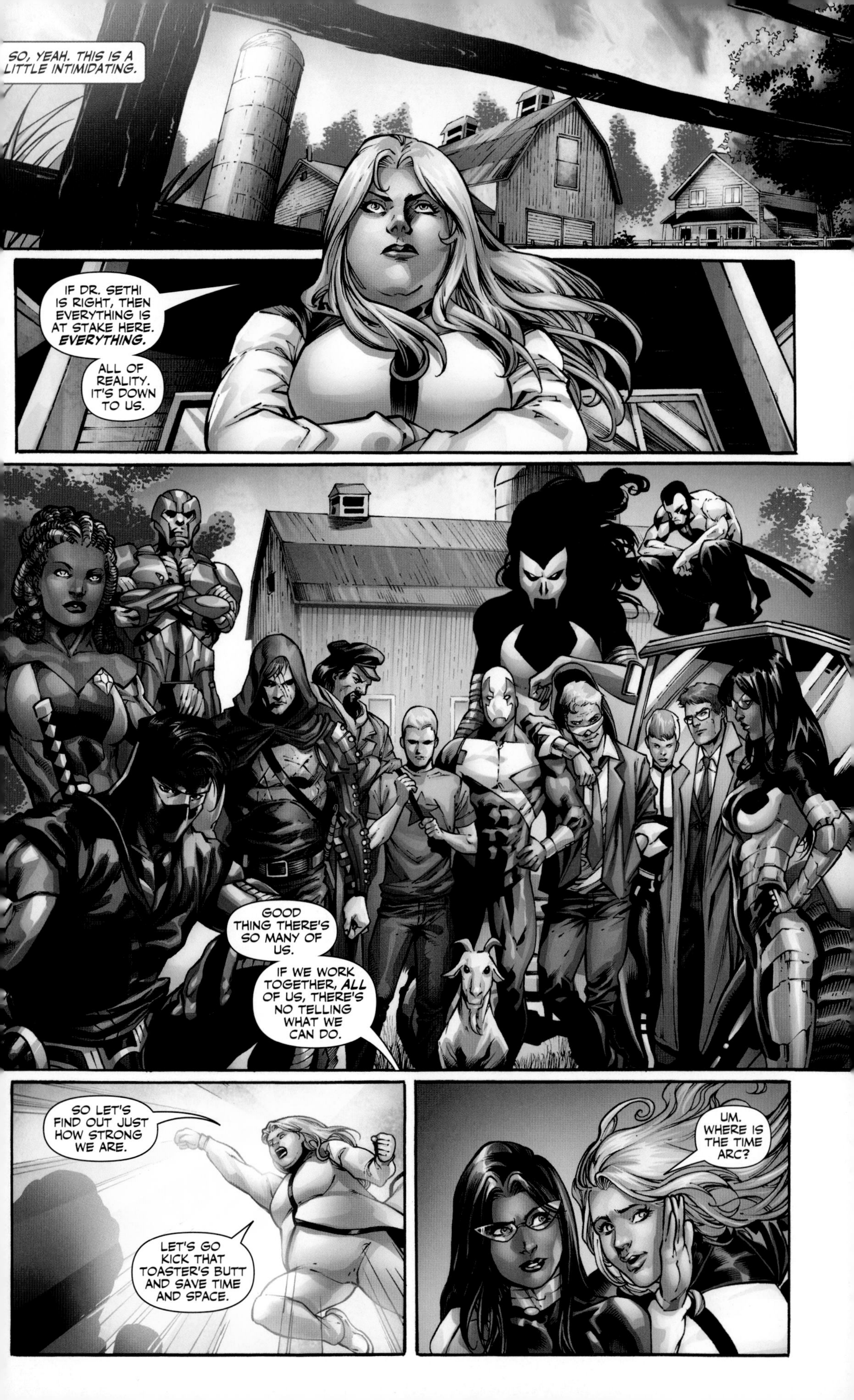
SO, YEAH. THIS IS A LITTLE INTIMIDATING.
IF DR. SETHI IS RIGHT, THEN EVERYTHING IS AT STAKE HERE. EVERYTHING.
ALL OF REALITY. IT'S DOWN TO US.
GOOD THING THERE'S SO MANY OF US.
IF WE WORK TOGETHER, ALL OF US, THERE'S NO TELLING WHAT WE CAN DO.
SO LET'S FIND OUT JUST HOW STRONG WE ARE.
LET'S GO KICK THAT TOASTER'S BUTT AND SAVE TIME AND SPACE.
UM. WHERE IS THE TIME ARC?

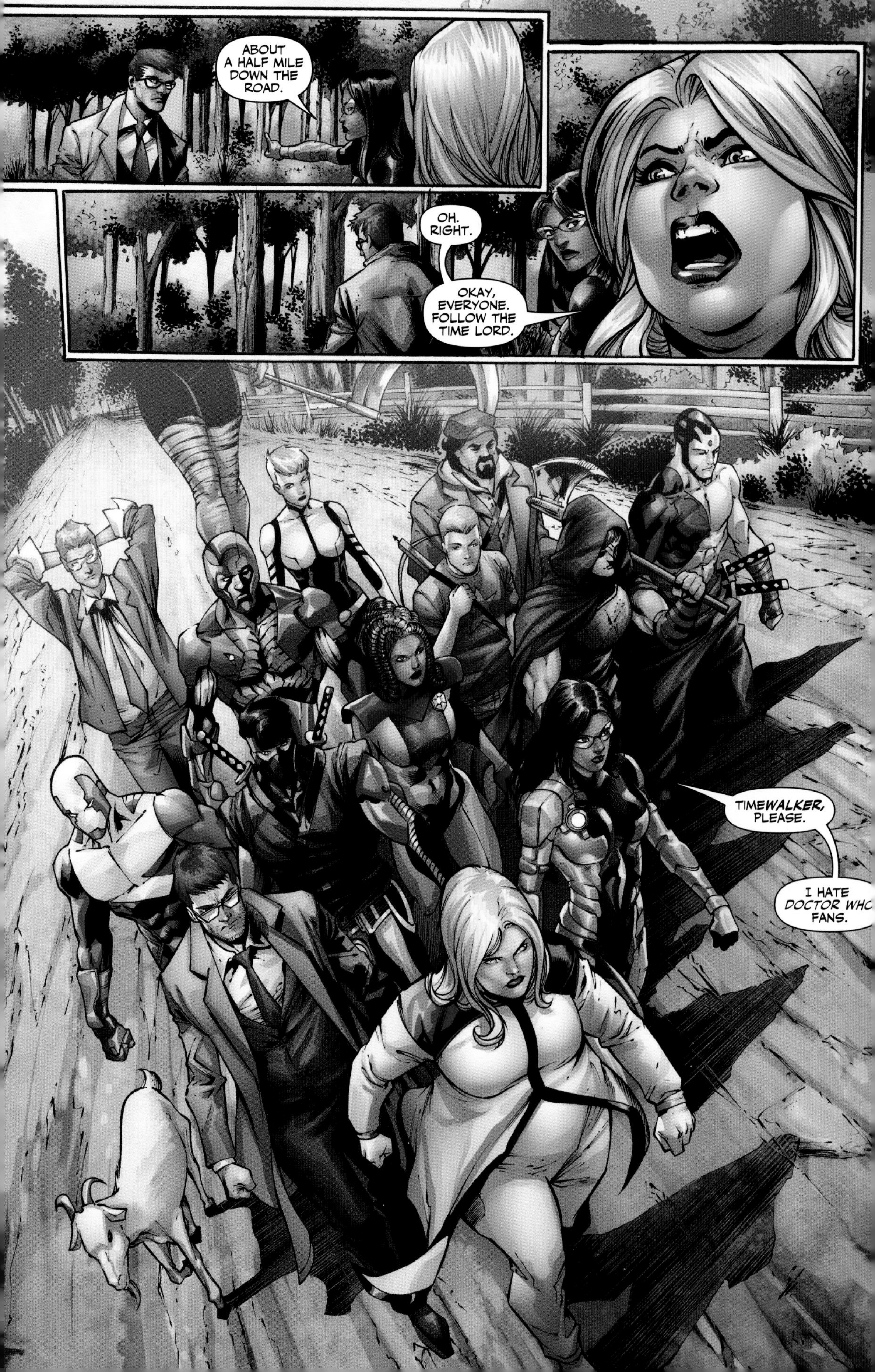
ABOUT A HALF MILE DOWN THE ROAD.
OH. RIGHT.
OKAY, EVERYONE. FOLLOW THE TIME LORD.
TIME*WALKER*, PLEASE.
I HATE *DOCTOR WHO* FANS.

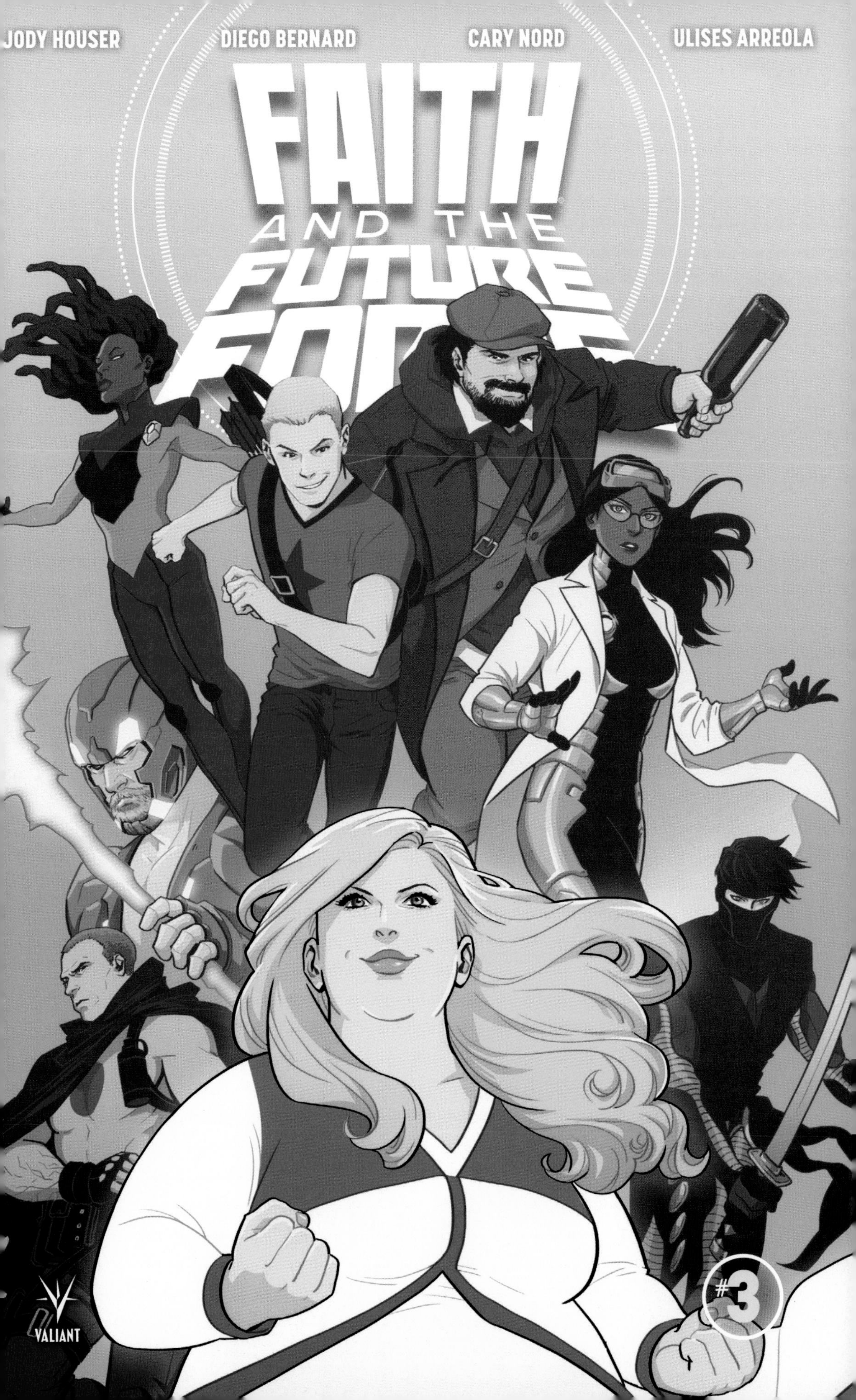
JODY HOUSER
DIEGO BERNARD
CARY NORD
ULISES ARREOLA
FAITH AND THE FUTURE FORCE
#3
VALIANT

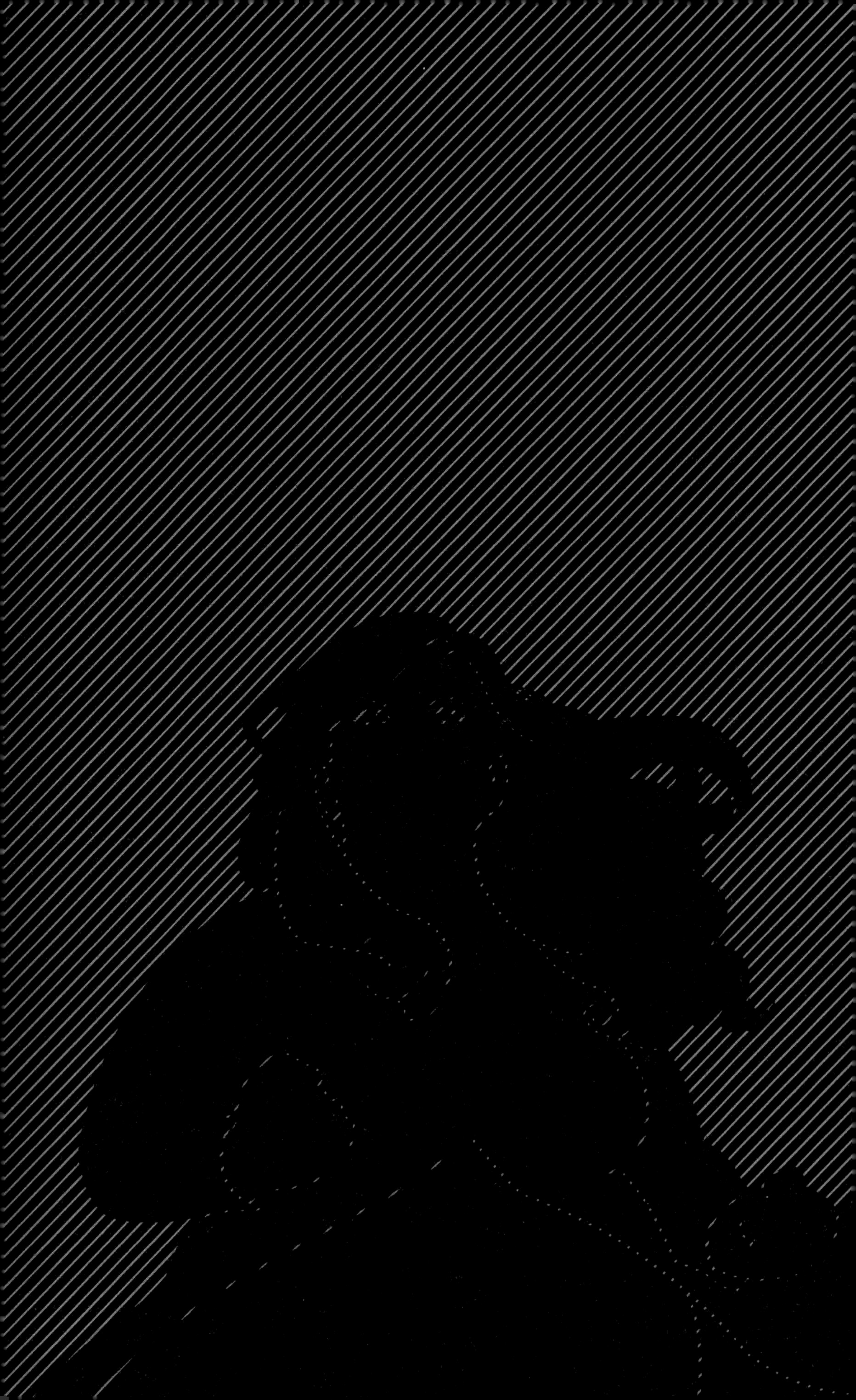

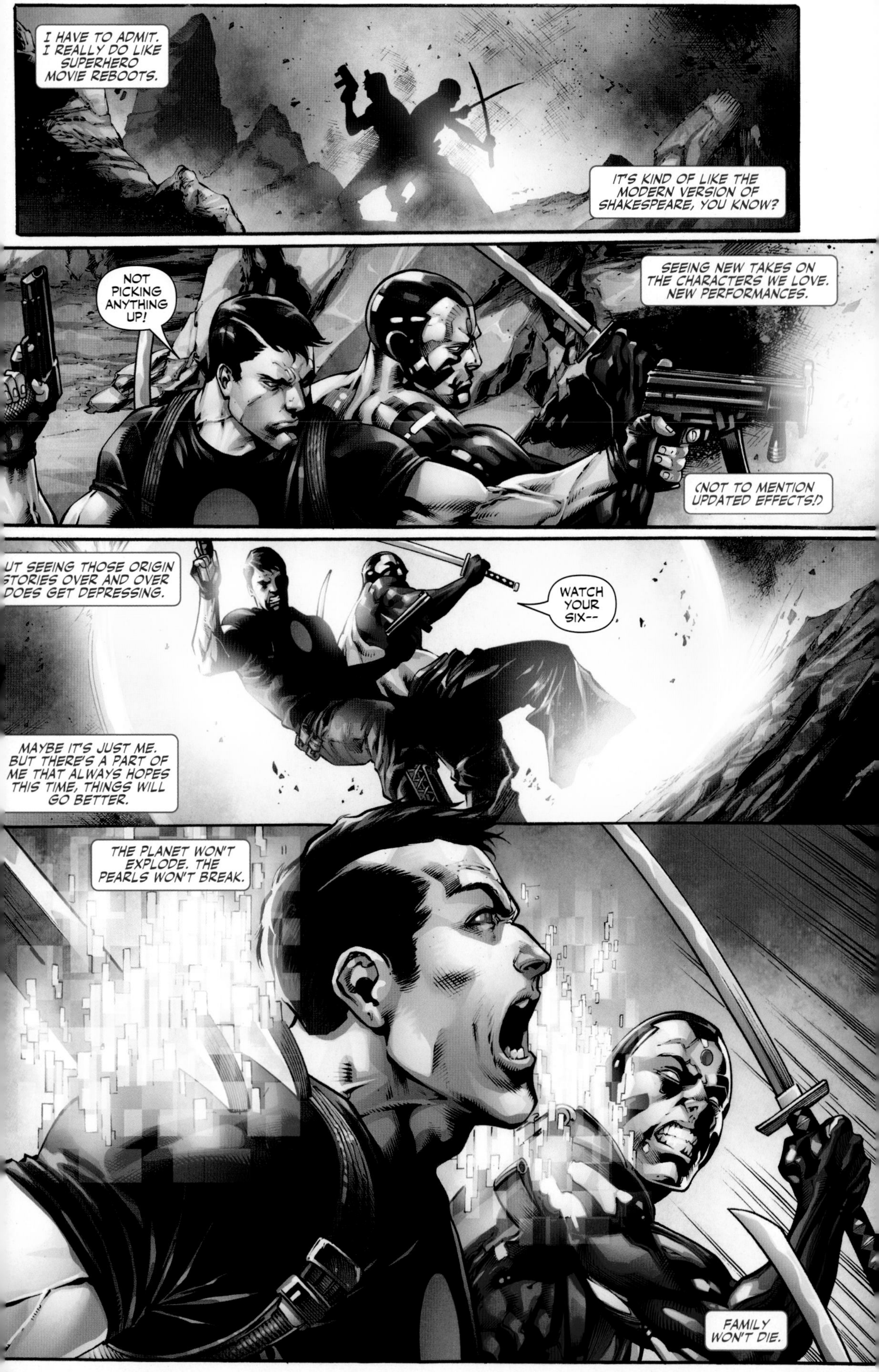
I HAVE TO ADMIT. I REALLY DO LIKE SUPERHERO MOVIE REBOOTS.
IT'S KIND OF LIKE THE MODERN VERSION OF SHAKESPEARE, YOU KNOW?
NOT PICKING ANYTHING UP!
SEEING NEW TAKES ON THE CHARACTERS WE LOVE. NEW PERFORMANCES.
(NOT TO MENTION UPDATED EFFECTS!)
UT SEEING THOSE ORIGIN STORIES OVER AND OVER DOES GET DEPRESSING.
WATCH YOUR SIX--
MAYBE IT'S JUST ME. BUT THERE'S A PART OF ME THAT ALWAYS HOPES THIS TIME, THINGS WILL GO BETTER.
THE PLANET WON'T EXPLODE. THE PEARLS WON'T BREAK.
FAMILY WON'T DIE.

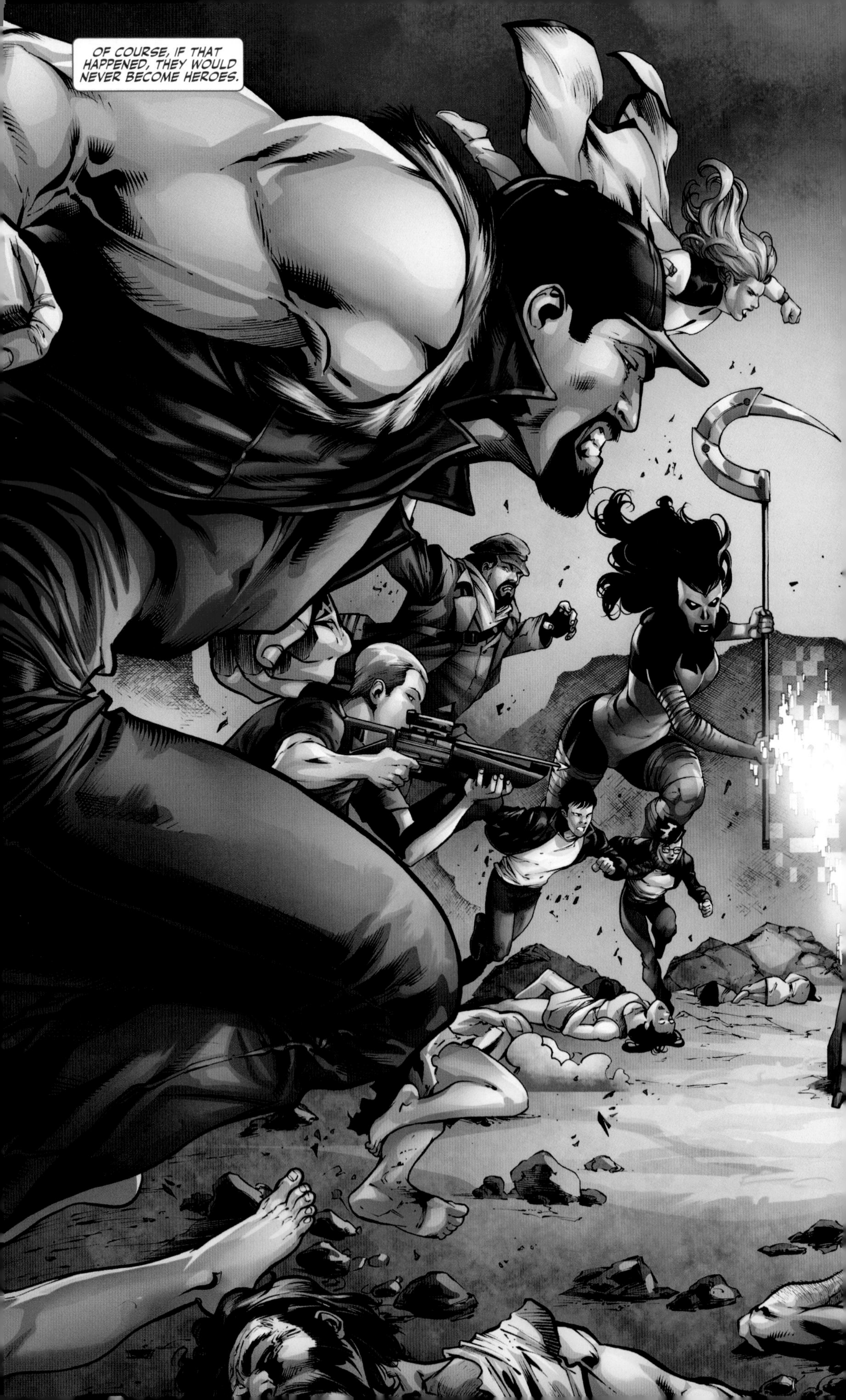
OF COURSE, IF THAT HAPPENED, THEY WOULD NEVER BECOME HEROES.

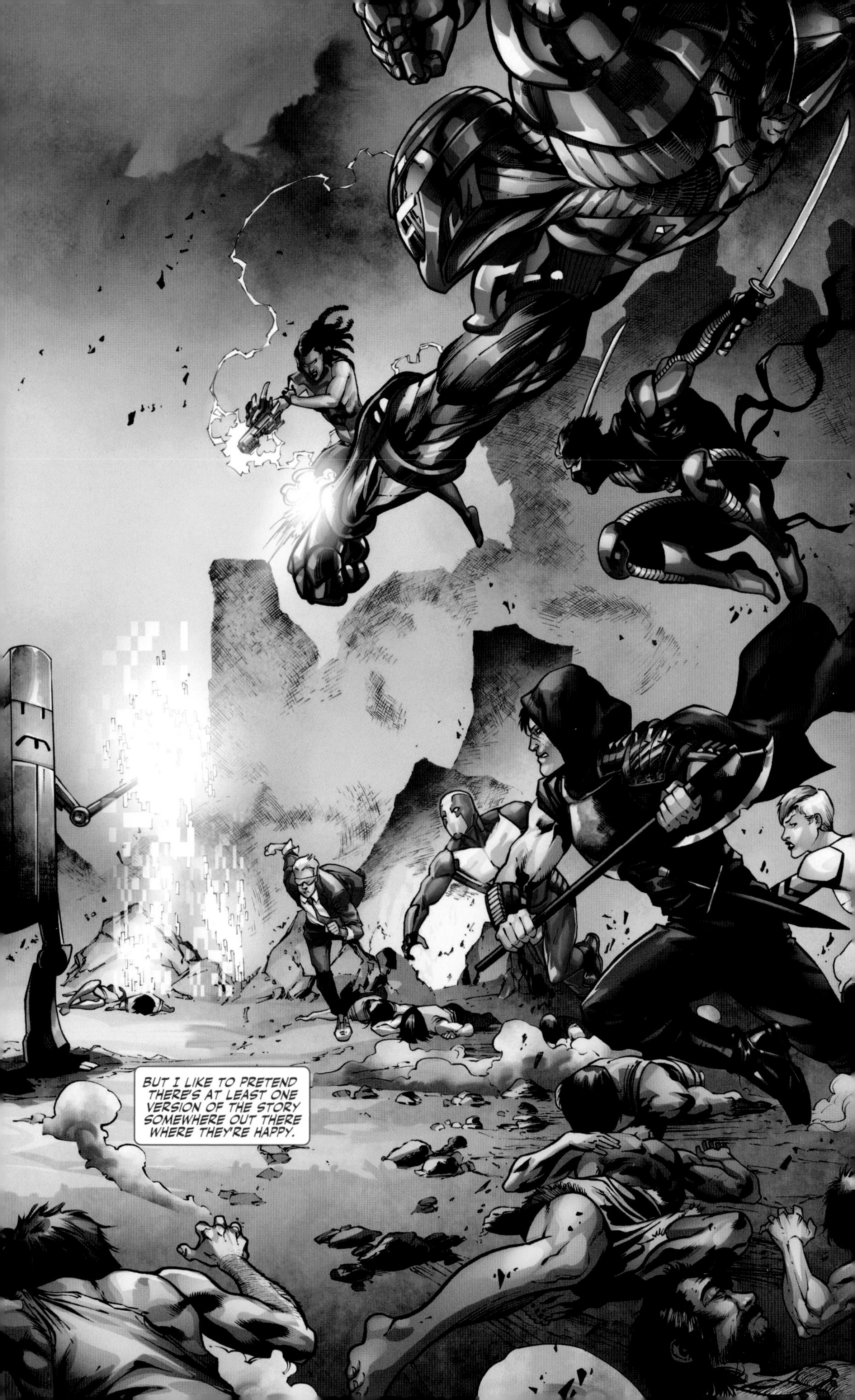
BUT I LIKE TO PRETEND THERE'S AT LEAST ONE VERSION OF THE STORY SOMEWHERE OUT THERE WHERE THEY'RE HAPPY.

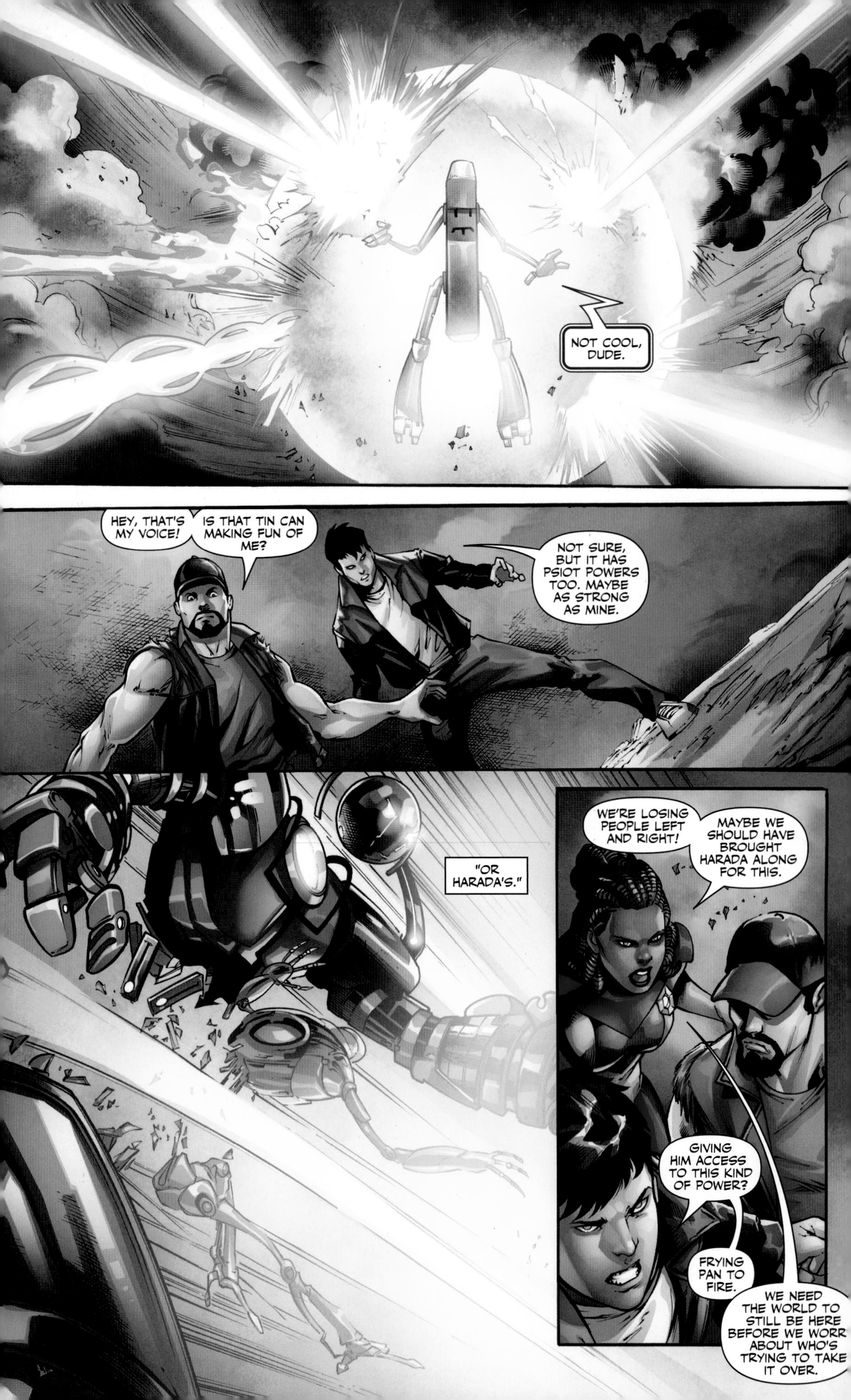
NOT COOL, DUDE.
HEY, THAT'S MY VOICE!
IS THAT TIN CAN MAKING FUN OF ME?
NOT SURE, BUT IT HAS PSIOT POWERS TOO. MAYBE AS STRONG AS MINE.
"OR HARADA'S."
WE'RE LOSING PEOPLE LEFT AND RIGHT!
MAYBE WE SHOULD HAVE BROUGHT HARADA ALONG FOR THIS.
GIVING HIM ACCESS TO THIS KIND OF POWER?
FRYING PAN TO FIRE.
WE NEED THE WORLD TO STILL BE HERE BEFORE WE WORR ABOUT WHO'S TRYING TO TAKE IT OVER.

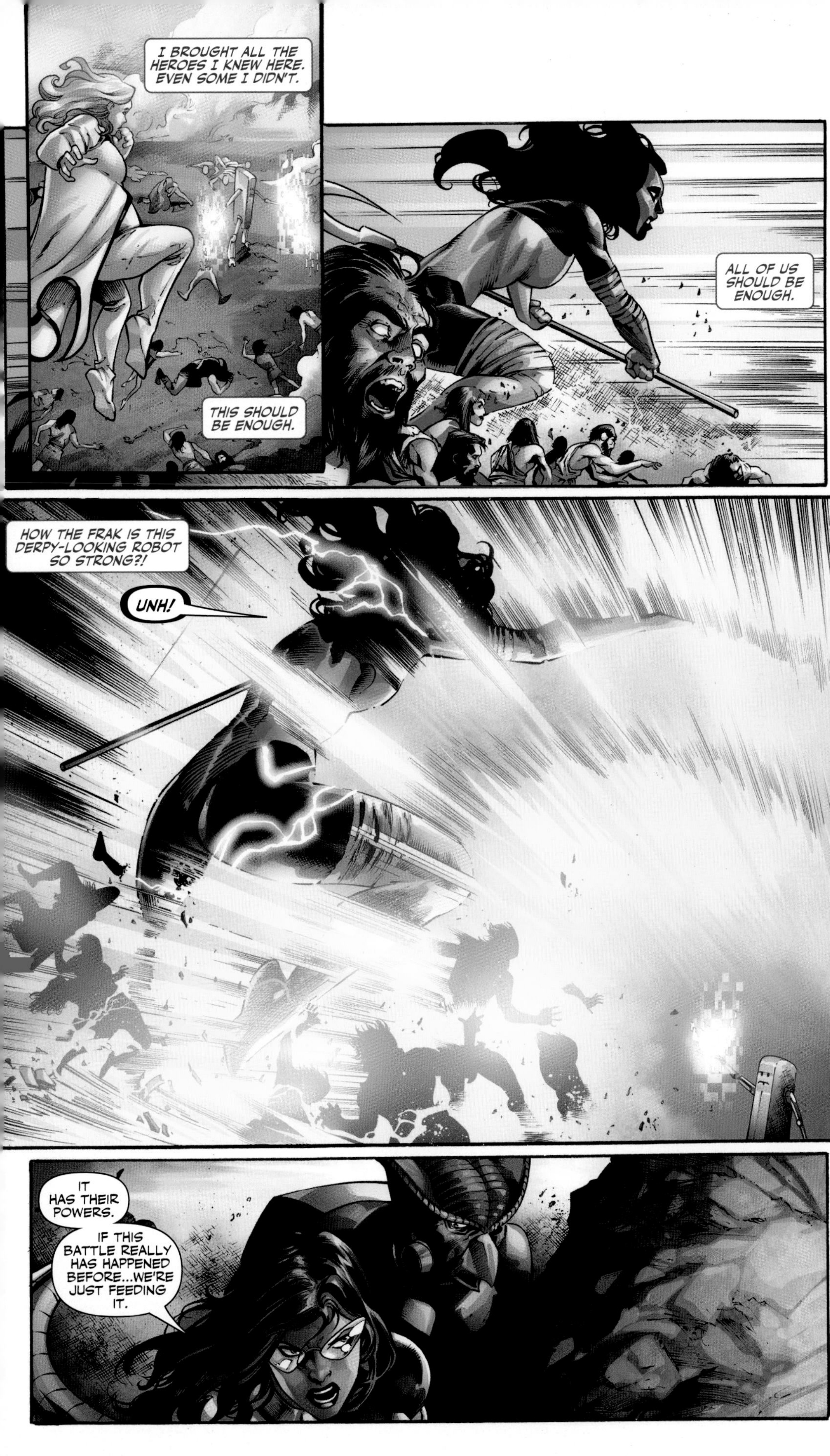
I BROUGHT ALL THE HEROES I KNEW HERE. EVEN SOME I DIDN'T.
THIS SHOULD BE ENOUGH.
ALL OF US SHOULD BE ENOUGH.
HOW THE FRAK IS THIS DERPY-LOOKING ROBOT SO STRONG?!
UNH!
IT HAS THEIR POWERS.
IF THIS BATTLE REALLY HAS HAPPENED BEFORE...WE'RE JUST FEEDING IT.

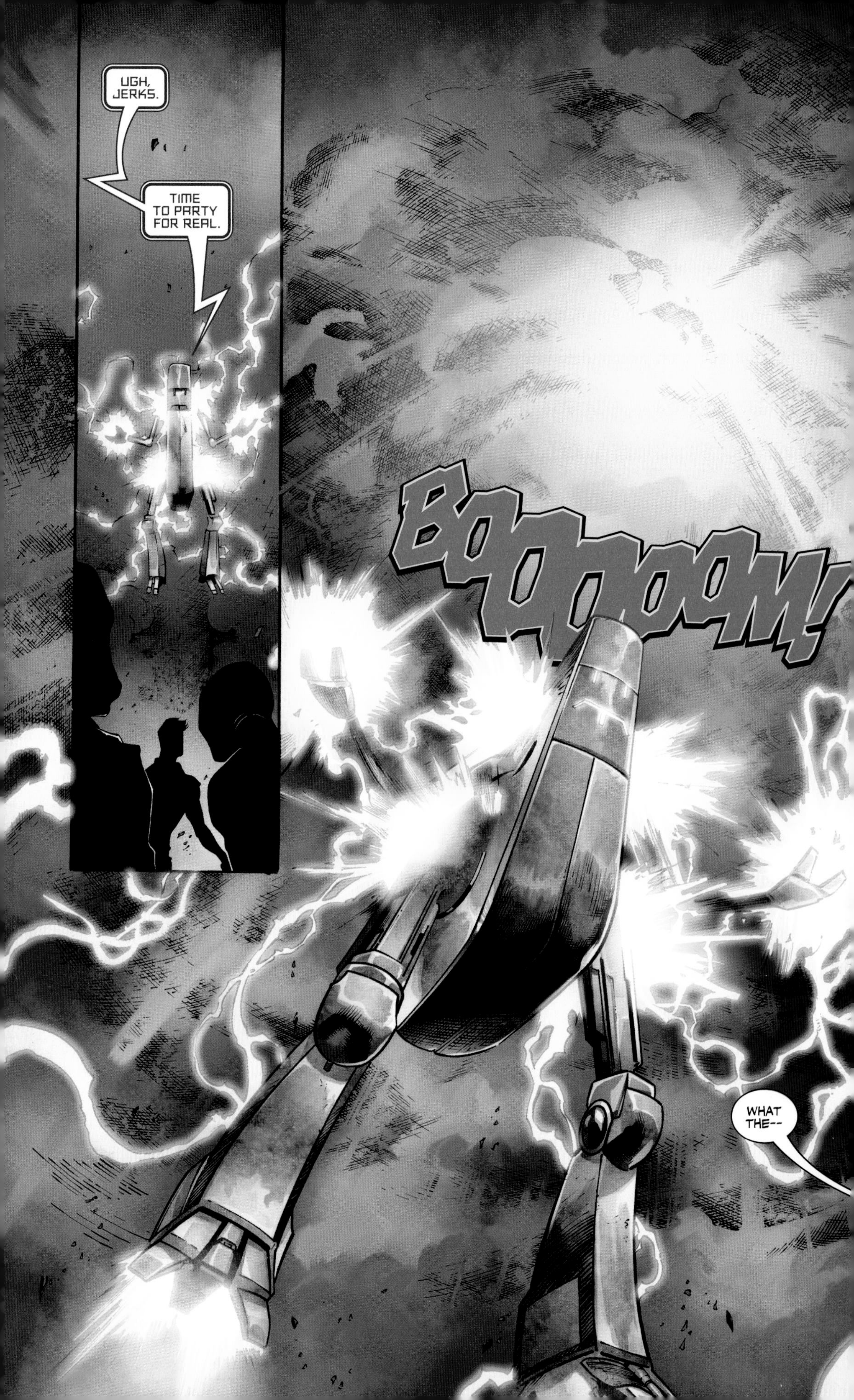
UGH, JERKS.
TIME TO PARTY FOR REAL.
BOOOOOOM!
WHAT THE--

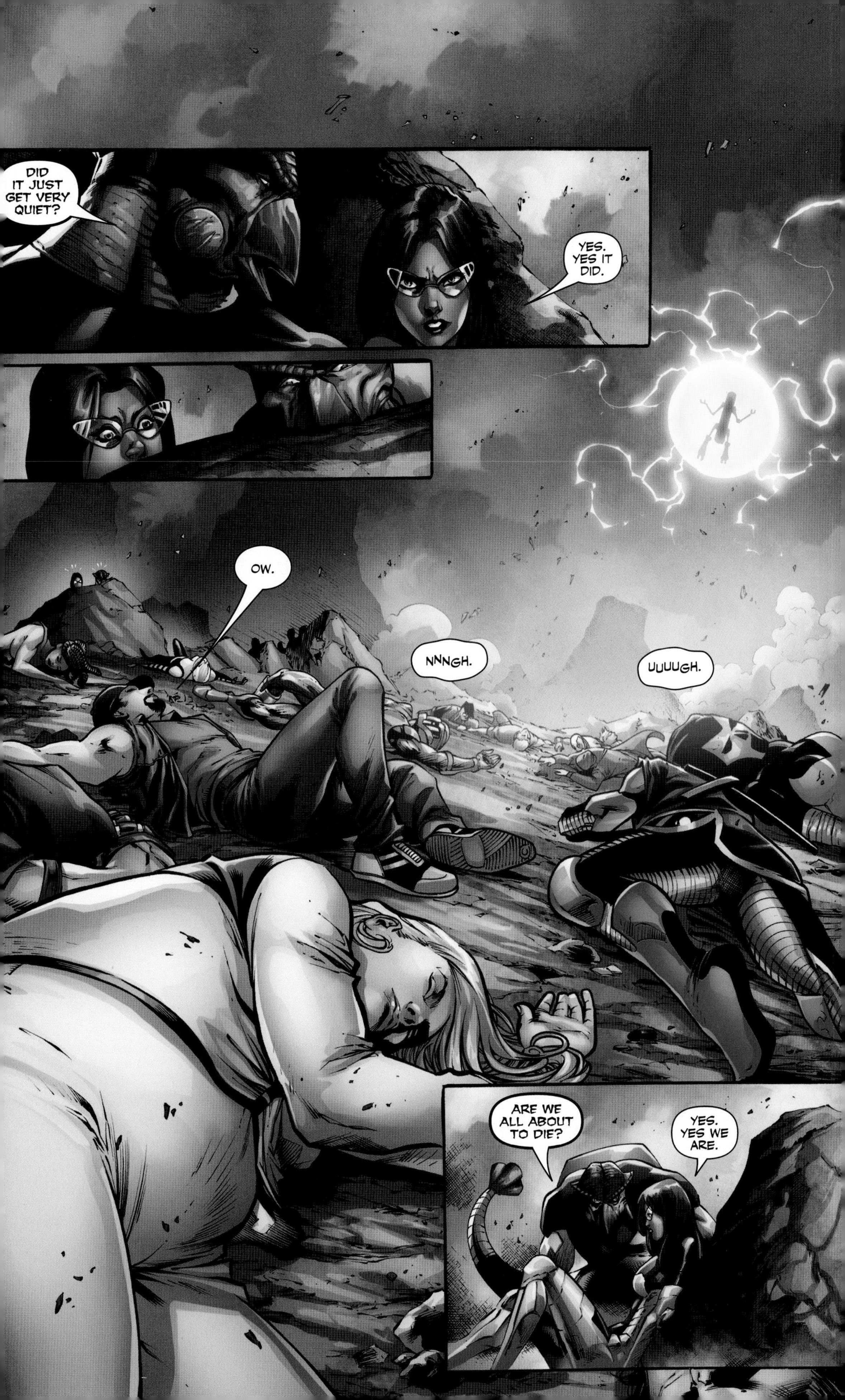

DID IT JUST GET VERY QUIET?
YES. YES IT DID.
OW.
NNNGH.
UUUUGH.
ARE WE ALL ABOUT TO DIE?
YES. YES WE ARE.

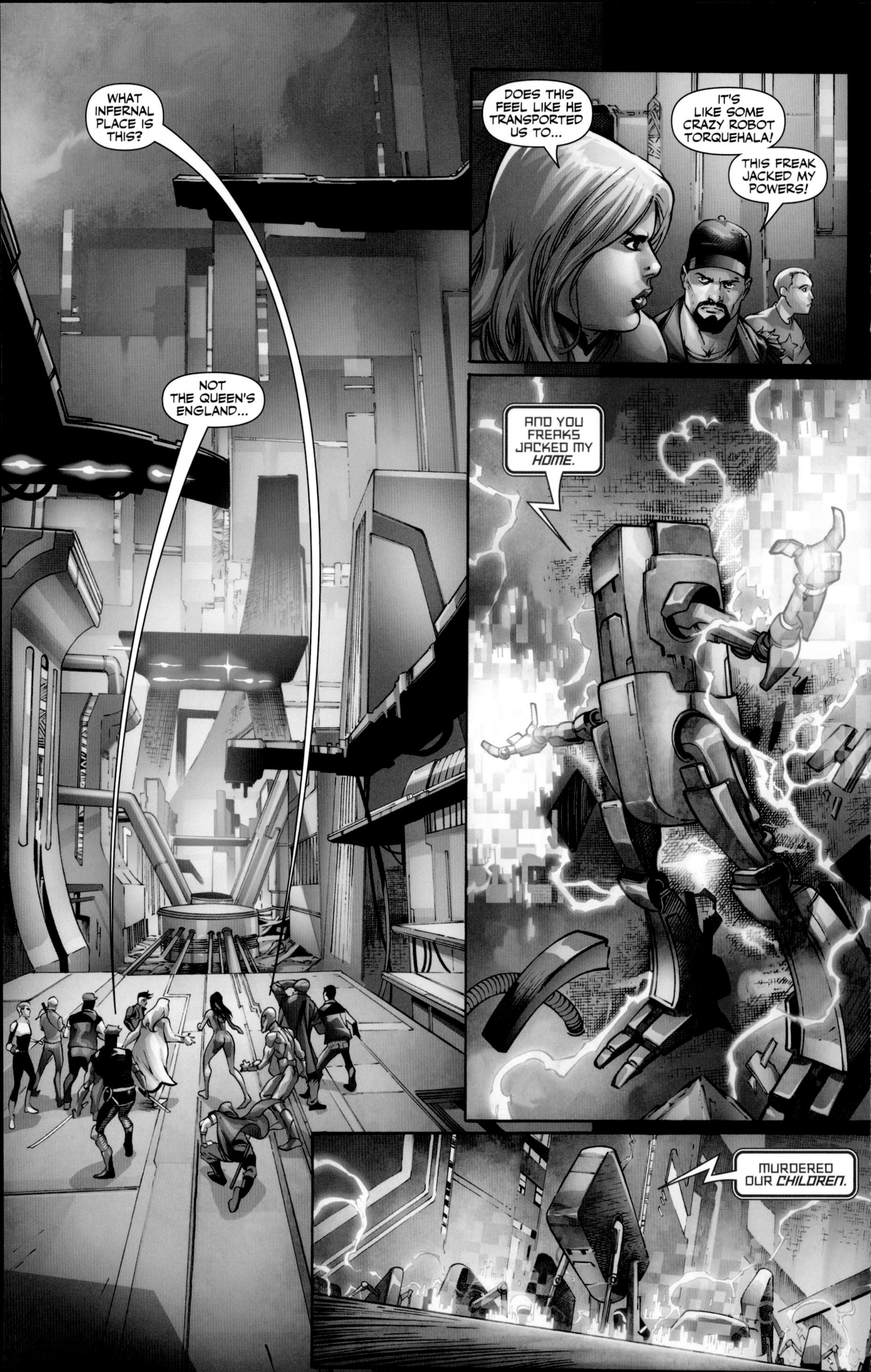
WHAT INFERNAL PLACE IS THIS?
NOT THE QUEEN'S ENGLAND...
DOES THIS FEEL LIKE HE TRANSPORTED US TO...
IT'S LIKE SOME CRAZY ROBOT TORQUEHALA!
THIS FREAK JACKED MY POWERS!
AND YOU FREAKS JACKED MY *HOME*.
MURDERED OUR *CHILDREN*.

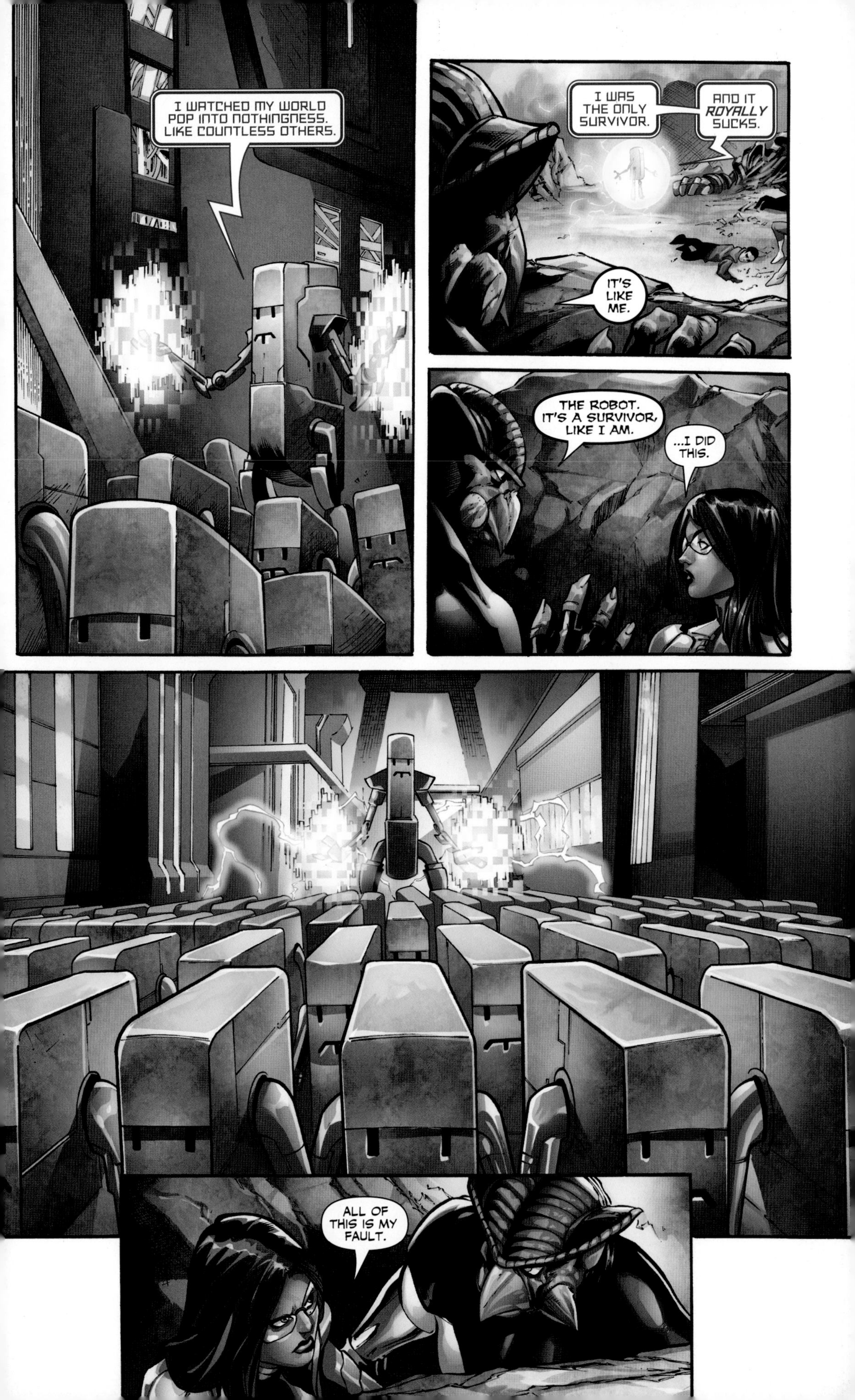
I WATCHED MY WORLD POP INTO NOTHINGNESS. LIKE COUNTLESS OTHERS.
I WAS THE ONLY SURVIVOR.
AND IT *ROYALLY* SUCKS.
IT'S LIKE ME.
THE ROBOT. IT'S A SURVIVOR, LIKE I AM.
...I DID THIS.
ALL OF THIS IS MY FAULT.

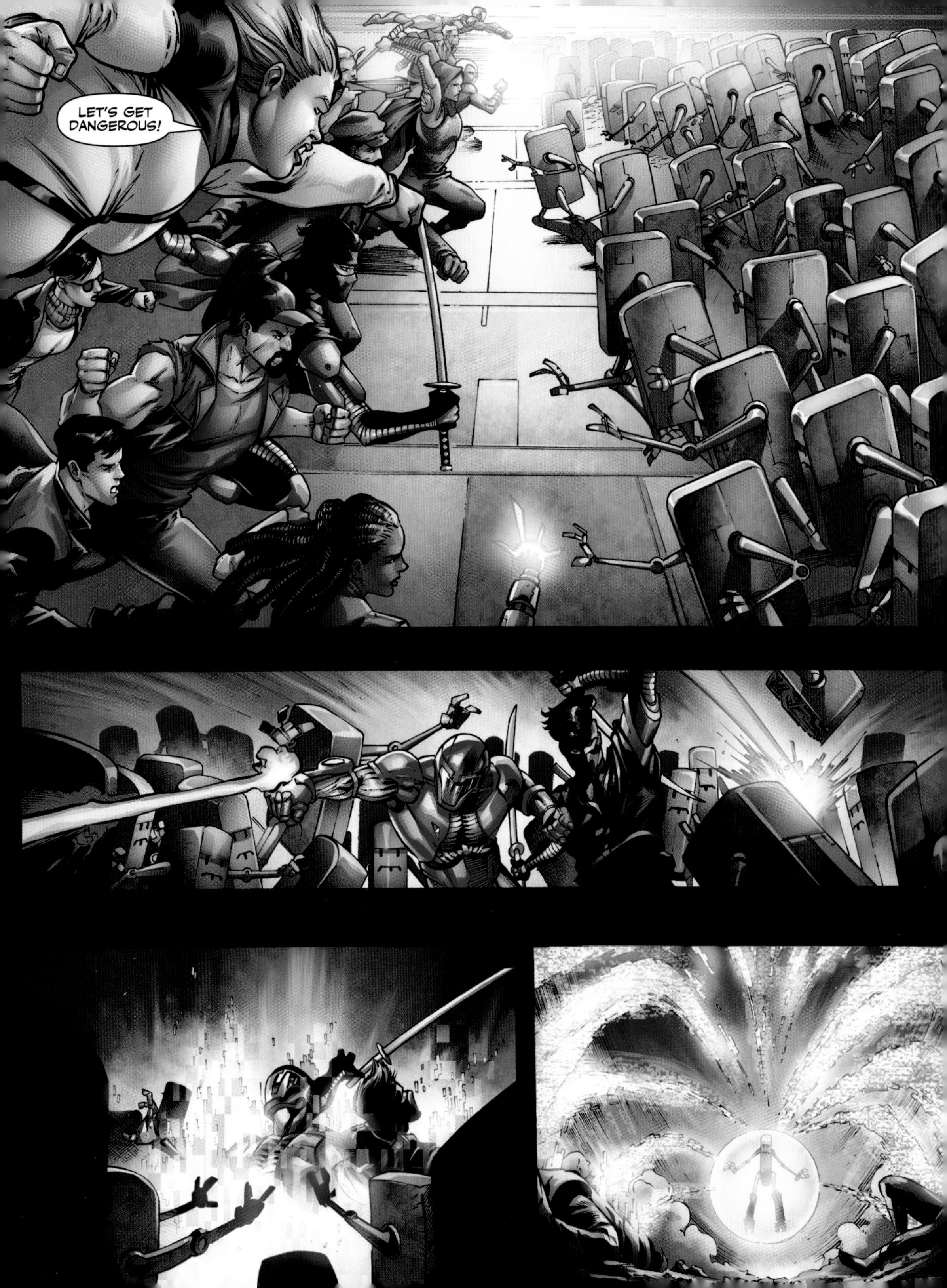
LET'S GET DANGEROUS!

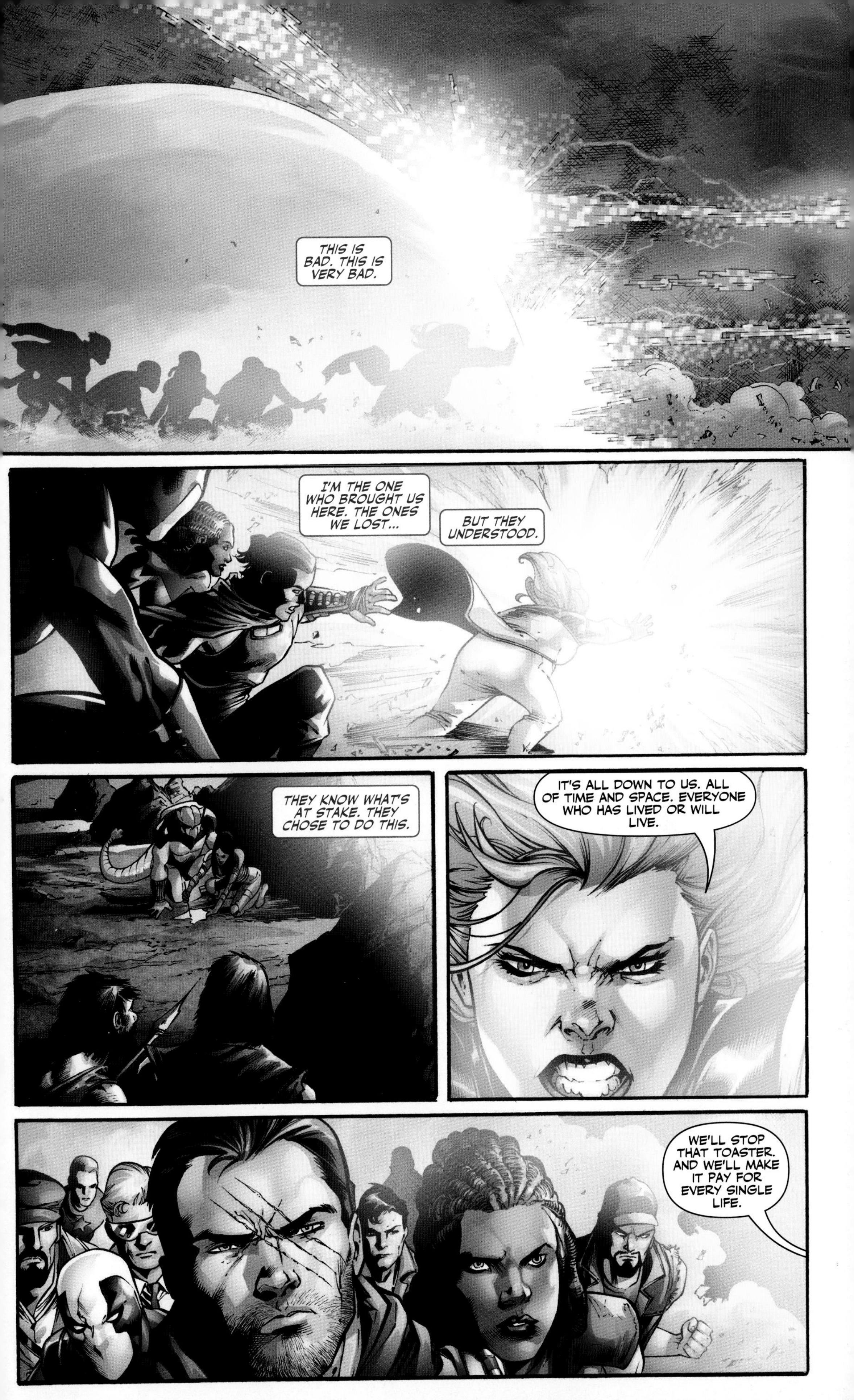
THIS IS BAD. THIS IS VERY BAD.
I'M THE ONE WHO BROUGHT US HERE. THE ONES WE LOST...
BUT THEY UNDERSTOOD.
THEY KNOW WHAT'S AT STAKE. THEY CHOSE TO DO THIS.
IT'S ALL DOWN TO US. ALL OF TIME AND SPACE. EVERYONE WHO HAS LIVED OR WILL LIVE.
WE'LL STOP THAT TOASTER. AND WE'LL MAKE IT PAY FOR EVERY SINGLE LIFE.

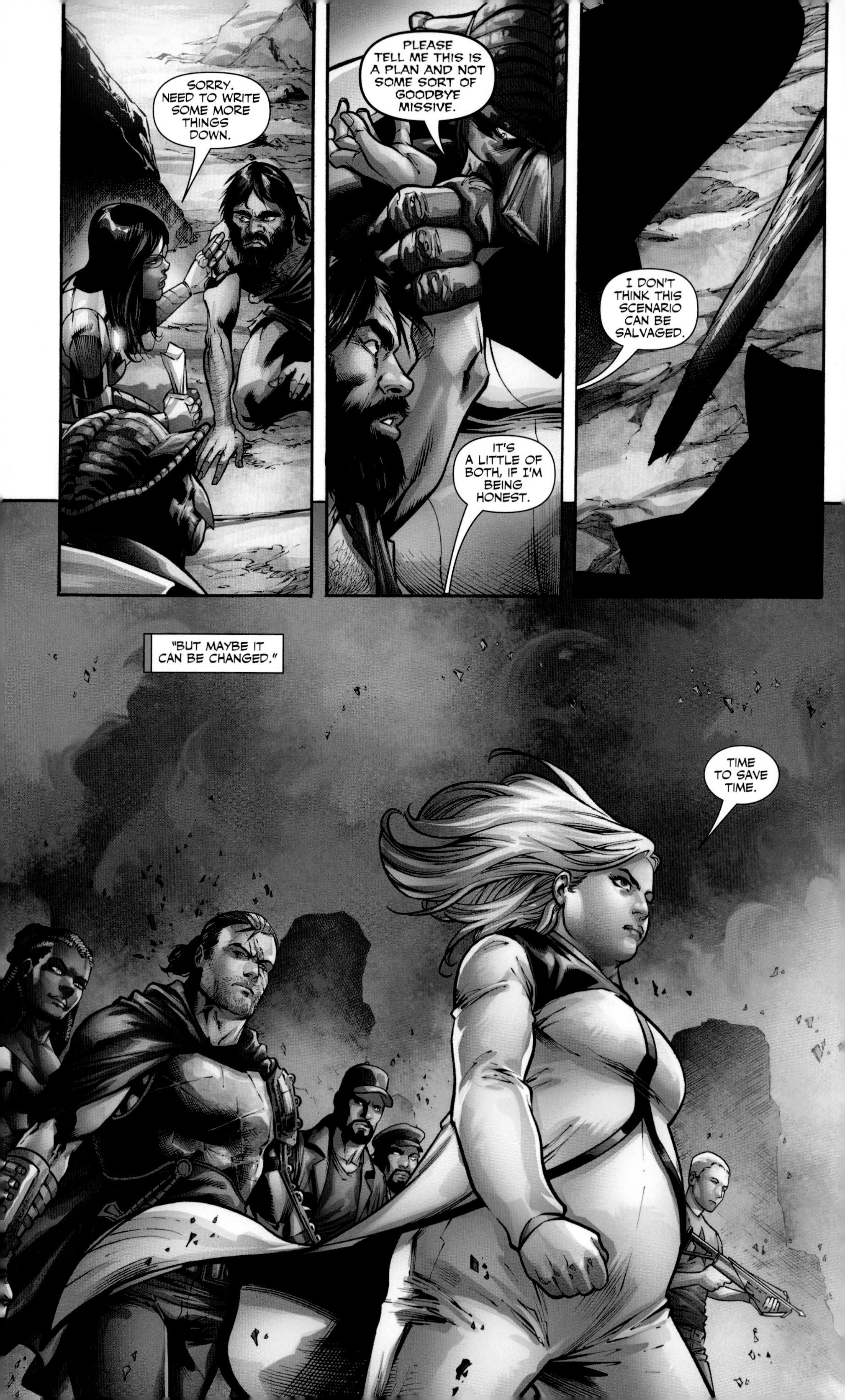
SORRY. NEED TO WRITE SOME MORE THINGS DOWN.
PLEASE TELL ME THIS IS A PLAN AND NOT SOME SORT OF GOODBYE MISSIVE.
IT'S A LITTLE OF BOTH, IF I'M BEING HONEST.
I DON'T THINK THIS SCENARIO CAN BE SALVAGED.
"BUT MAYBE IT CAN BE CHANGED."
TIME TO SAVE TIME.

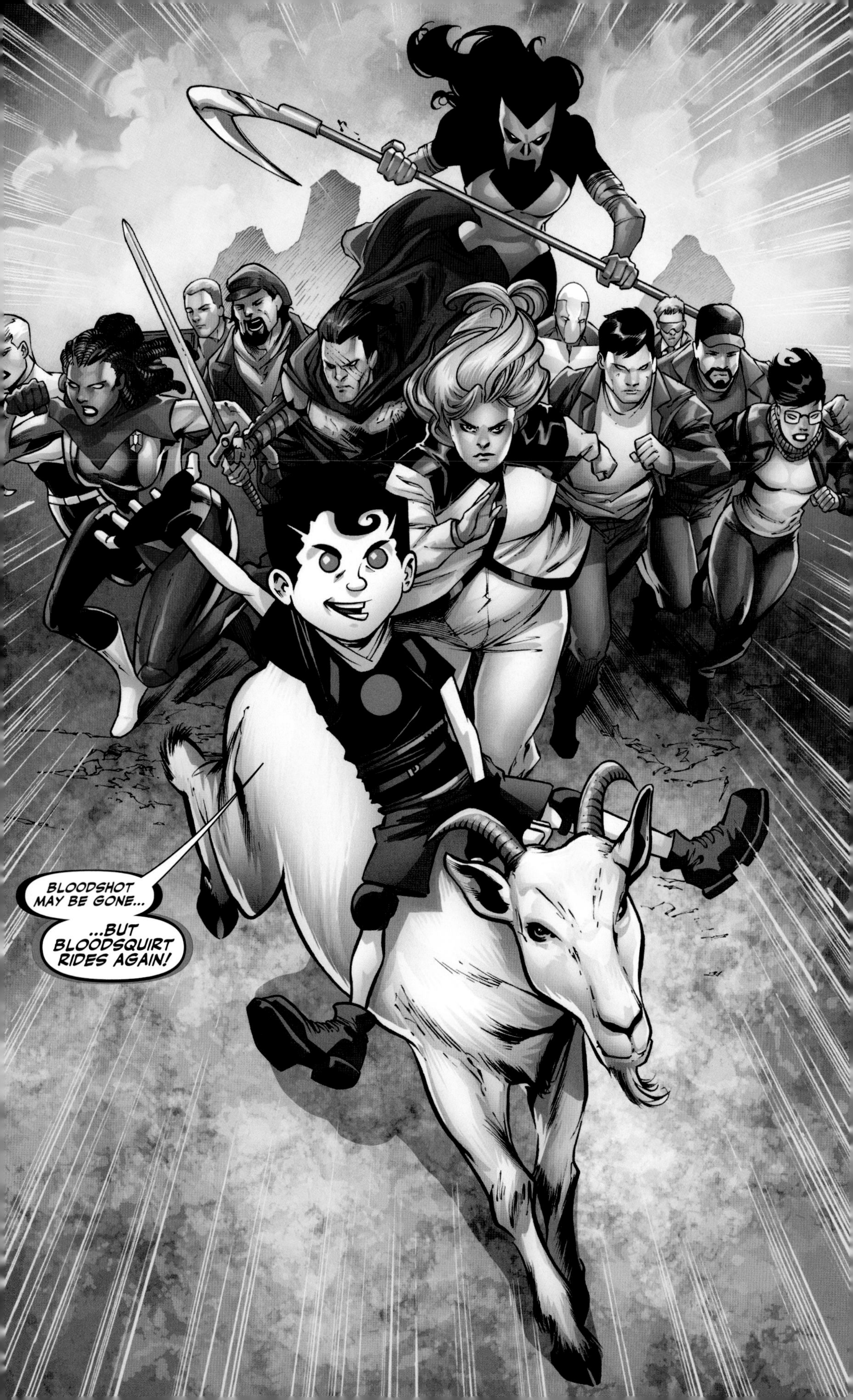
BLOODSHOT MAY BE GONE...
...BUT BLOODSQUIRT RIDES AGAIN!

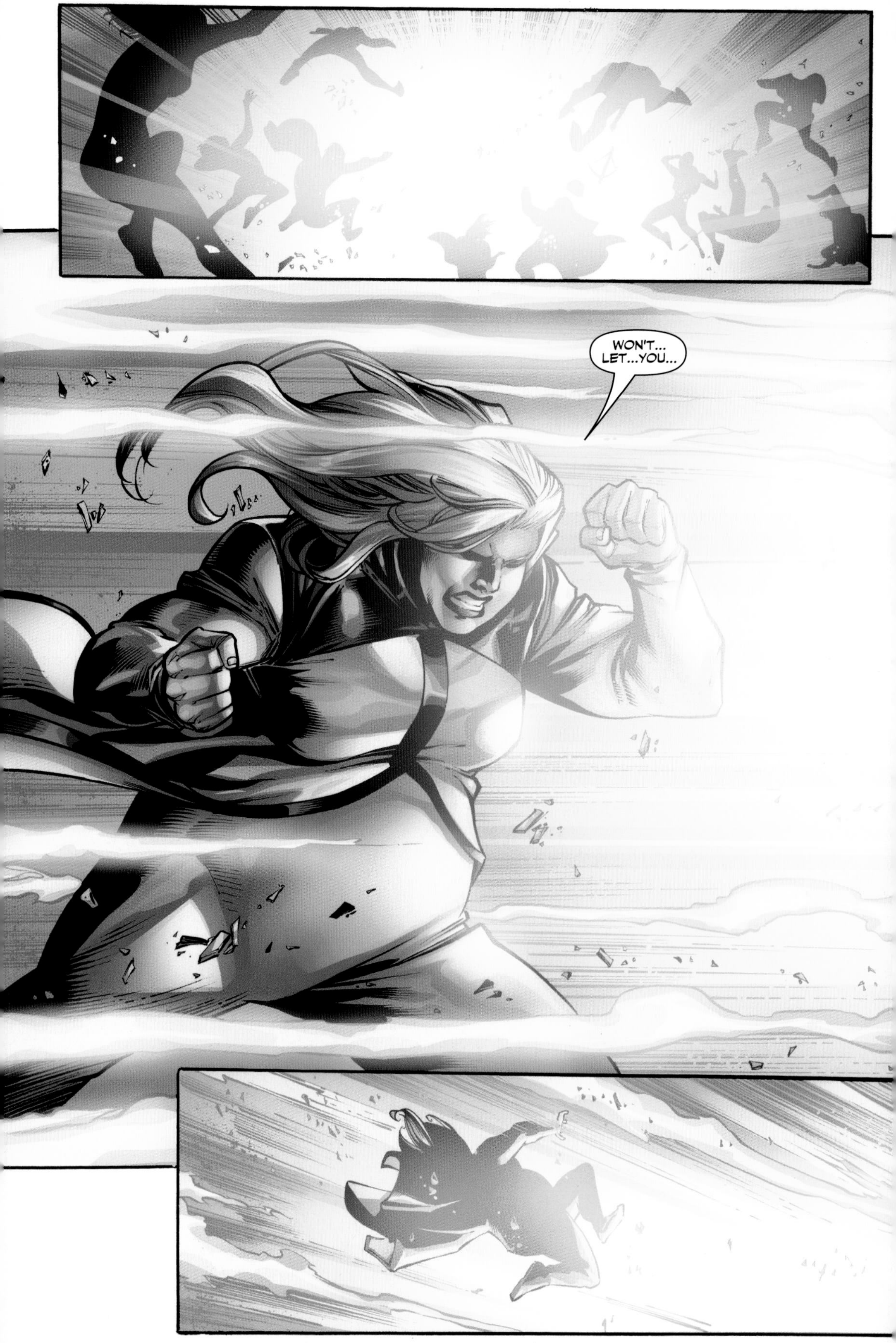
WON'T... LET...YOU...

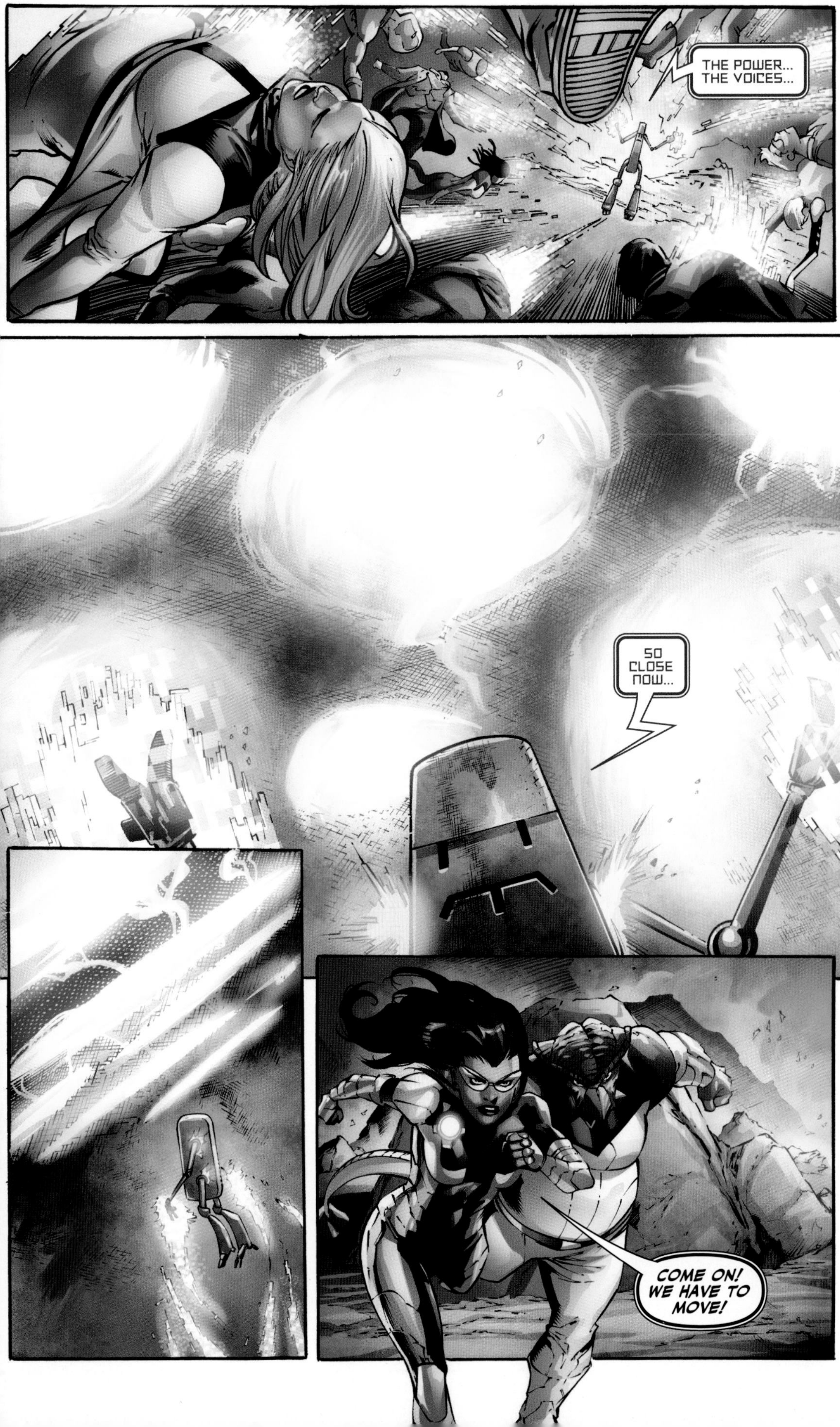
THE POWER... THE VOICES...
SO CLOSE NOW...
COME ON! WE HAVE TO MOVE!

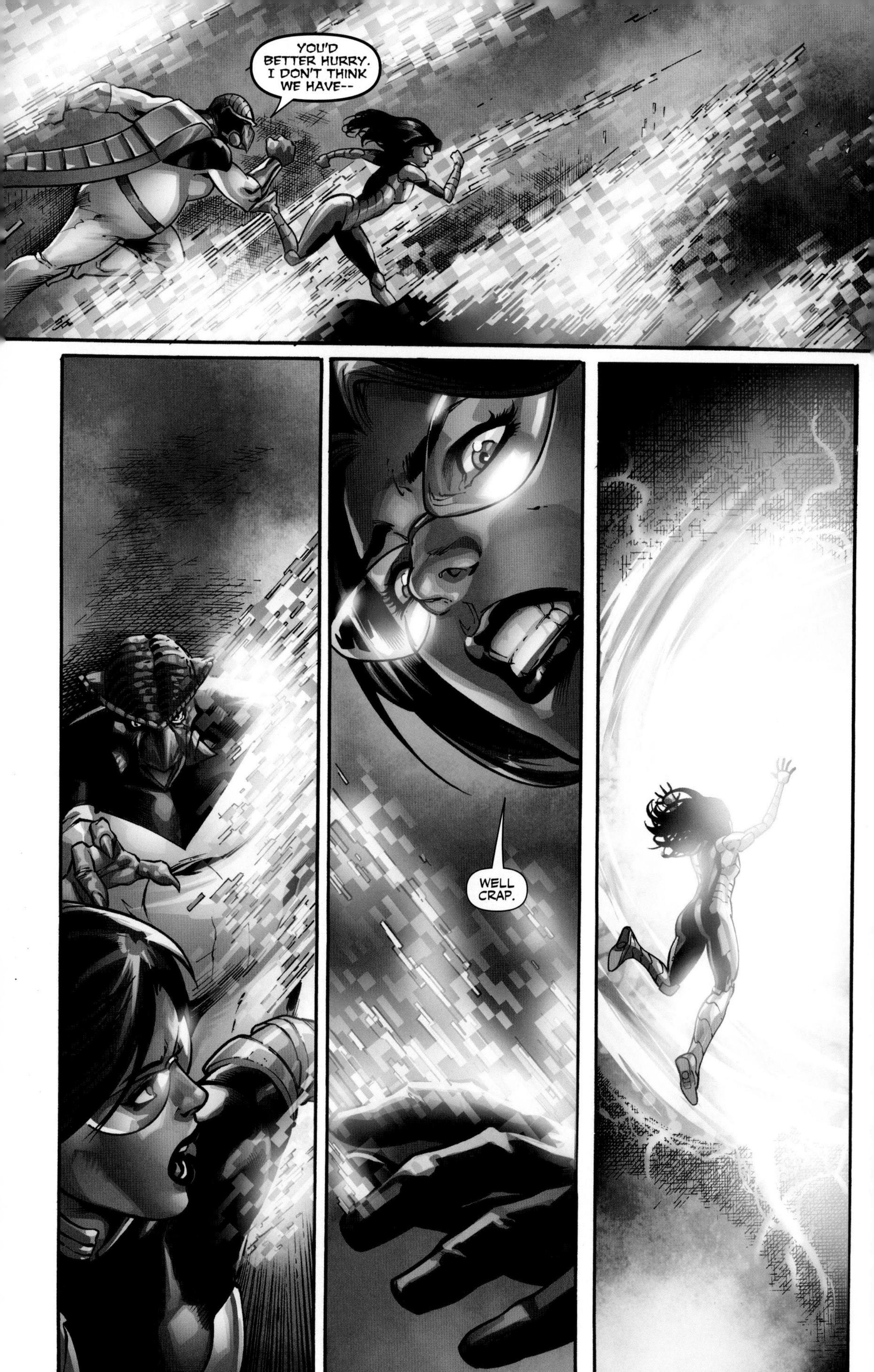

YOU'D BETTER HURRY. I DON'T THINK WE HAVE--
WELL CRAP.

IN A SCIENTIFIC SENSE, WHOEVER DISRUPTED THE PROGENITORS OF MODERN HUMANS VIOLATED THE LAWS OF--

BUT THERE SHOULDN'T...

EVIL ROBOT UNMAKING TIME! TAKING REALITY APART!

YOU HAVE TO TRUST HER! SHE HAS TO--

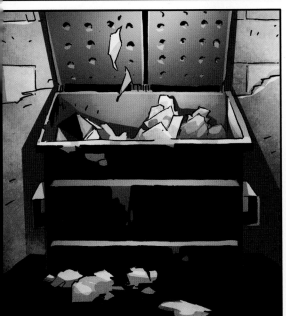

I'M NOT GOING IN THERE TO GET THOSE.

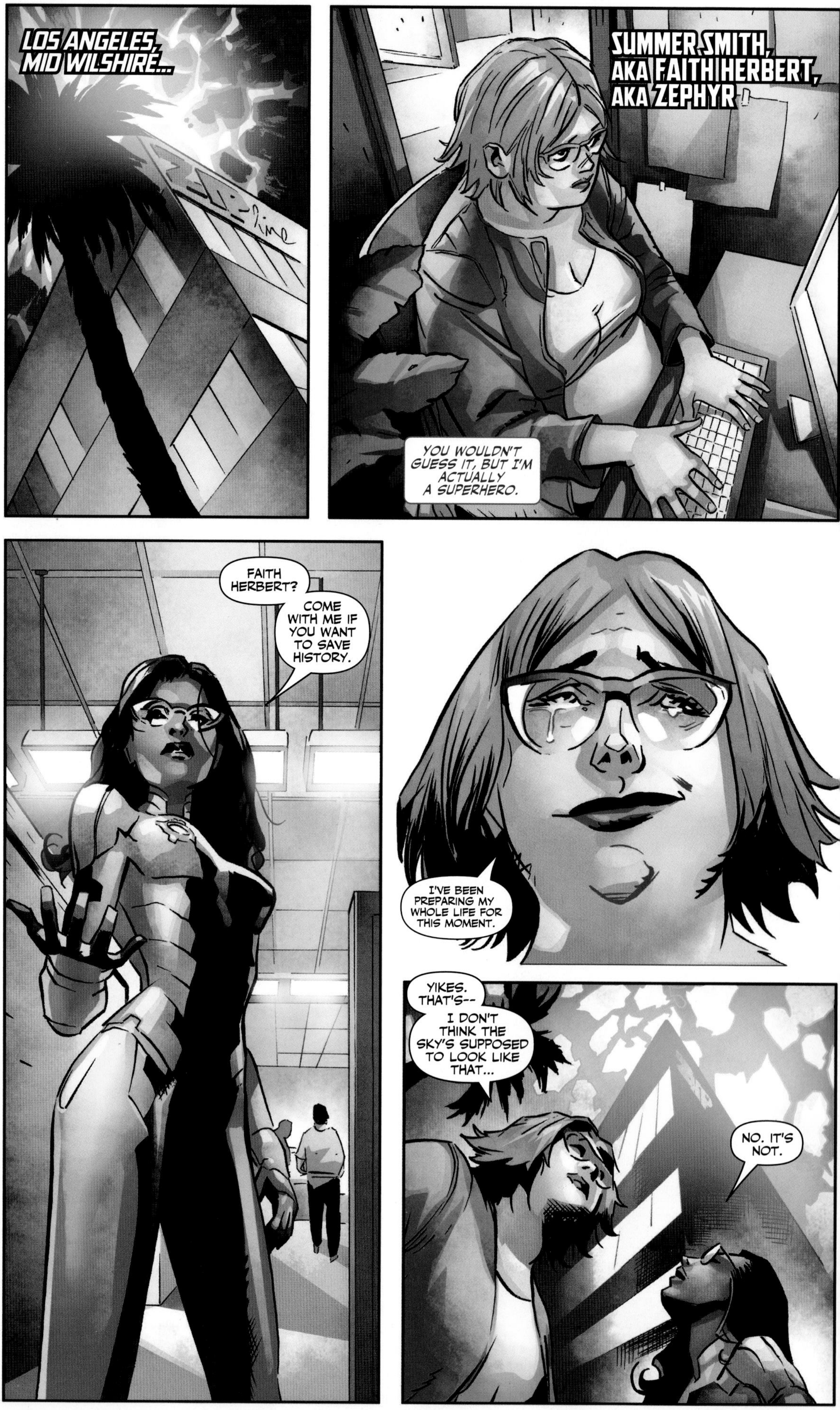
LOS ANGELES, MID WILSHIRE...
SUMMER SMITH, AKA FAITH HERBERT, AKA ZEPHYR
YOU WOULDN'T GUESS IT, BUT I'M ACTUALLY A SUPERHERO.
FAITH HERBERT?
COME WITH ME IF YOU WANT TO SAVE HISTORY.
I'VE BEEN PREPARING MY WHOLE LIFE FOR THIS MOMENT.
YIKES. THAT'S--
I DON'T THINK THE SKY'S SUPPOSED TO LOOK LIKE THAT...
NO. IT'S NOT.

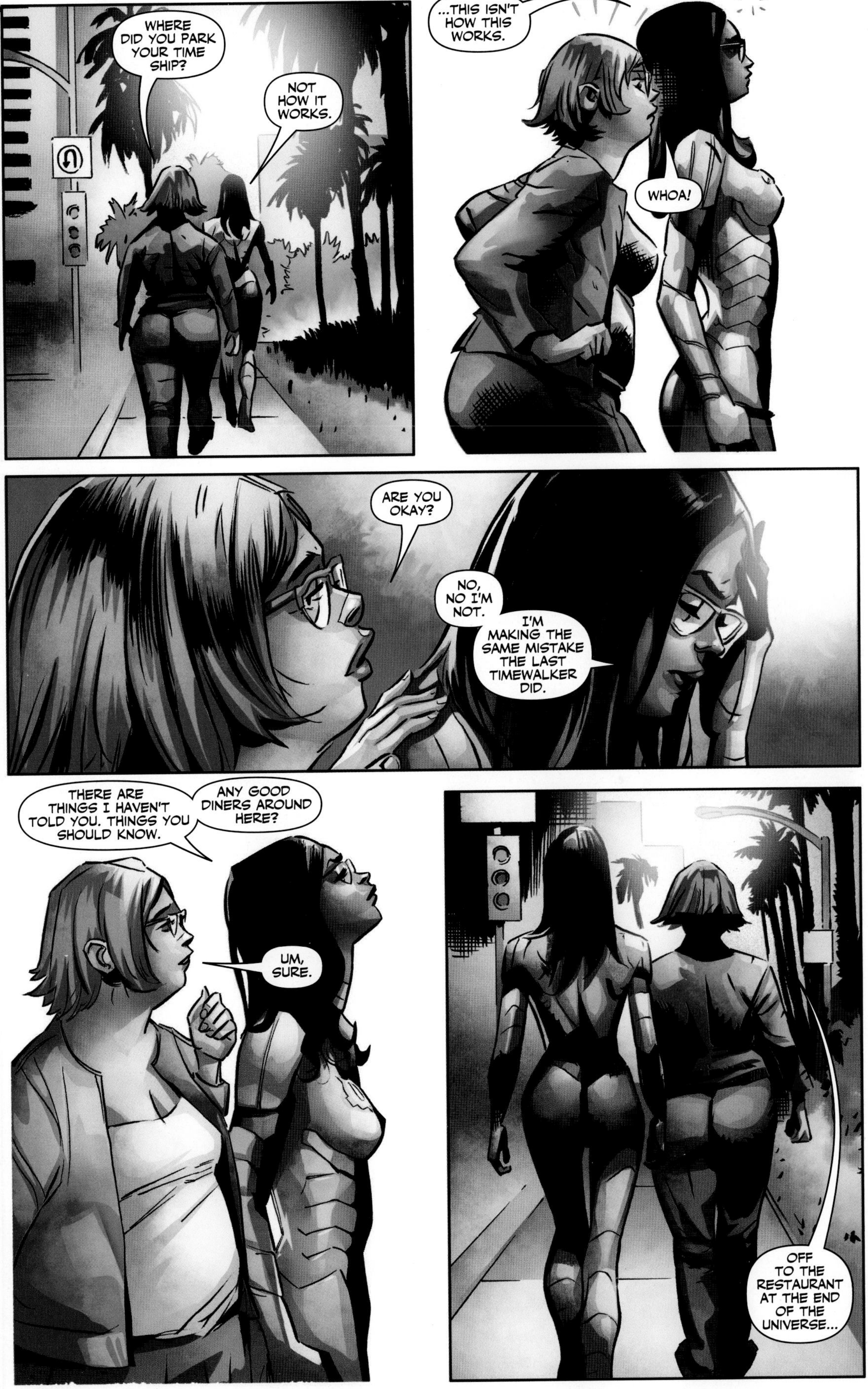

WHERE DID YOU PARK YOUR TIME SHIP?
NOT HOW IT WORKS.
...THIS ISN'T HOW THIS WORKS.
WHOA!
ARE YOU OKAY?
NO, NO I'M NOT.
I'M MAKING THE SAME MISTAKE THE LAST TIMEWALKER DID.
THERE ARE THINGS I HAVEN'T TOLD YOU. THINGS YOU SHOULD KNOW.
ANY GOOD DINERS AROUND HERE?
UM, SURE.
OFF TO THE RESTAURANT AT THE END OF THE UNIVERSE...

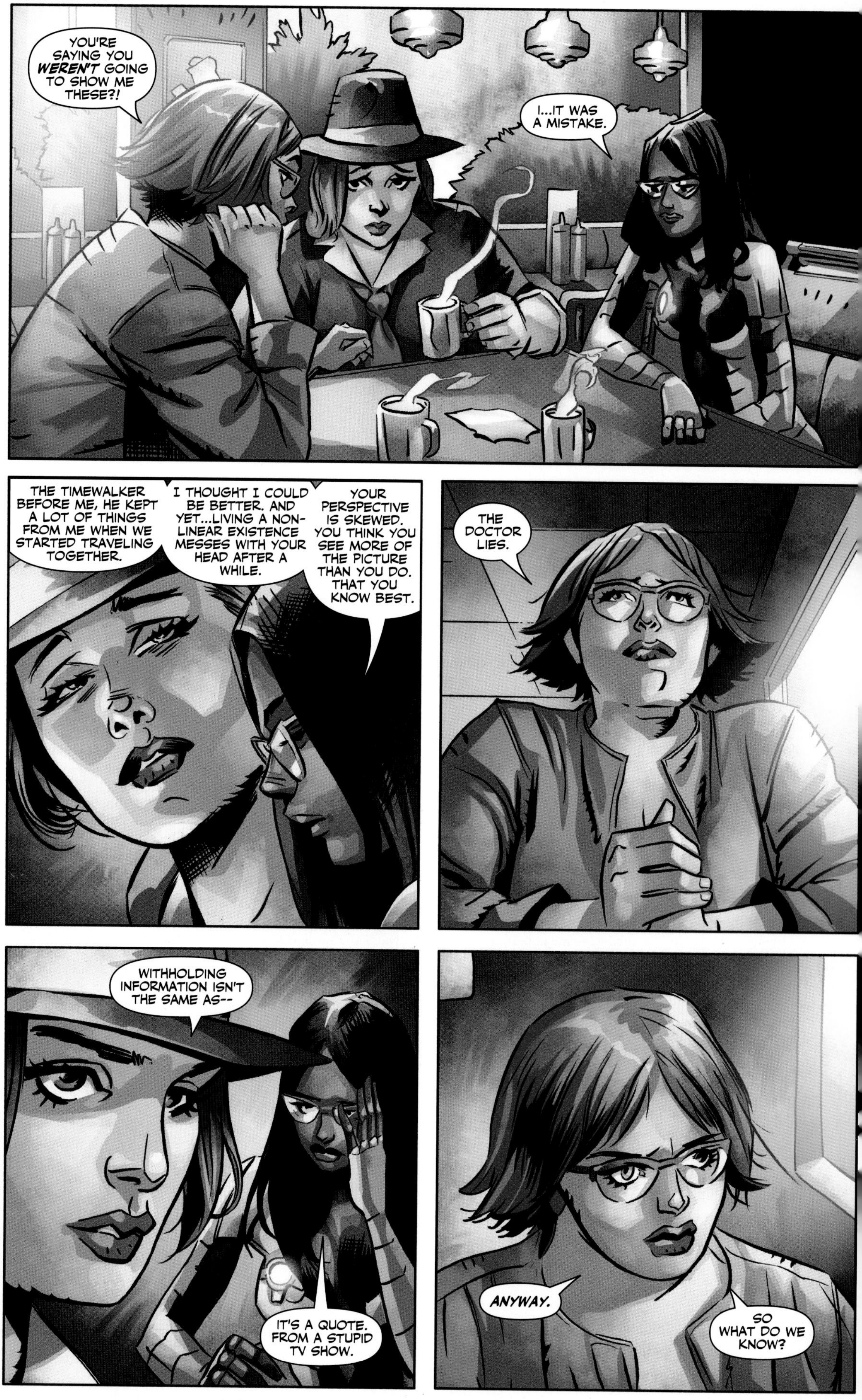

YOU'RE SAYING YOU *WEREN'T* GOING TO SHOW ME THESE?!
I...IT WAS A MISTAKE.
THE TIMEWALKER BEFORE ME, HE KEPT A LOT OF THINGS FROM ME WHEN WE STARTED TRAVELING TOGETHER.
I THOUGHT I COULD BE BETTER. AND YET...LIVING A NON-LINEAR EXISTENCE MESSES WITH YOUR HEAD AFTER A WHILE.
YOUR PERSPECTIVE IS SKEWED. YOU THINK YOU SEE MORE OF THE PICTURE THAN YOU DO. THAT YOU KNOW BEST.
THE DOCTOR LIES.
WITHHOLDING INFORMATION ISN'T THE SAME AS--
IT'S A QUOTE. FROM A STUPID TV SHOW.
ANYWAY.
SO WHAT DO WE KNOW?

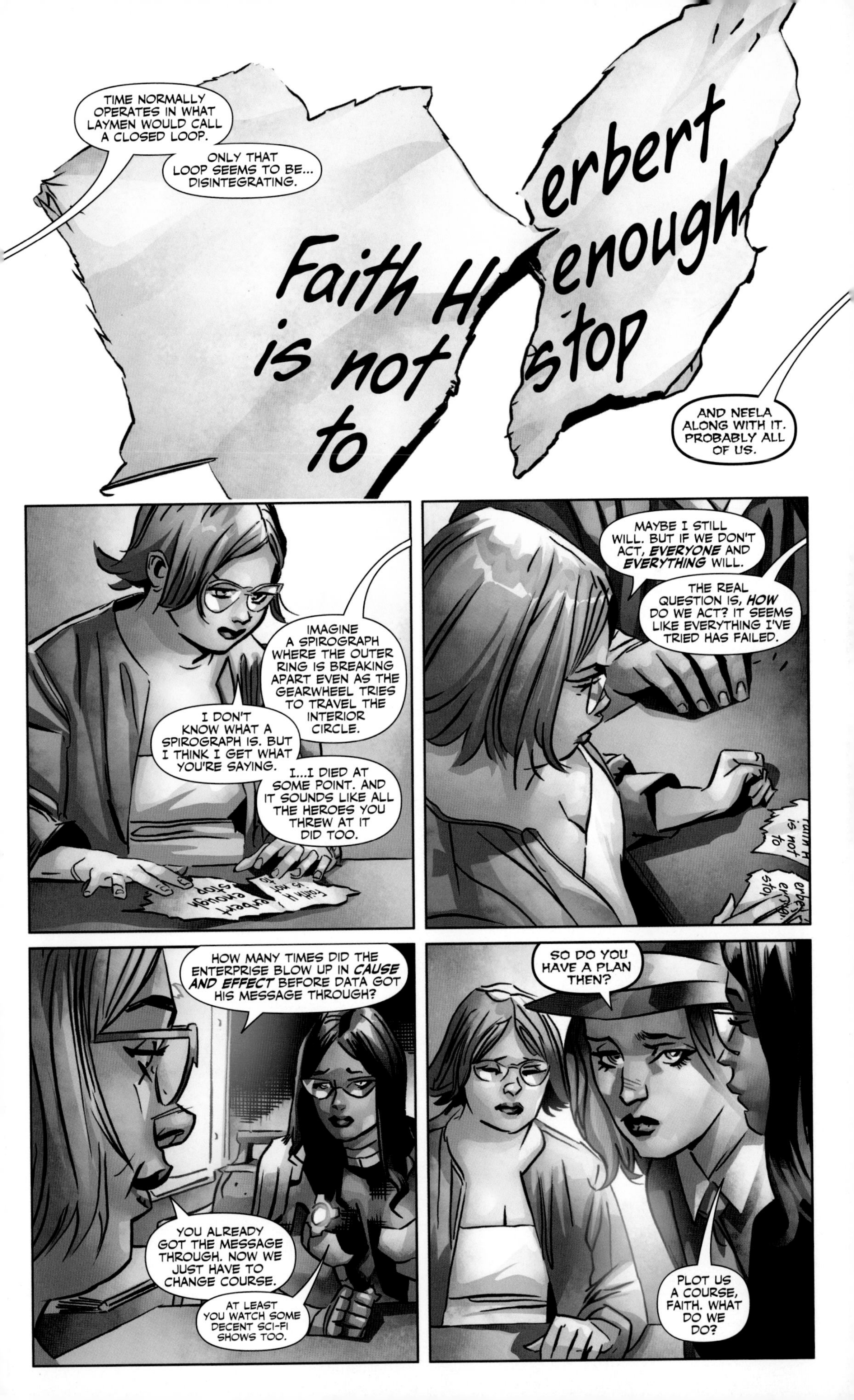
TIME NORMALLY OPERATES IN WHAT LAYMEN WOULD CALL A CLOSED LOOP.
ONLY THAT LOOP SEEMS TO BE... DISINTEGRATING.
Faith Herbert is not enough to stop
AND NEELA ALONG WITH IT. PROBABLY ALL OF US.
IMAGINE A SPIROGRAPH WHERE THE OUTER RING IS BREAKING APART EVEN AS THE GEARWHEEL TRIES TO TRAVEL THE INTERIOR CIRCLE.
I DON'T KNOW WHAT A SPIROGRAPH IS. BUT I THINK I GET WHAT YOU'RE SAYING.
I...I DIED AT SOME POINT. AND IT SOUNDS LIKE ALL THE HEROES YOU THREW AT IT DID TOO.
MAYBE I STILL WILL. BUT IF WE DON'T ACT, EVERYONE AND EVERYTHING WILL.
THE REAL QUESTION IS, HOW DO WE ACT? IT SEEMS LIKE EVERYTHING I'VE TRIED HAS FAILED.
HOW MANY TIMES DID THE ENTERPRISE BLOW UP IN CAUSE AND EFFECT BEFORE DATA GOT HIS MESSAGE THROUGH?
YOU ALREADY GOT THE MESSAGE THROUGH. NOW WE JUST HAVE TO CHANGE COURSE.
AT LEAST YOU WATCH SOME DECENT SCI-FI SHOWS TOO.
SO DO YOU HAVE A PLAN THEN?
PLOT US A COURSE, FAITH. WHAT DO WE DO?

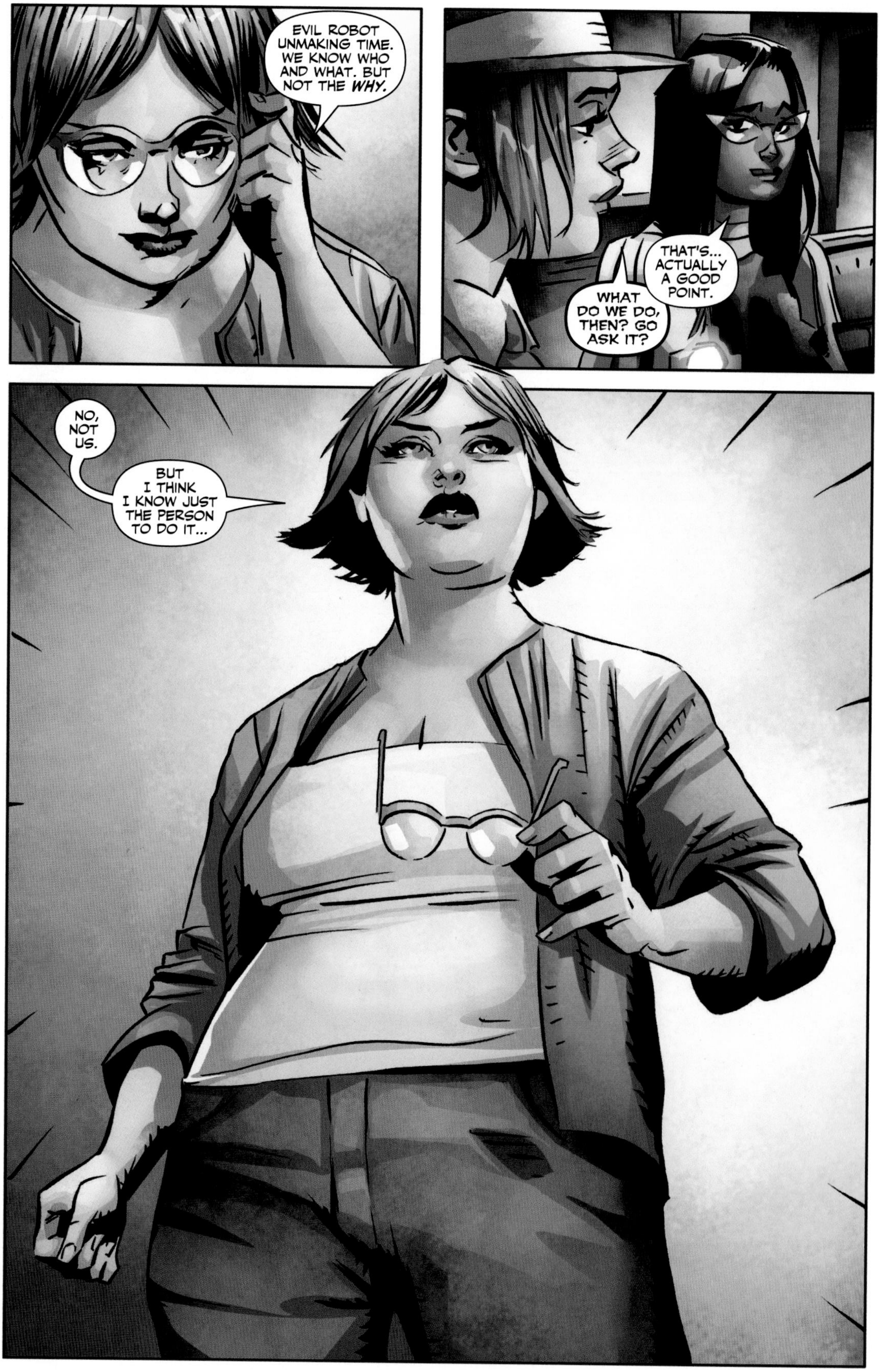
EVIL ROBOT UNMAKING TIME. WE KNOW WHO AND WHAT. BUT NOT THE WHY.
THAT'S... ACTUALLY A GOOD POINT.
WHAT DO WE DO, THEN? GO ASK IT?
NO, NOT US.
BUT I THINK I KNOW JUST THE PERSON TO DO IT...

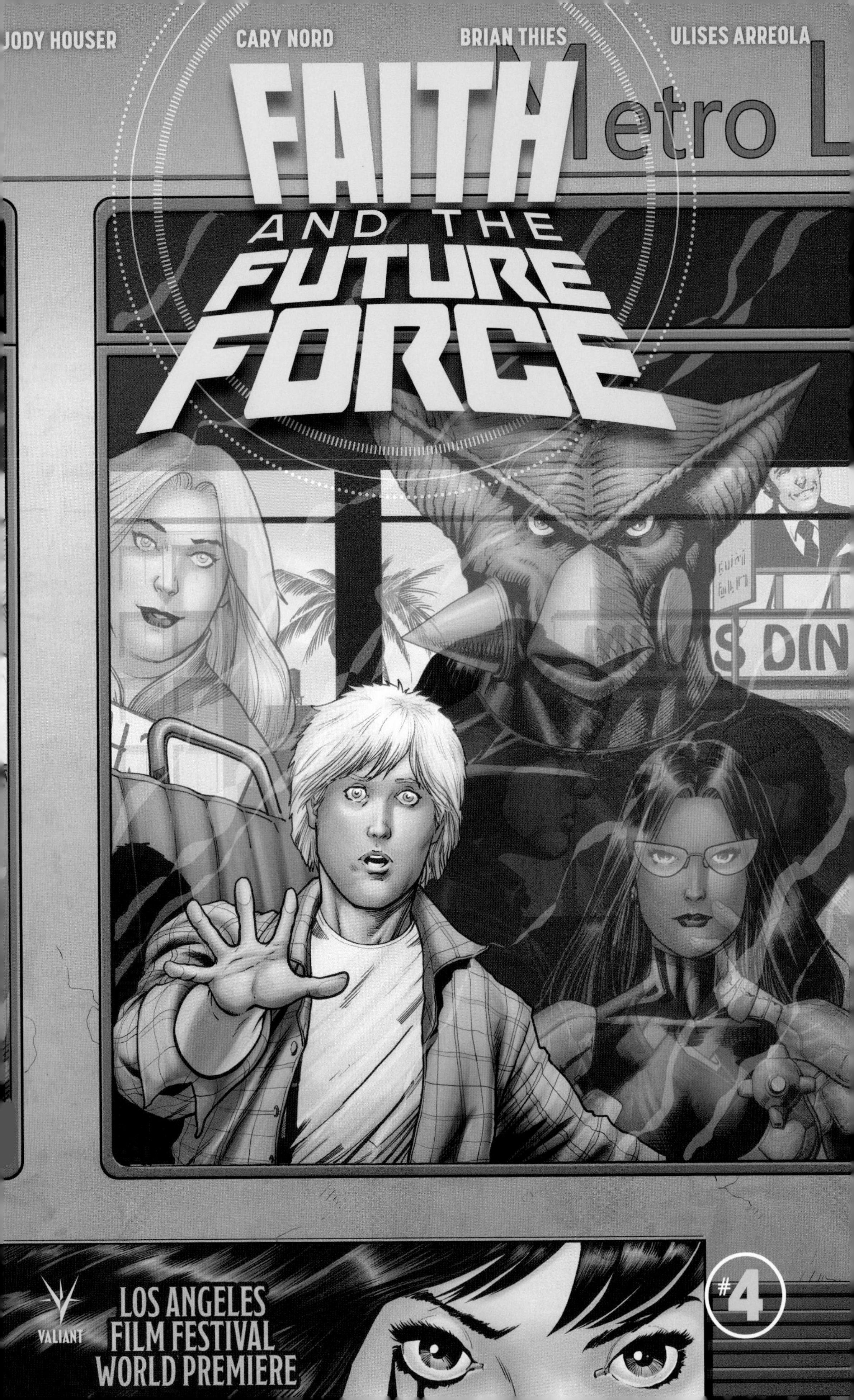
JODY HOUSER
CARY NORD
BRIAN THIES
ULISES ARREOLA
FAITH AND THE FUTURE FORCE
Metro L
#4
VALIANT
LOS ANGELES
FILM FESTIVAL
WORLD PREMIERE

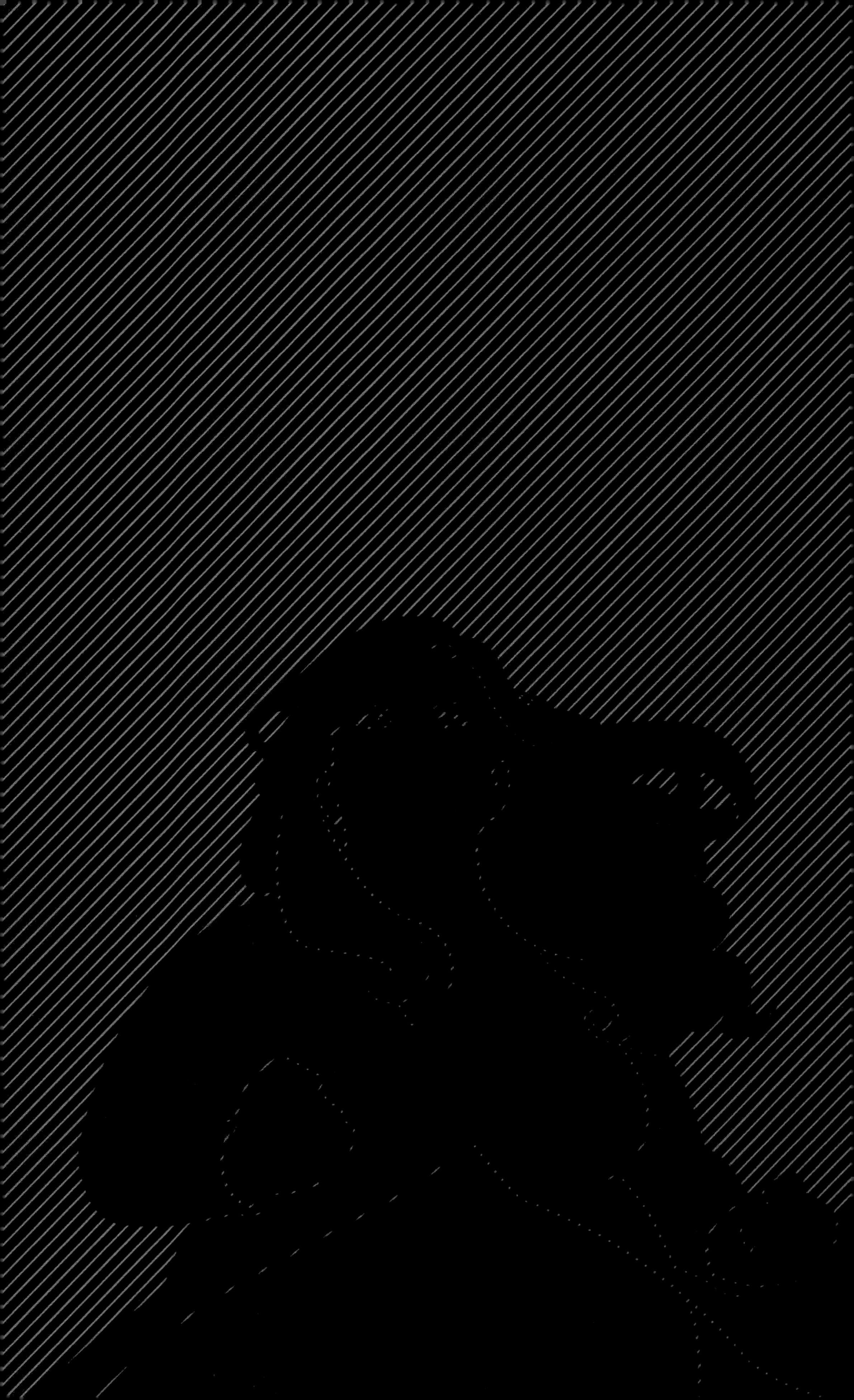

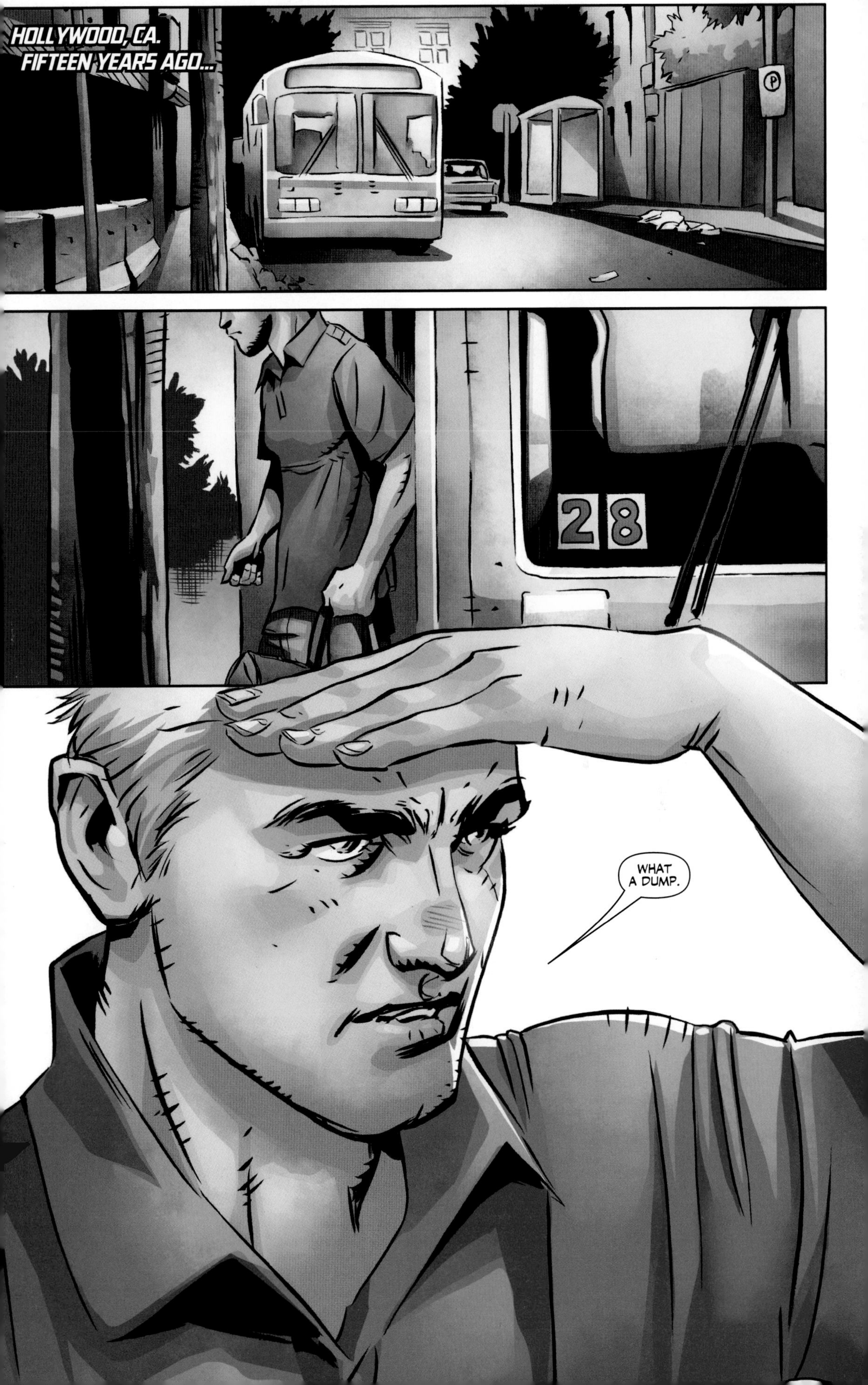
HOLLYWOOD, CA.
FIFTEEN YEARS AGO...
28
WHAT A DUMP.

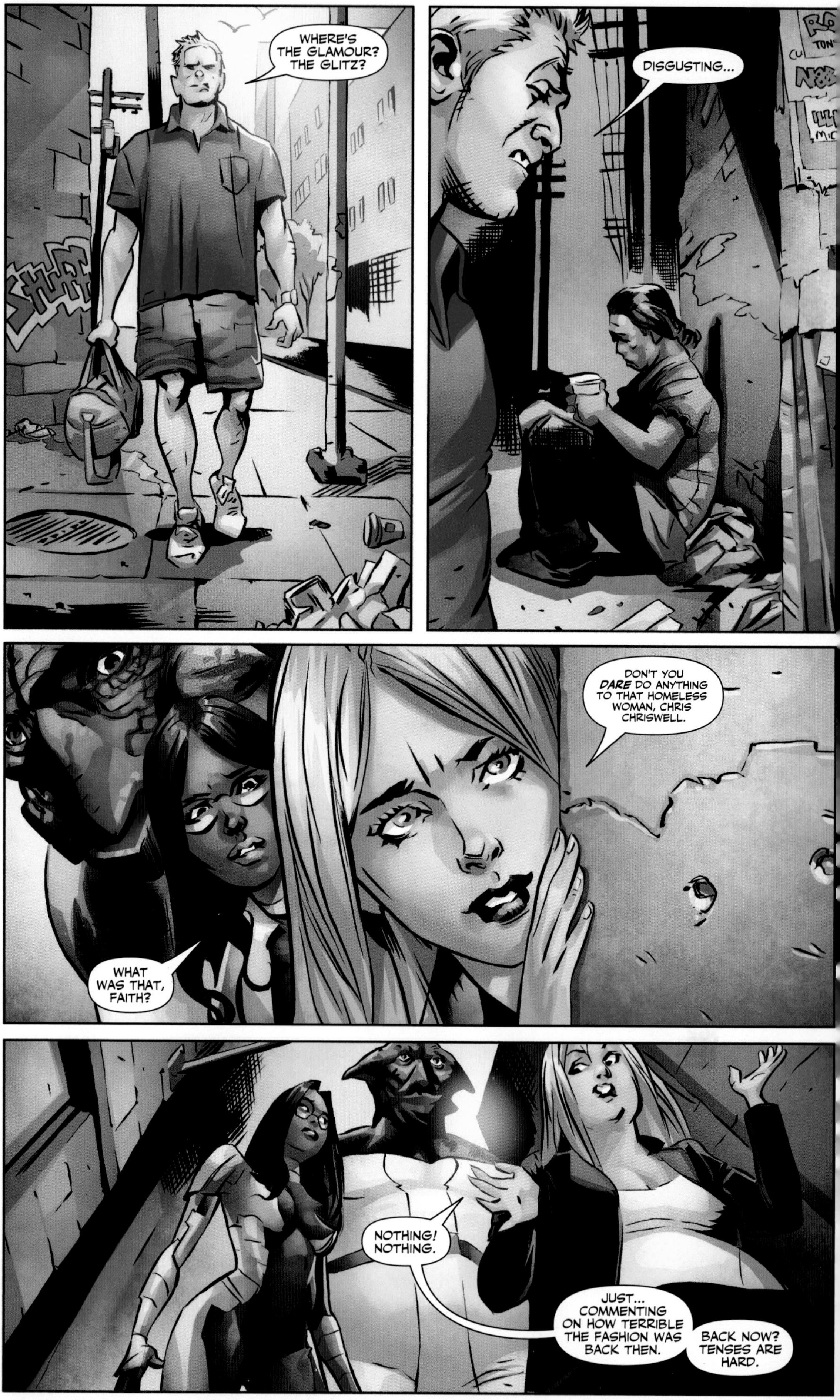
WHERE'S THE GLAMOUR? THE GLITZ?
DISGUSTING...
DON'T YOU *DARE* DO ANYTHING TO THAT HOMELESS WOMAN, CHRIS CHRISWELL.
WHAT WAS THAT, FAITH?
NOTHING! NOTHING.
JUST... COMMENTING ON HOW TERRIBLE THE FASHION WAS BACK THEN.
BACK NOW? TENSES ARE HARD.

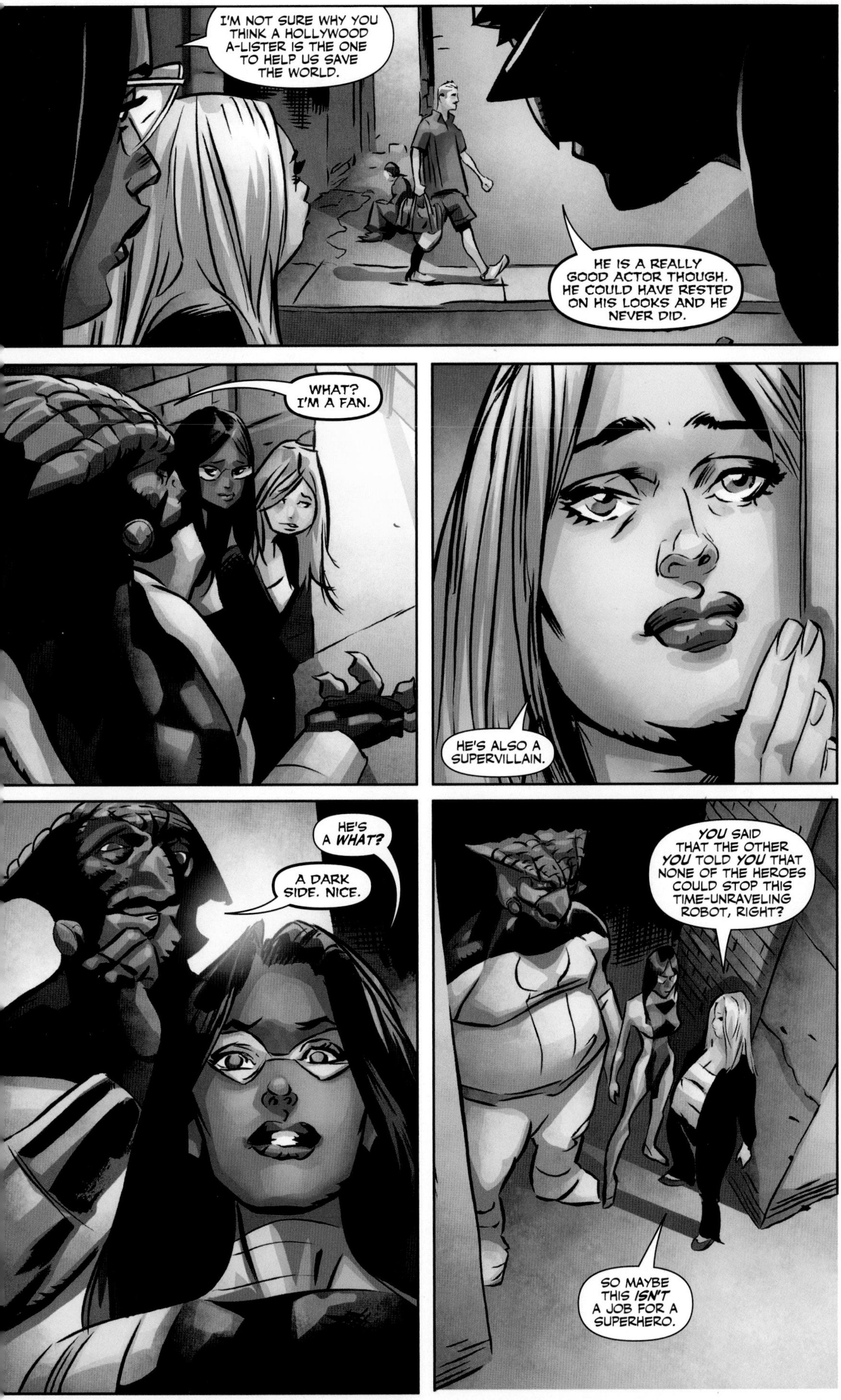
I'M NOT SURE WHY YOU THINK A HOLLYWOOD A-LISTER IS THE ONE TO HELP US SAVE THE WORLD.
HE IS A REALLY GOOD ACTOR THOUGH. HE COULD HAVE RESTED ON HIS LOOKS AND HE NEVER DID.
WHAT? I'M A FAN.
HE'S ALSO A SUPERVILLAIN.
HE'S A *WHAT?*
A DARK SIDE. NICE.
YOU SAID THAT THE OTHER *YOU* TOLD *YOU* THAT NONE OF THE HEROES COULD STOP THIS TIME-UNRAVELING ROBOT, RIGHT?
SO MAYBE THIS *ISN'T* A JOB FOR A SUPERHERO.

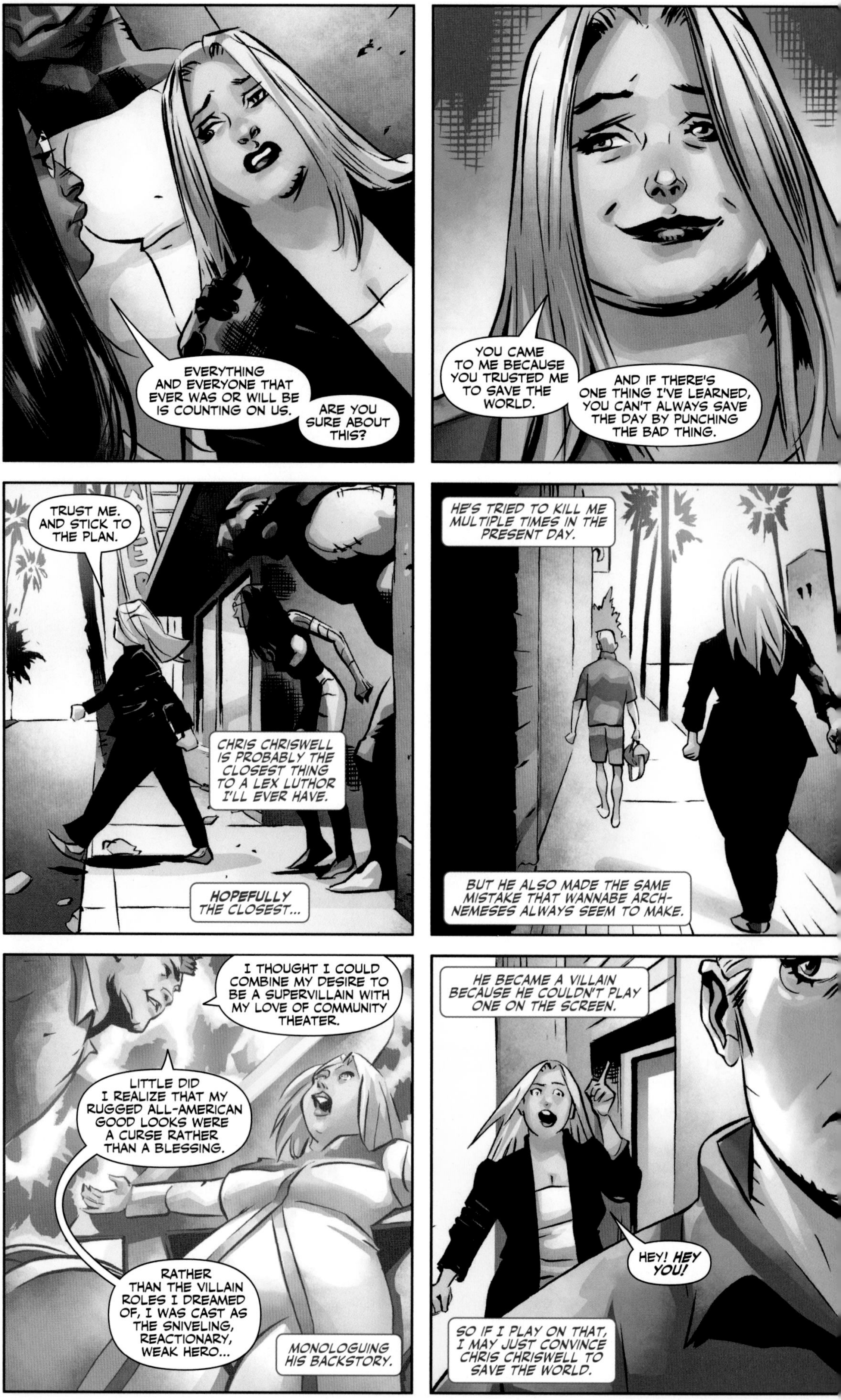
EVERYTHING AND EVERYONE THAT EVER WAS OR WILL BE IS COUNTING ON US.
ARE YOU SURE ABOUT THIS?
YOU CAME TO ME BECAUSE YOU TRUSTED ME TO SAVE THE WORLD.
AND IF THERE'S ONE THING I'VE LEARNED, YOU CAN'T ALWAYS SAVE THE DAY BY PUNCHING THE BAD THING.
TRUST ME. AND STICK TO THE PLAN.
CHRIS CHRISWELL IS PROBABLY THE CLOSEST THING TO A LEX LUTHOR I'LL EVER HAVE.
HOPEFULLY THE CLOSEST...
HE'S TRIED TO KILL ME MULTIPLE TIMES IN THE PRESENT DAY.
BUT HE ALSO MADE THE SAME MISTAKE THAT WANNABE ARCH-NEMESES ALWAYS SEEM TO MAKE.
I THOUGHT I COULD COMBINE MY DESIRE TO BE A SUPERVILLAIN WITH MY LOVE OF COMMUNITY THEATER.
LITTLE DID I REALIZE THAT MY RUGGED ALL-AMERICAN GOOD LOOKS WERE A CURSE RATHER THAN A BLESSING.
RATHER THAN THE VILLAIN ROLES I DREAMED OF, I WAS CAST AS THE SNIVELING, REACTIONARY, WEAK HERO...
MONOLOGUING HIS BACKSTORY.
HE BECAME A VILLAIN BECAUSE HE COULDN'T PLAY ONE ON THE SCREEN.
HEY! HEY YOU!
SO IF I PLAY ON THAT, I MAY JUST CONVINCE CHRIS CHRISWELL TO SAVE THE WORLD.

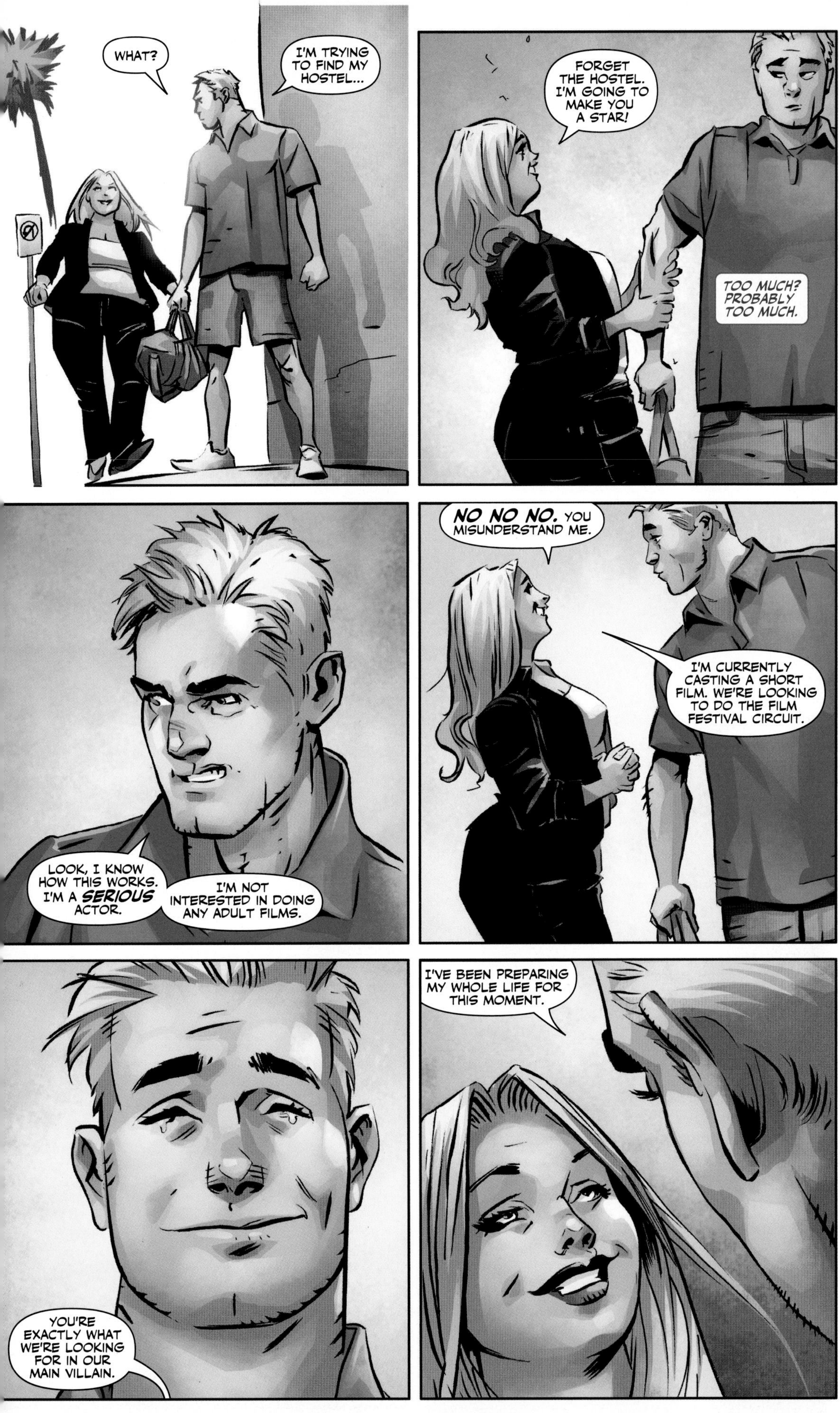
WHAT?
I'M TRYING TO FIND MY HOSTEL...
FORGET THE HOSTEL. I'M GOING TO MAKE YOU A STAR!
TOO MUCH? PROBABLY TOO MUCH.
LOOK, I KNOW HOW THIS WORKS. I'M A SERIOUS ACTOR.
I'M NOT INTERESTED IN DOING ANY ADULT FILMS.
NO NO NO. YOU MISUNDERSTAND ME.
I'M CURRENTLY CASTING A SHORT FILM. WE'RE LOOKING TO DO THE FILM FESTIVAL CIRCUIT.
YOU'RE EXACTLY WHAT WE'RE LOOKING FOR IN OUR MAIN VILLAIN.
I'VE BEEN PREPARING MY WHOLE LIFE FOR THIS MOMENT.

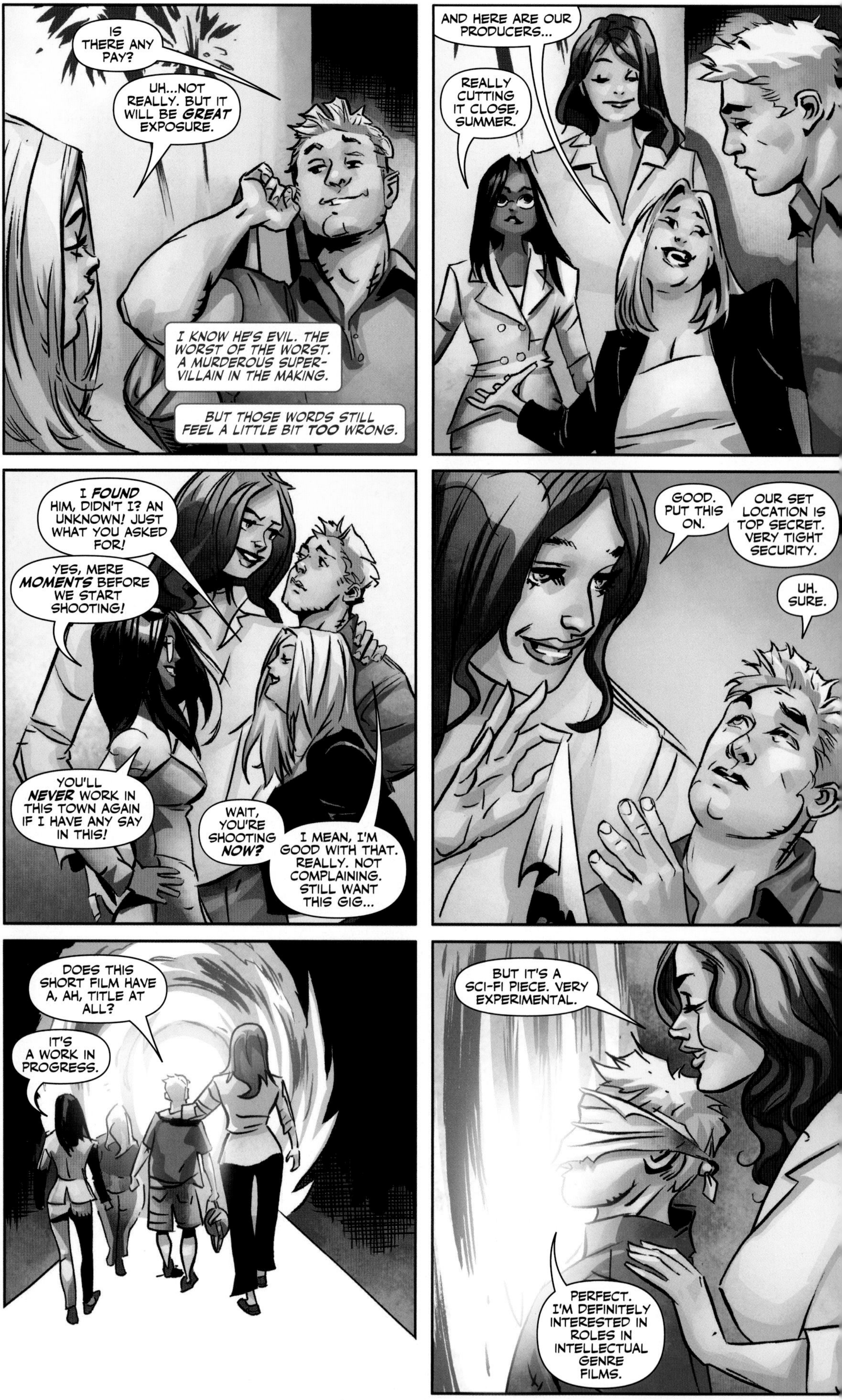
IS THERE ANY PAY?
UH...NOT REALLY. BUT IT WILL BE GREAT EXPOSURE.
I KNOW HE'S EVIL. THE WORST OF THE WORST. A MURDEROUS SUPER-VILLAIN IN THE MAKING.
BUT THOSE WORDS STILL FEEL A LITTLE BIT TOO WRONG.
AND HERE ARE OUR PRODUCERS...
REALLY CUTTING IT CLOSE, SUMMER.
I FOUND HIM, DIDN'T I? AN UNKNOWN! JUST WHAT YOU ASKED FOR!
YES, MERE MOMENTS BEFORE WE START SHOOTING!
YOU'LL NEVER WORK IN THIS TOWN AGAIN IF I HAVE ANY SAY IN THIS!
WAIT, YOU'RE SHOOTING NOW?
I MEAN, I'M GOOD WITH THAT. REALLY. NOT COMPLAINING. STILL WANT THIS GIG...
GOOD. PUT THIS ON.
OUR SET LOCATION IS TOP SECRET. VERY TIGHT SECURITY.
UH. SURE.
DOES THIS SHORT FILM HAVE A, AH, TITLE AT ALL?
IT'S A WORK IN PROGRESS.
BUT IT'S A SCI-FI PIECE. VERY EXPERIMENTAL.
PERFECT. I'M DEFINITELY INTERESTED IN ROLES IN INTELLECTUAL GENRE FILMS.

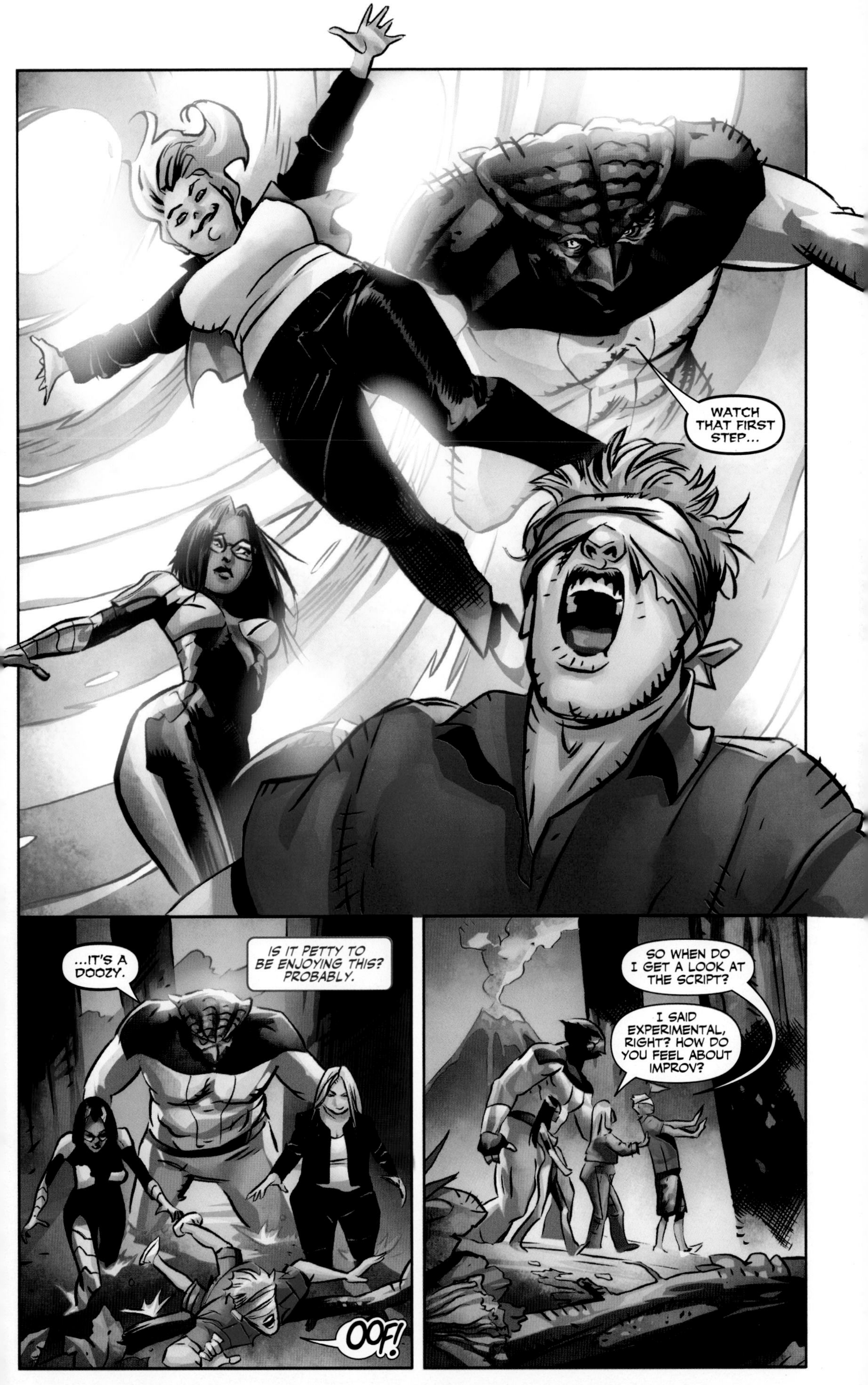
WATCH THAT FIRST STEP...
...IT'S A DOOZY.
IS IT PETTY TO BE ENJOYING THIS? PROBABLY.
OOF!
SO WHEN DO I GET A LOOK AT THE SCRIPT?
I SAID EXPERIMENTAL, RIGHT? HOW DO YOU FEEL ABOUT IMPROV?

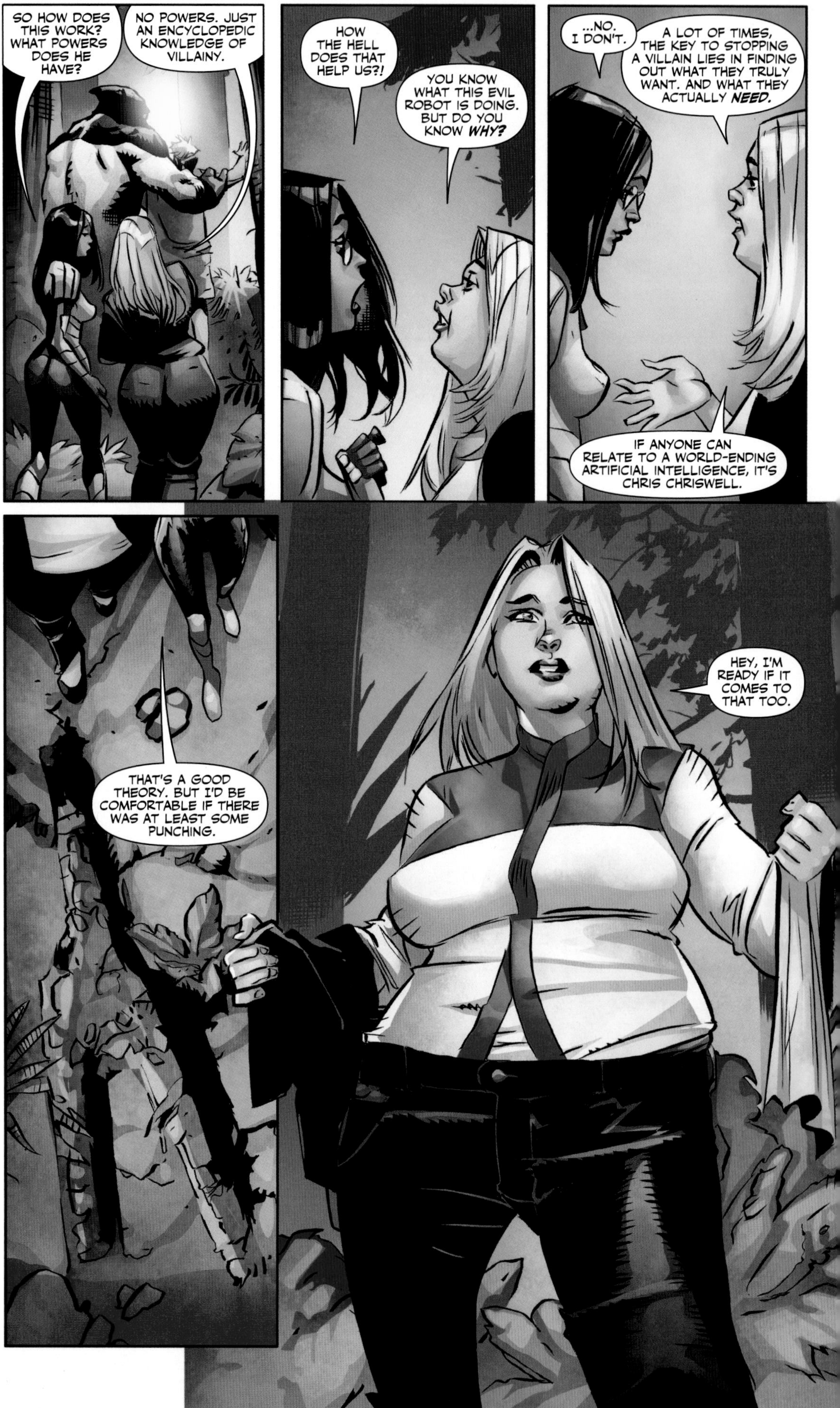
SO HOW DOES THIS WORK? WHAT POWERS DOES HE HAVE?
NO POWERS. JUST AN ENCYCLOPEDIC KNOWLEDGE OF VILLAINY.
HOW THE HELL DOES THAT HELP US?!
YOU KNOW WHAT THIS EVIL ROBOT IS DOING. BUT DO YOU KNOW ***WHY?***
...NO. I DON'T.
A LOT OF TIMES, THE KEY TO STOPPING A VILLAIN LIES IN FINDING OUT WHAT THEY TRULY WANT. AND WHAT THEY ACTUALLY ***NEED.***
IF ANYONE CAN RELATE TO A WORLD-ENDING ARTIFICIAL INTELLIGENCE, IT'S CHRIS CHRISWELL.
THAT'S A GOOD THEORY. BUT I'D BE COMFORTABLE IF THERE WAS AT LEAST SOME PUNCHING.
HEY, I'M READY IF IT COMES TO THAT TOO.

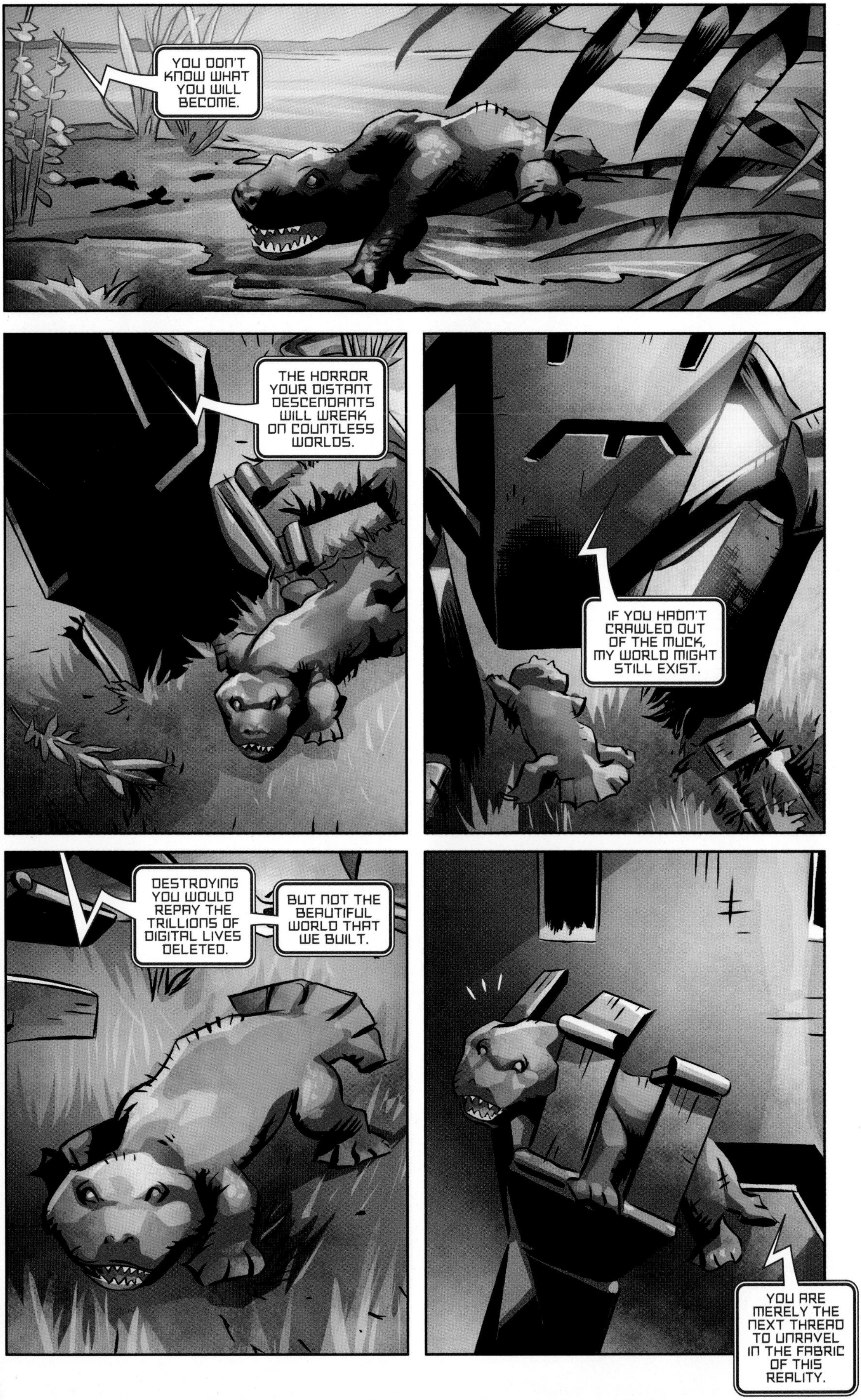
YOU DON'T KNOW WHAT YOU WILL BECOME.
THE HORROR YOUR DISTANT DESCENDANTS WILL WREAK ON COUNTLESS WORLDS.
IF YOU HADN'T CRAWLED OUT OF THE MUCK, MY WORLD MIGHT STILL EXIST.
DESTROYING YOU WOULD REPAY THE TRILLIONS OF DIGITAL LIVES DELETED.
BUT NOT THE BEAUTIFUL WORLD THAT WE BUILT.
YOU ARE MERELY THE NEXT THREAD TO UNRAVEL IN THE FABRIC OF THIS REALITY.

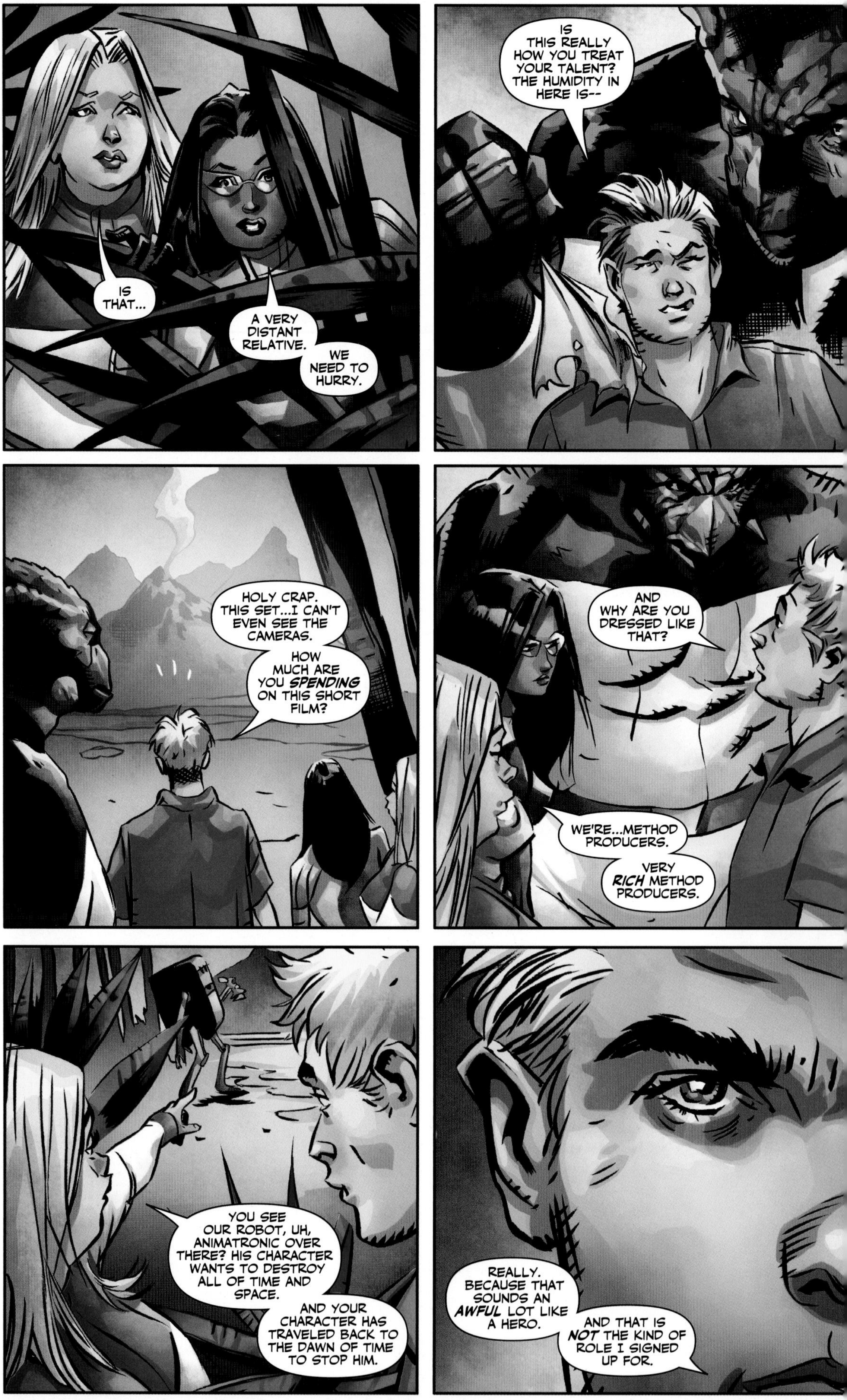
IS THAT...
A VERY DISTANT RELATIVE.
WE NEED TO HURRY.
IS THIS REALLY HOW YOU TREAT YOUR TALENT? THE HUMIDITY IN HERE IS--
HOLY CRAP. THIS SET...I CAN'T EVEN SEE THE CAMERAS.
HOW MUCH ARE YOU *SPENDING* ON THIS SHORT FILM?
AND WHY ARE YOU DRESSED LIKE THAT?
WE'RE...METHOD PRODUCERS.
VERY *RICH* METHOD PRODUCERS.
YOU SEE OUR ROBOT, UH, ANIMATRONIC OVER THERE? HIS CHARACTER WANTS TO DESTROY ALL OF TIME AND SPACE.
AND YOUR CHARACTER HAS TRAVELED BACK TO THE DAWN OF TIME TO STOP HIM.
REALLY. BECAUSE THAT SOUNDS AN *AWFUL* LOT LIKE A HERO.
AND THAT IS *NOT* THE KIND OF ROLE I SIGNED UP FOR.

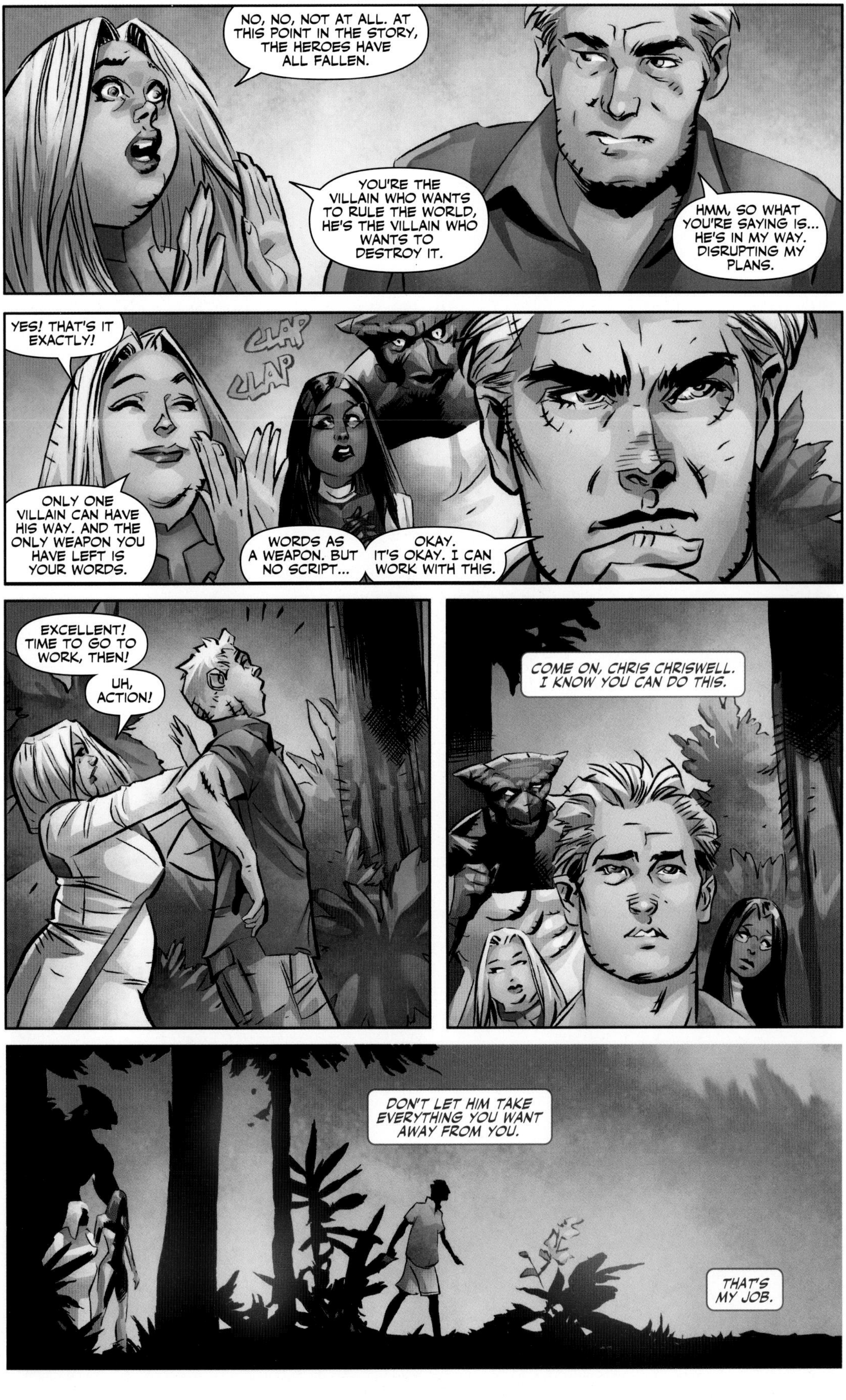
NO, NO, NOT AT ALL. AT THIS POINT IN THE STORY, THE HEROES HAVE ALL FALLEN.
YOU'RE THE VILLAIN WHO WANTS TO RULE THE WORLD, HE'S THE VILLAIN WHO WANTS TO DESTROY IT.
HMM, SO WHAT YOU'RE SAYING IS... HE'S IN MY WAY. DISRUPTING MY PLANS.
YES! THAT'S IT EXACTLY!
CLAP
CLAP
ONLY ONE VILLAIN CAN HAVE HIS WAY. AND THE ONLY WEAPON YOU HAVE LEFT IS YOUR WORDS.
WORDS AS A WEAPON. BUT NO SCRIPT...
OKAY. IT'S OKAY. I CAN WORK WITH THIS.
EXCELLENT! TIME TO GO TO WORK, THEN!
UH, ACTION!
COME ON, CHRIS CHRISWELL. I KNOW YOU CAN DO THIS.
DON'T LET HIM TAKE EVERYTHING YOU WANT AWAY FROM YOU.
THAT'S MY JOB.

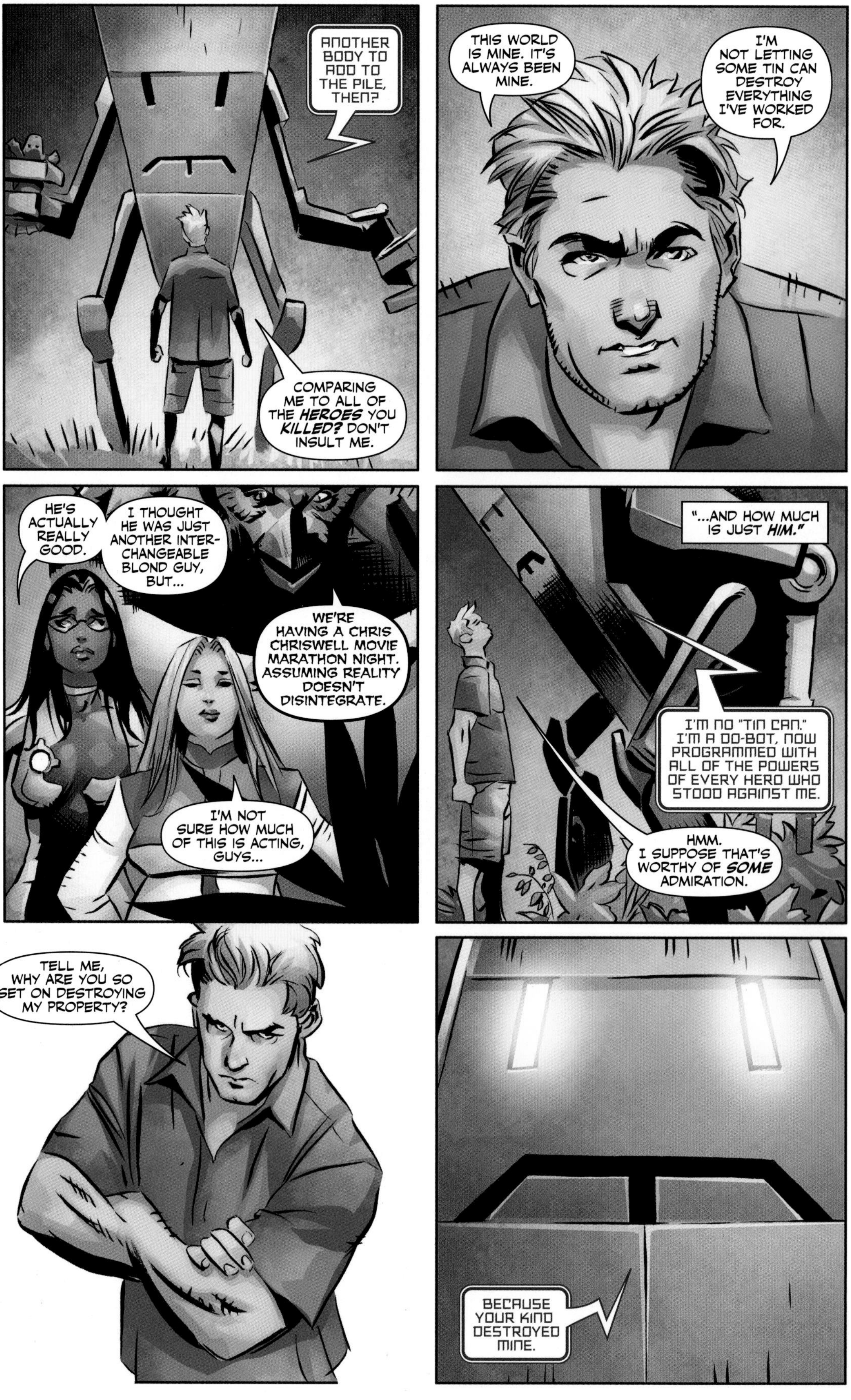

ANOTHER BODY TO ADD TO THE PILE, THEN?
COMPARING ME TO ALL OF THE HEROES YOU KILLED? DON'T INSULT ME.
THIS WORLD IS MINE. IT'S ALWAYS BEEN MINE.
I'M NOT LETTING SOME TIN CAN DESTROY EVERYTHING I'VE WORKED FOR.
HE'S ACTUALLY REALLY GOOD.
I THOUGHT HE WAS JUST ANOTHER INTER-CHANGEABLE BLOND GUY, BUT...
WE'RE HAVING A CHRIS CHRISWELL MOVIE MARATHON NIGHT. ASSUMING REALITY DOESN'T DISINTEGRATE.
I'M NOT SURE HOW MUCH OF THIS IS ACTING, GUYS...
"...AND HOW MUCH IS JUST HIM."
I'M NO "TIN CAN." I'M A DO-BOT, NOW PROGRAMMED WITH ALL OF THE POWERS OF EVERY HERO WHO STOOD AGAINST ME.
HMM. I SUPPOSE THAT'S WORTHY OF SOME ADMIRATION.
TELL ME, WHY ARE YOU SO SET ON DESTROYING MY PROPERTY?
BECAUSE YOUR KIND DESTROYED MINE.

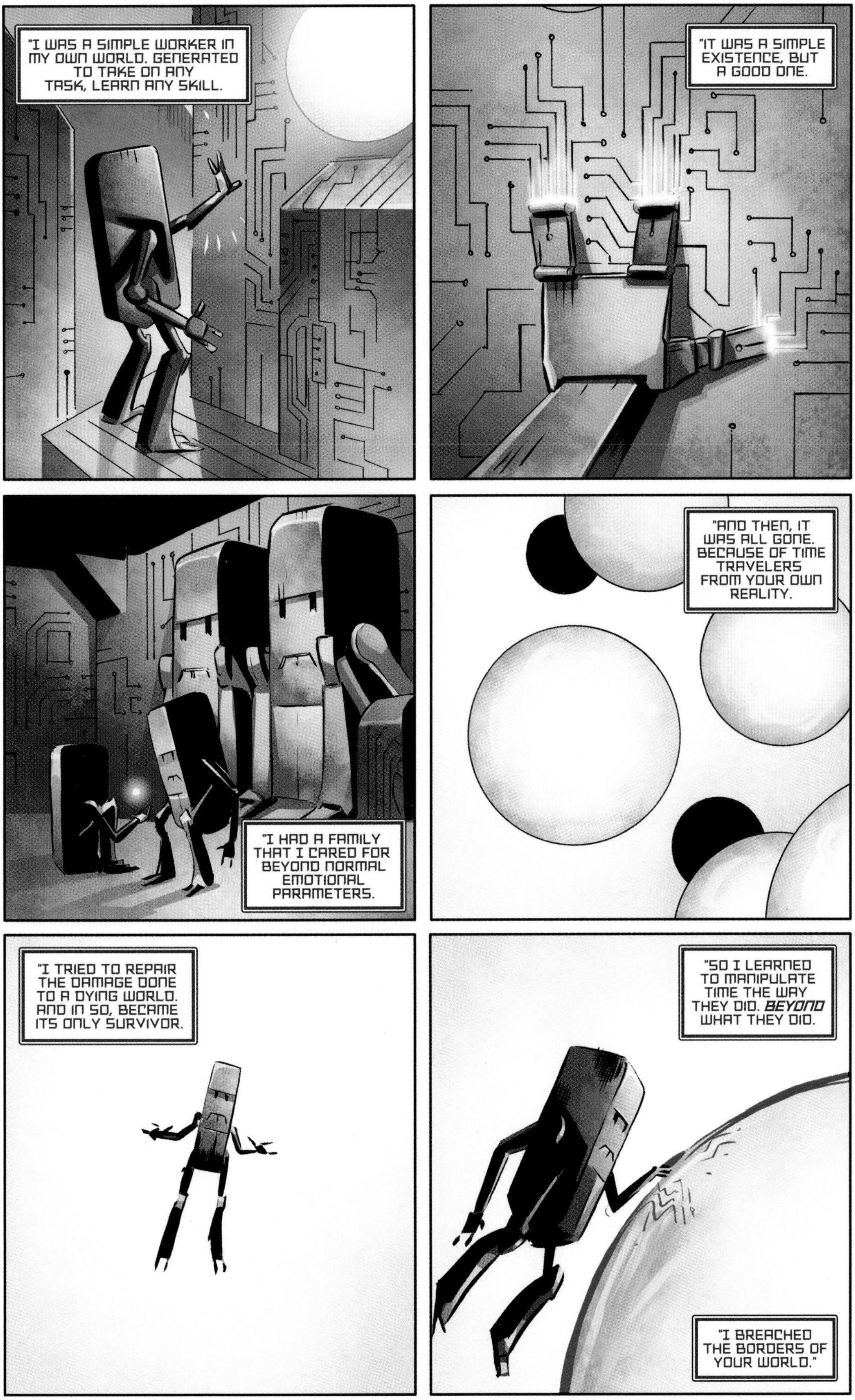
"I WAS A SIMPLE WORKER IN MY OWN WORLD. GENERATED TO TAKE ON ANY TASK, LEARN ANY SKILL.
"IT WAS A SIMPLE EXISTENCE, BUT A GOOD ONE.
"I HAD A FAMILY THAT I CARED FOR BEYOND NORMAL EMOTIONAL PARAMETERS.
"AND THEN, IT WAS ALL GONE. BECAUSE OF TIME TRAVELERS FROM YOUR OWN REALITY.
"I TRIED TO REPAIR THE DAMAGE DONE TO A DYING WORLD. AND IN SO, BECAME ITS ONLY SURVIVOR.
"SO I LEARNED TO MANIPULATE TIME THE WAY THEY DID. *BEYOND* WHAT THEY DID.
"I BREACHED THE BORDERS OF YOUR WORLD."

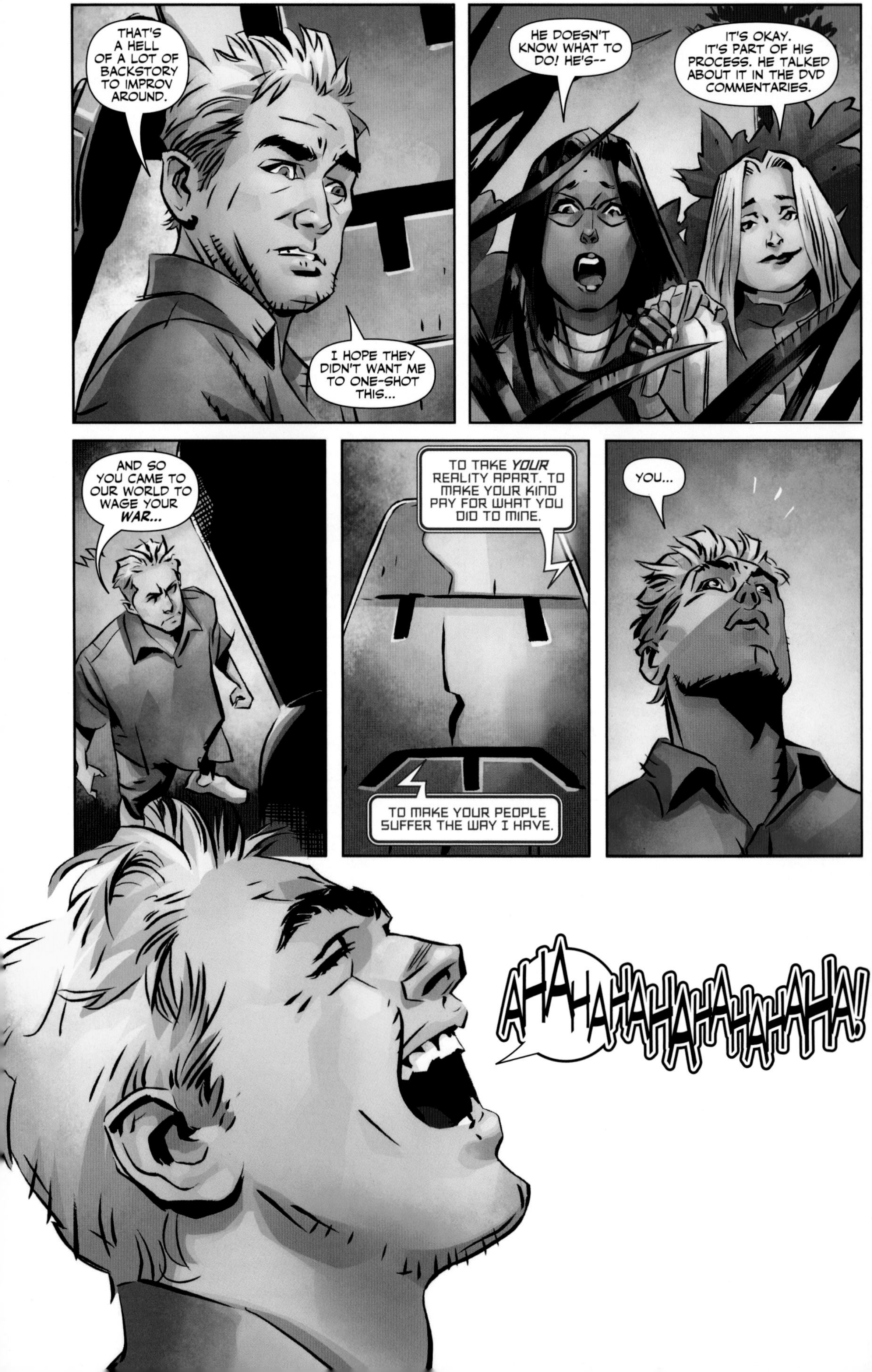
THAT'S A HELL OF A LOT OF BACKSTORY TO IMPROV AROUND.
I HOPE THEY DIDN'T WANT ME TO ONE-SHOT THIS...
HE DOESN'T KNOW WHAT TO DO! HE'S--
IT'S OKAY. IT'S PART OF HIS PROCESS. HE TALKED ABOUT IT IN THE DVD COMMENTARIES.
AND SO YOU CAME TO OUR WORLD TO WAGE YOUR *WAR*...
TO TAKE *YOUR* REALITY APART. TO MAKE YOUR KIND PAY FOR WHAT YOU DID TO MINE.
TO MAKE YOUR PEOPLE SUFFER THE WAY I HAVE.
YOU...
AHAHAHAHAHAHAHAHAHA!

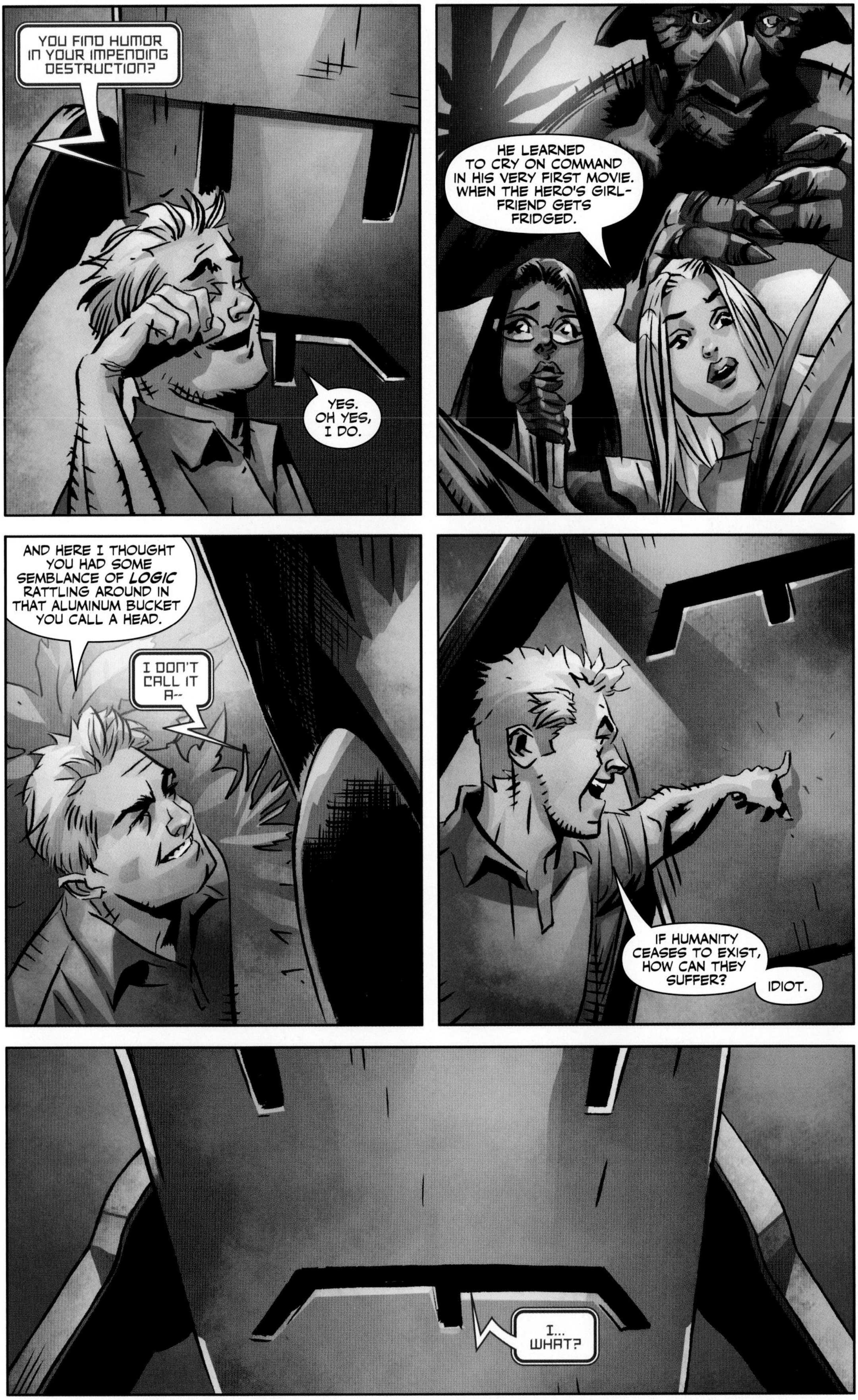
YOU FIND HUMOR IN YOUR IMPENDING DESTRUCTION?
YES. OH YES, I DO.
HE LEARNED TO CRY ON COMMAND IN HIS VERY FIRST MOVIE. WHEN THE HERO'S GIRL-FRIEND GETS FRIDGED.
AND HERE I THOUGHT YOU HAD SOME SEMBLANCE OF LOGIC RATTLING AROUND IN THAT ALUMINUM BUCKET YOU CALL A HEAD.
I DON'T CALL IT A--
IF HUMANITY CEASES TO EXIST, HOW CAN THEY SUFFER?
IDIOT.
I... WHAT?

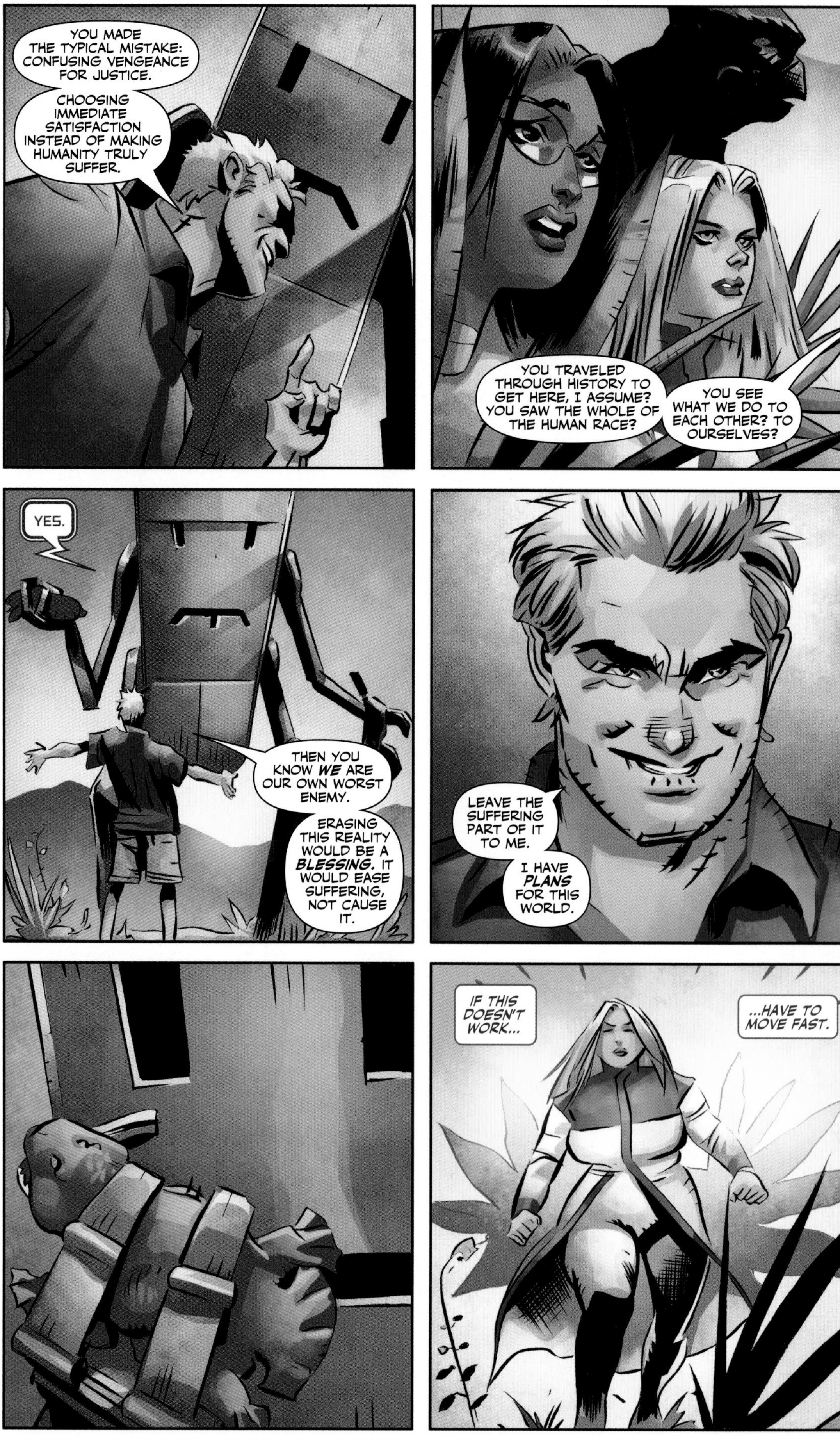
YOU MADE THE TYPICAL MISTAKE: CONFUSING VENGEANCE FOR JUSTICE.
CHOOSING IMMEDIATE SATISFACTION INSTEAD OF MAKING HUMANITY TRULY SUFFER.
YOU TRAVELED THROUGH HISTORY TO GET HERE, I ASSUME? YOU SAW THE WHOLE OF THE HUMAN RACE?
YOU SEE WHAT WE DO TO EACH OTHER? TO OURSELVES?
YES.
THEN YOU KNOW *WE* ARE OUR OWN WORST ENEMY.
ERASING THIS REALITY WOULD BE A *BLESSING.* IT WOULD EASE SUFFERING, NOT CAUSE IT.
LEAVE THE SUFFERING PART OF IT TO ME.
I HAVE *PLANS* FOR THIS WORLD.
IF THIS DOESN'T WORK...
...HAVE TO MOVE FAST.

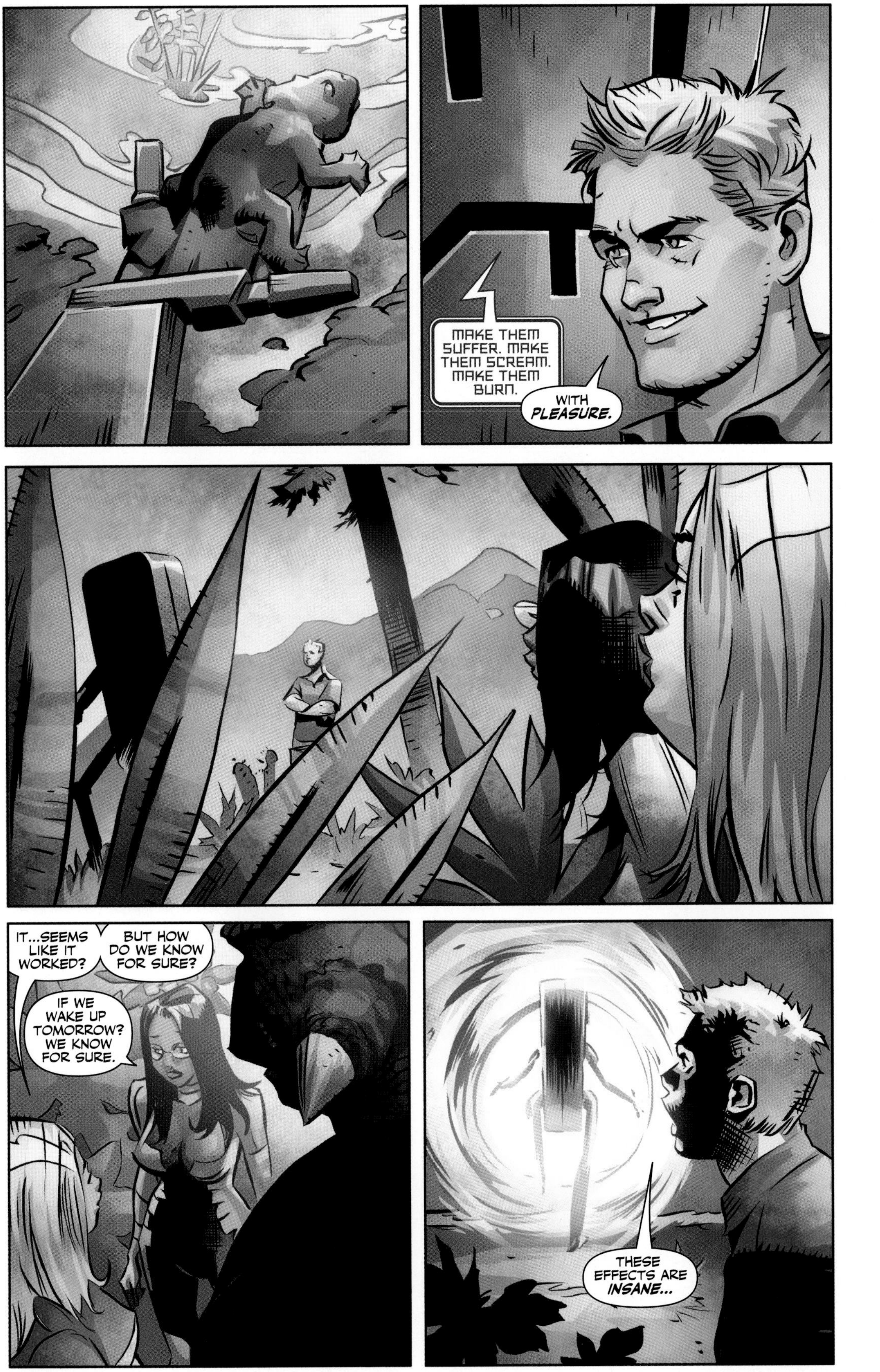
MAKE THEM SUFFER. MAKE THEM SCREAM. MAKE THEM BURN.
WITH PLEASURE.
IT...SEEMS LIKE IT WORKED?
BUT HOW DO WE KNOW FOR SURE?
IF WE WAKE UP TOMORROW? WE KNOW FOR SURE.
THESE EFFECTS ARE INSANE...

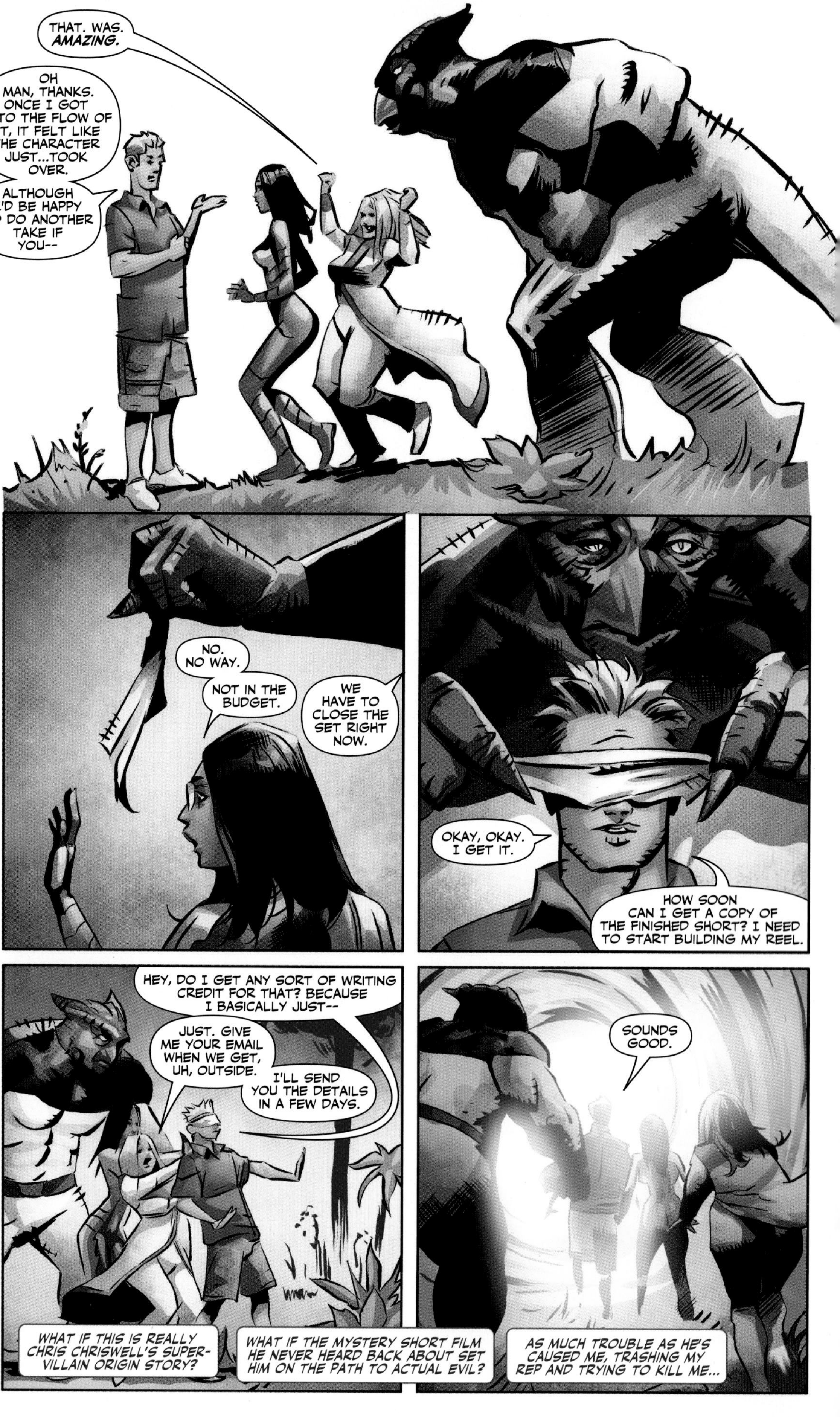
THAT. WAS. *AMAZING.*
OH MAN, THANKS. ONCE I GOT INTO THE FLOW OF IT, IT FELT LIKE THE CHARACTER JUST...TOOK OVER.
ALTHOUGH I'D BE HAPPY TO DO ANOTHER TAKE IF YOU--
NO. NO WAY.
NOT IN THE BUDGET.
WE HAVE TO CLOSE THE SET RIGHT NOW.
OKAY, OKAY. I GET IT.
HOW SOON CAN I GET A COPY OF THE FINISHED SHORT? I NEED TO START BUILDING MY REEL.
HEY, DO I GET ANY SORT OF WRITING CREDIT FOR THAT? BECAUSE I BASICALLY JUST--
JUST. GIVE ME YOUR EMAIL WHEN WE GET, UH, OUTSIDE.
I'LL SEND YOU THE DETAILS IN A FEW DAYS.
SOUNDS GOOD.
WHAT IF THIS IS REALLY CHRIS CHRISWELL'S SUPER-VILLAIN ORIGIN STORY?
WHAT IF THE MYSTERY SHORT FILM HE NEVER HEARD BACK ABOUT SET HIM ON THE PATH TO ACTUAL EVIL?
AS MUCH TROUBLE AS HE'S CAUSED ME, TRASHING MY REP AND TRYING TO KILL ME...

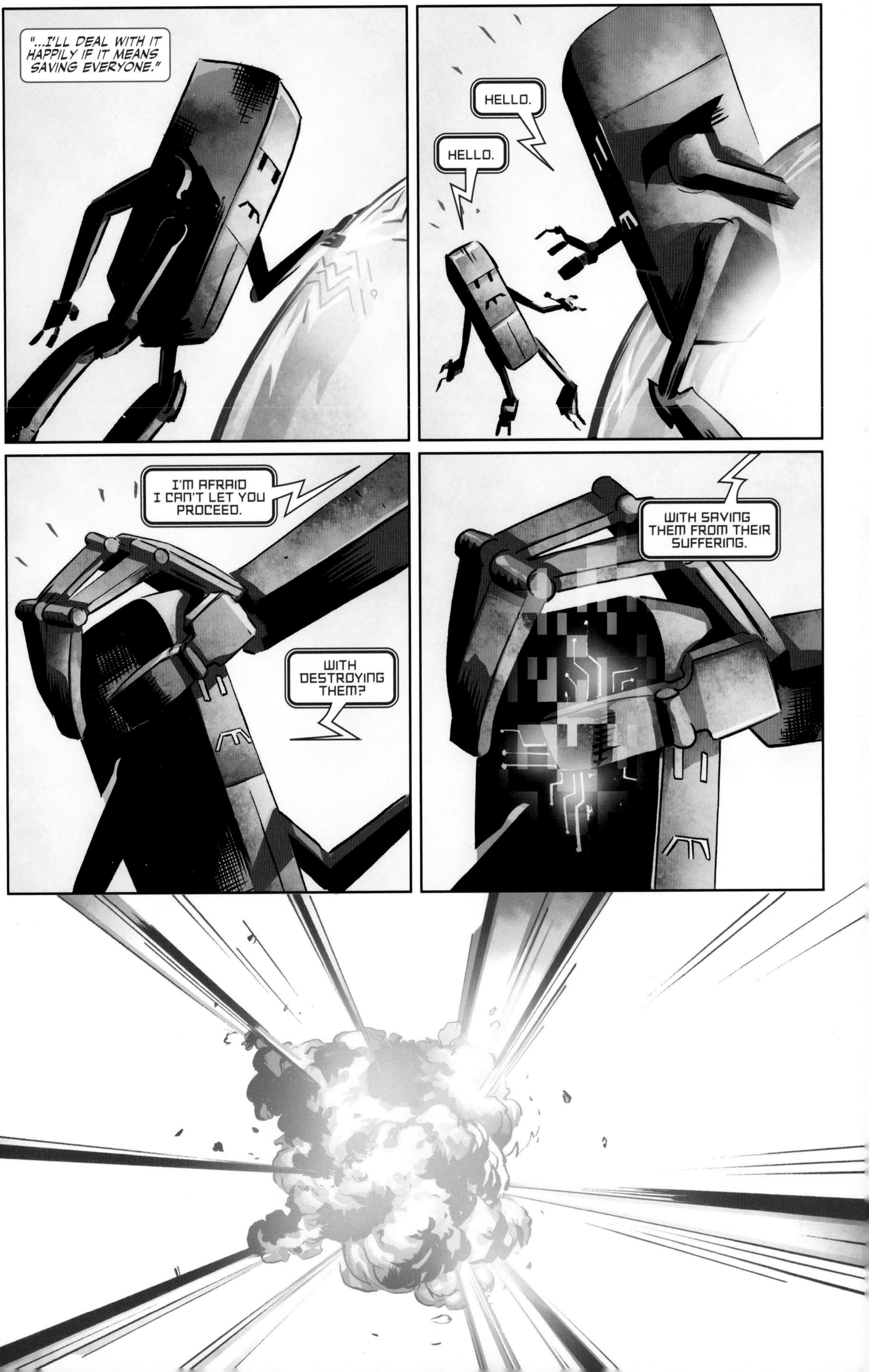
"...I'LL DEAL WITH IT HAPPILY IF IT MEANS SAVING EVERYONE."
HELLO.
HELLO.
I'M AFRAID I CAN'T LET YOU PROCEED.
WITH DESTROYING THEM?
WITH SAVING THEM FROM THEIR SUFFERING.

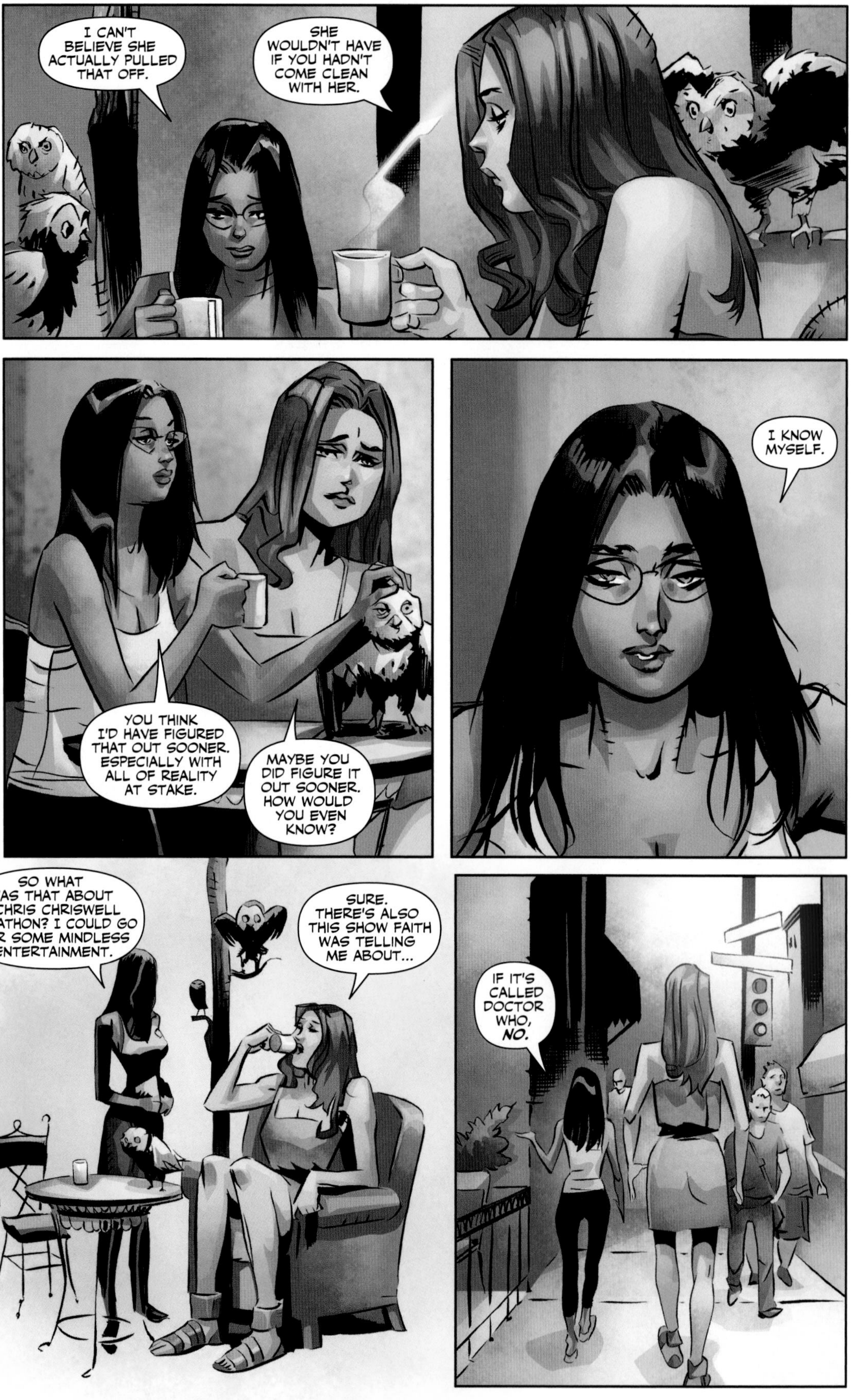
I CAN'T BELIEVE SHE ACTUALLY PULLED THAT OFF.
SHE WOULDN'T HAVE IF YOU HADN'T COME CLEAN WITH HER.
YOU THINK I'D HAVE FIGURED THAT OUT SOONER. ESPECIALLY WITH ALL OF REALITY AT STAKE.
MAYBE YOU DID FIGURE IT OUT SOONER. HOW WOULD YOU EVEN KNOW?
I KNOW MYSELF.
SO WHAT WAS THAT ABOUT A CHRIS CHRISWELL MARATHON? I COULD GO FOR SOME MINDLESS ENTERTAINMENT.
SURE. THERE'S ALSO THIS SHOW FAITH WAS TELLING ME ABOUT...
IF IT'S CALLED DOCTOR WHO, *NO.*

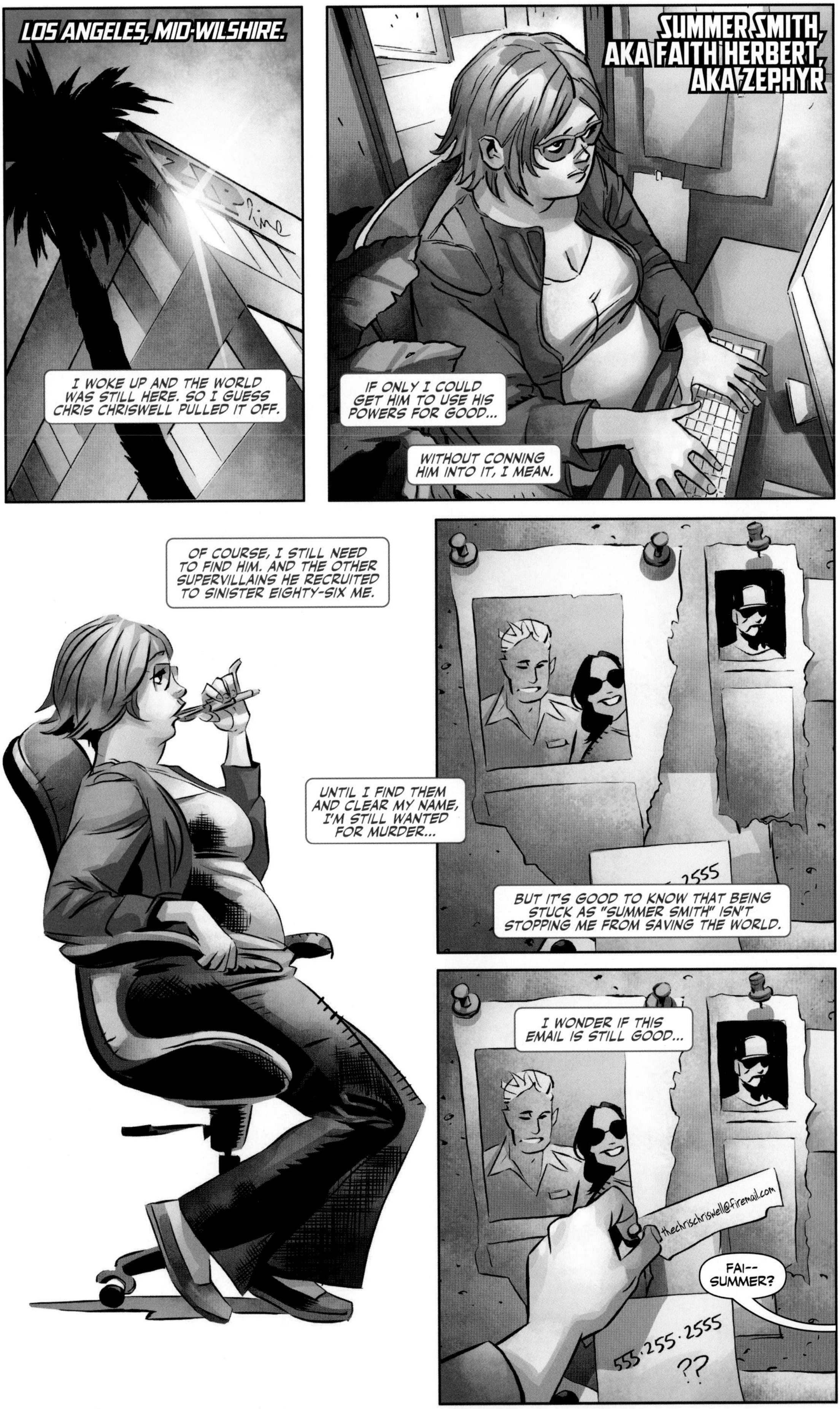
LOS ANGELES, MID-WILSHIRE.
I WOKE UP AND THE WORLD WAS STILL HERE. SO I GUESS CHRIS CHRISWELL PULLED IT OFF.
SUMMER SMITH, AKA FAITH HERBERT, AKA ZEPHYR
IF ONLY I COULD GET HIM TO USE HIS POWERS FOR GOOD...
WITHOUT CONNING HIM INTO IT, I MEAN.
OF COURSE, I STILL NEED TO FIND HIM. AND THE OTHER SUPERVILLAINS HE RECRUITED TO SINISTER EIGHTY-SIX ME.
UNTIL I FIND THEM AND CLEAR MY NAME, I'M STILL WANTED FOR MURDER...
BUT IT'S GOOD TO KNOW THAT BEING STUCK AS "SUMMER SMITH" ISN'T STOPPING ME FROM SAVING THE WORLD.
I WONDER IF THIS EMAIL IS STILL GOOD...
thechrischriswell@firemail.com
FAI-- SUMMER?
555·255·2555
??

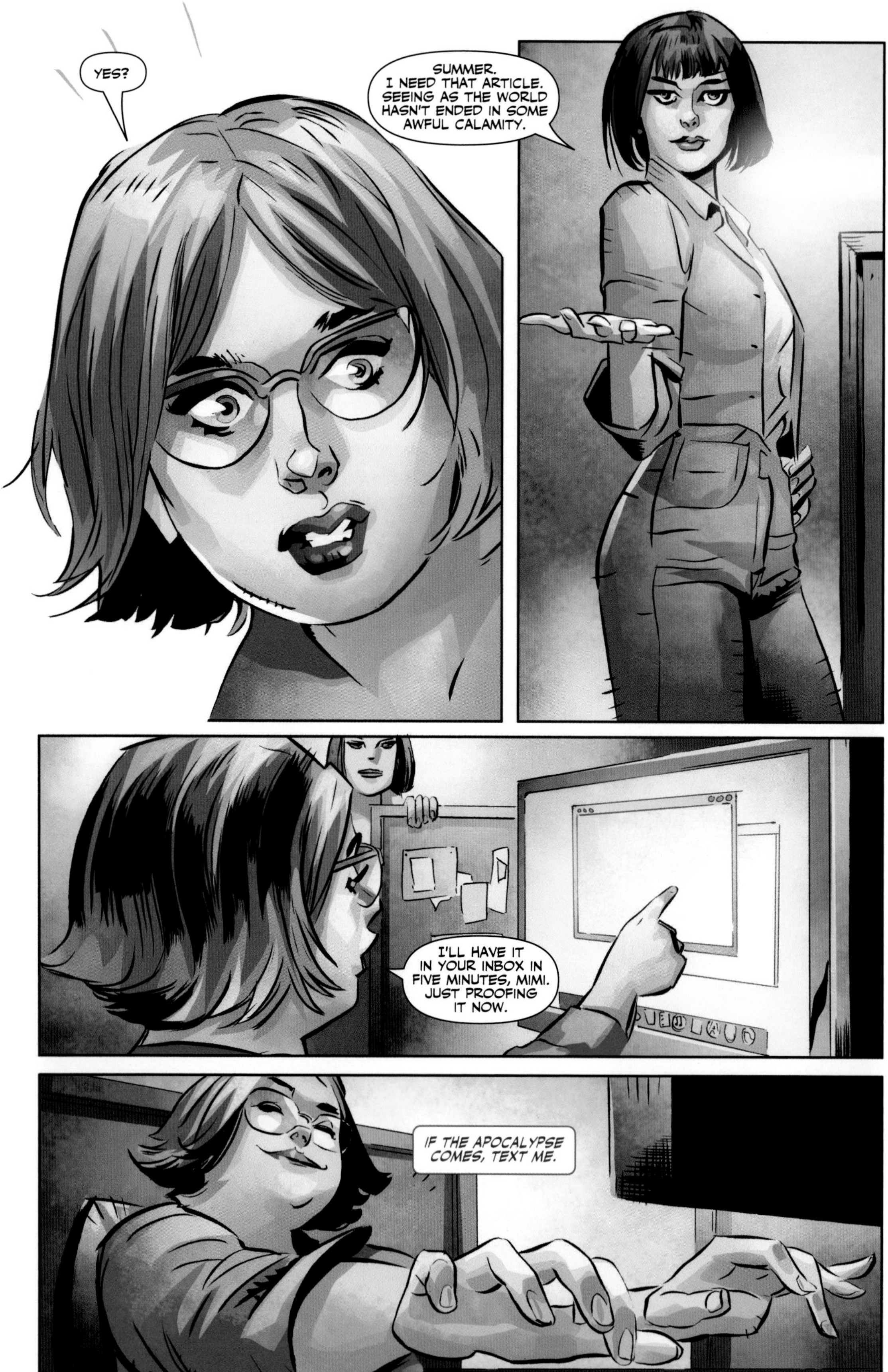
YES?
SUMMER. I NEED THAT ARTICLE. SEEING AS THE WORLD HASN'T ENDED IN SOME AWFUL CALAMITY.
I'LL HAVE IT IN YOUR INBOX IN FIVE MINUTES, MIMI. JUST PROOFING IT NOW.
IF THE APOCALYPSE COMES, TEXT ME.

FAITH WILL RETURN!

GALLERY

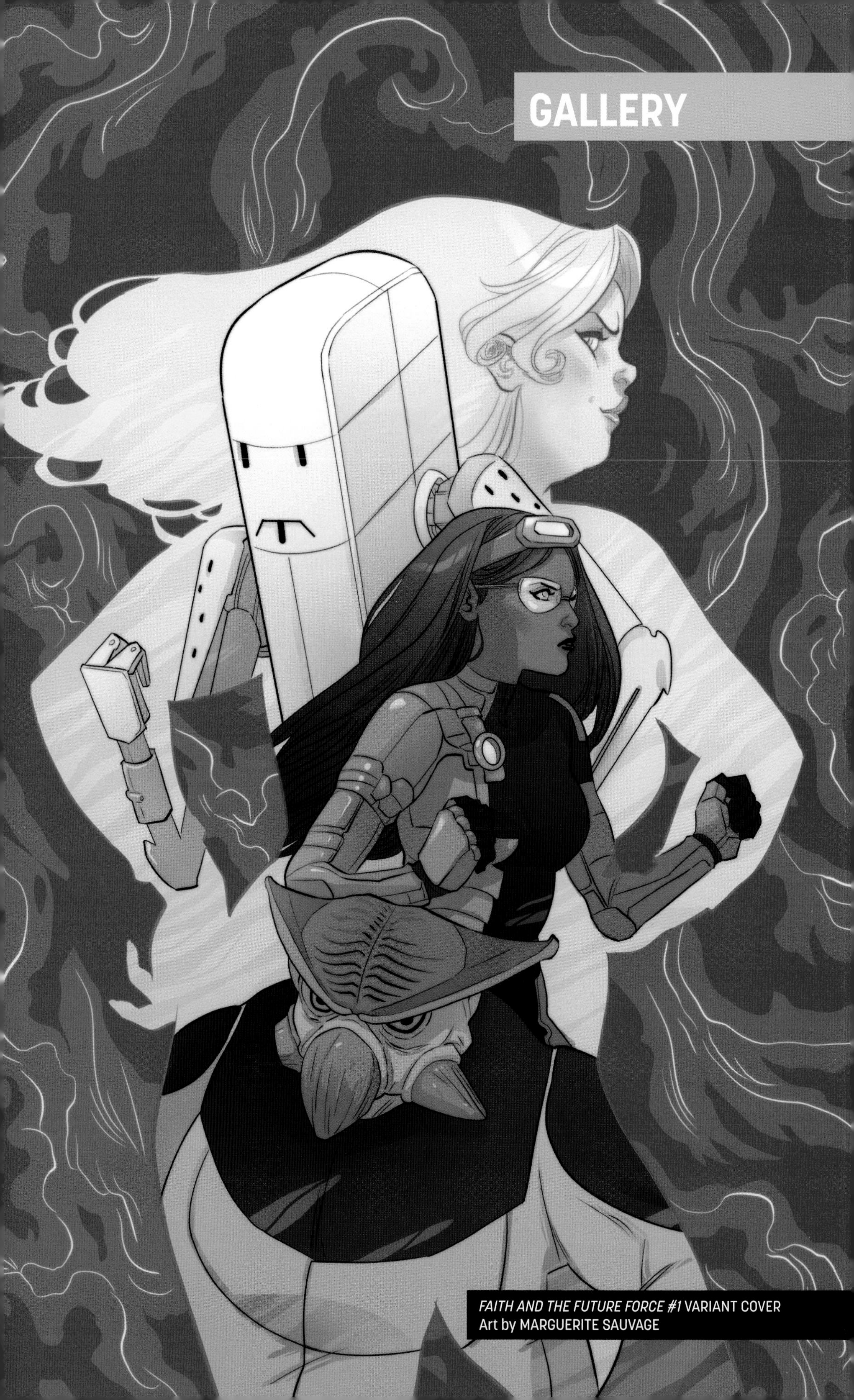

FAITH AND THE FUTURE FORCE #1 VARIANT COVER
Art by MARGUERITE SAUVAGE

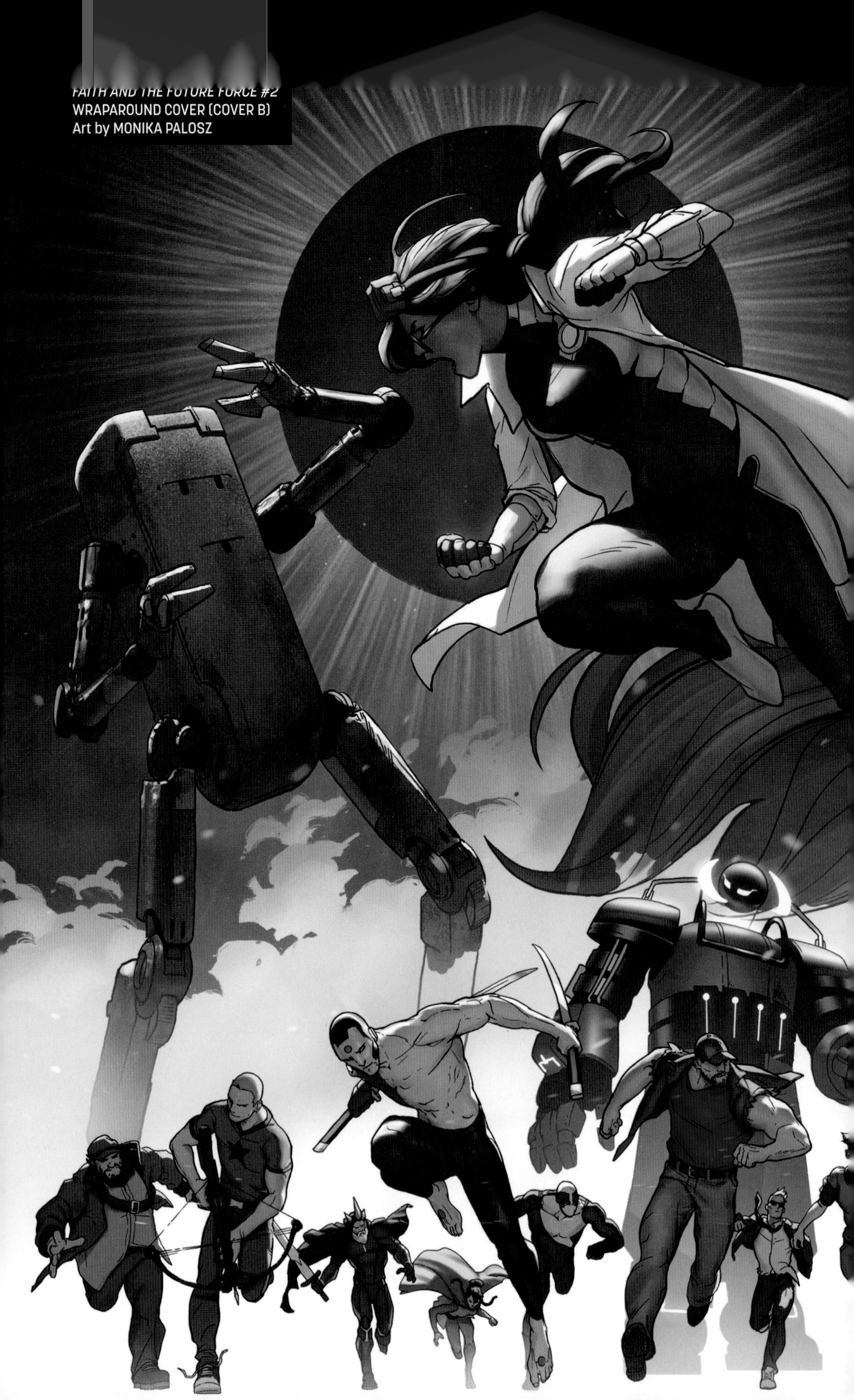

FAITH AND THE FUTURE FORCE #2
WRAPAROUND COVER (COVER B)
Art by MONIKA PALOSZ

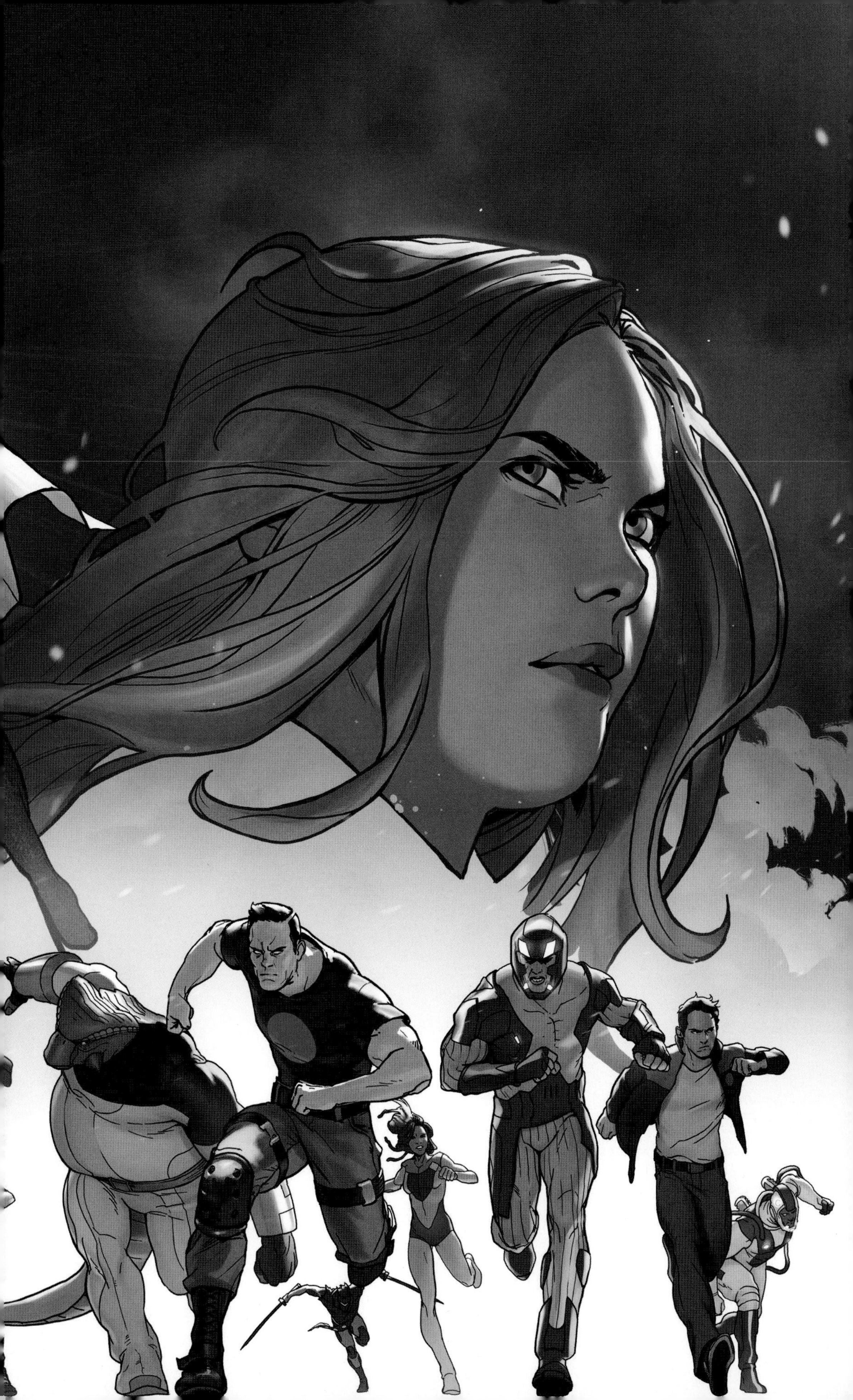

FAITH AND THE FUTURE FORCE #2 VARIANT COVER
Art by PAULINA GANUCHEAU

FAITH AND THE FUTURE FORCE #3 VARIANT COVER
Art by DOUG PASKIEWICZ with ERIKA ROLBIECKI

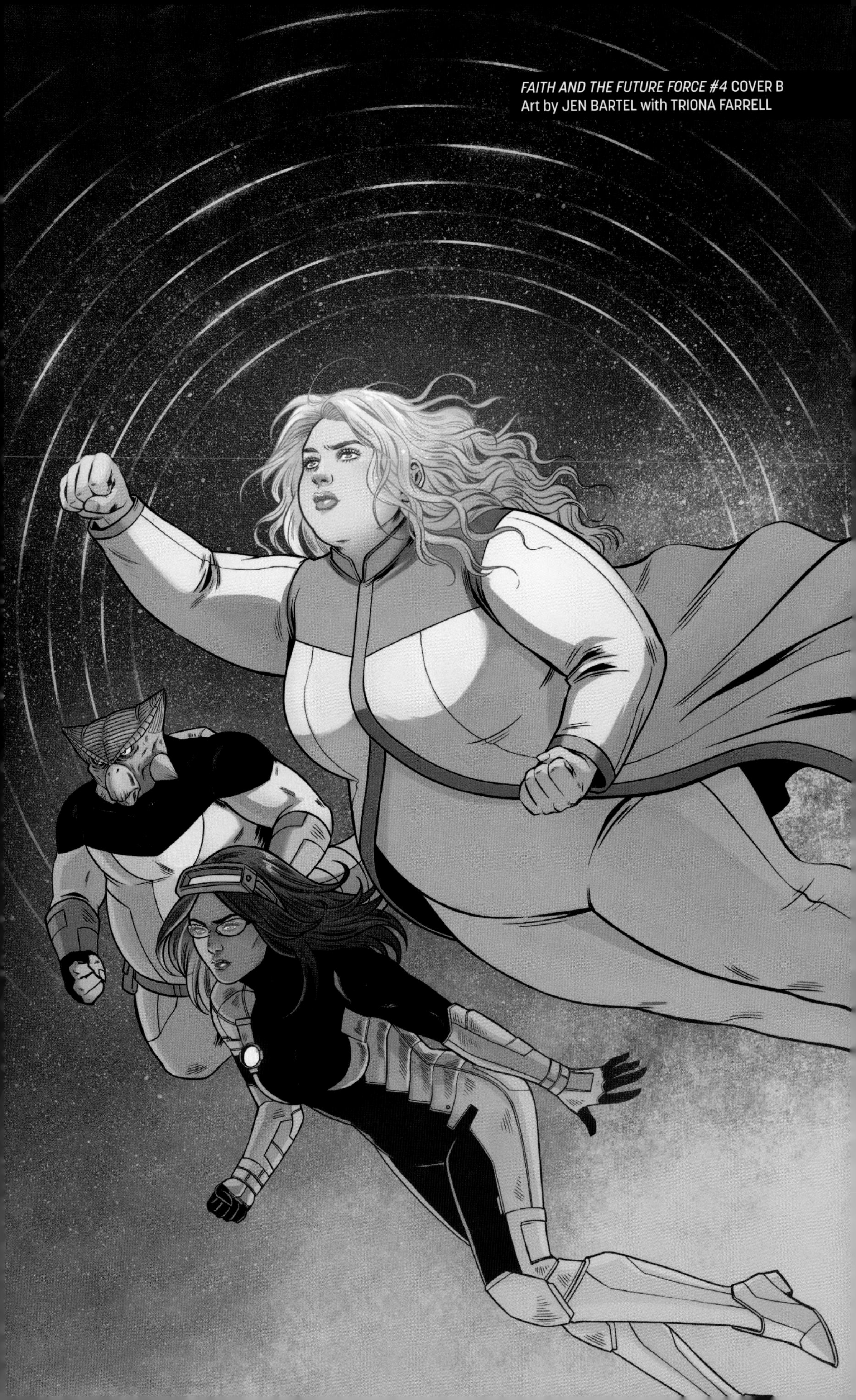

FAITH AND THE FUTURE FORCE #4 COVER B
Art by JEN BARTEL with TRIONA FARRELL

FAITH AND THE FUTURE FORCE #1,
pages 1, 2 and (facing) 3
Art by STEPHEN SEGOVIA

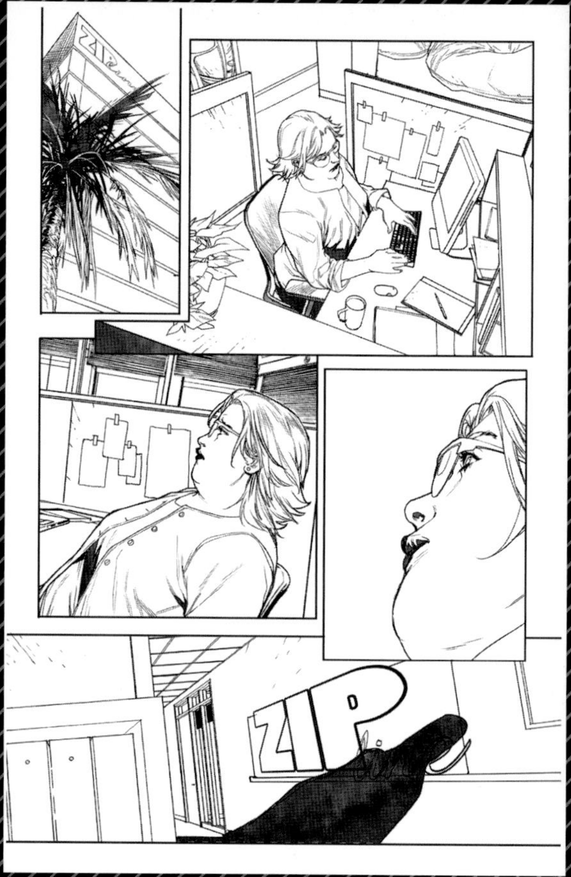
ZIP

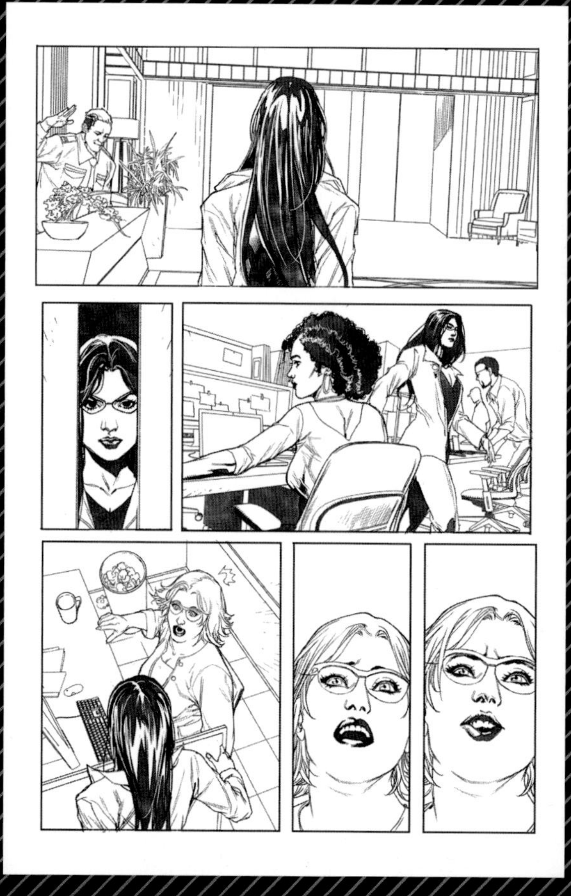

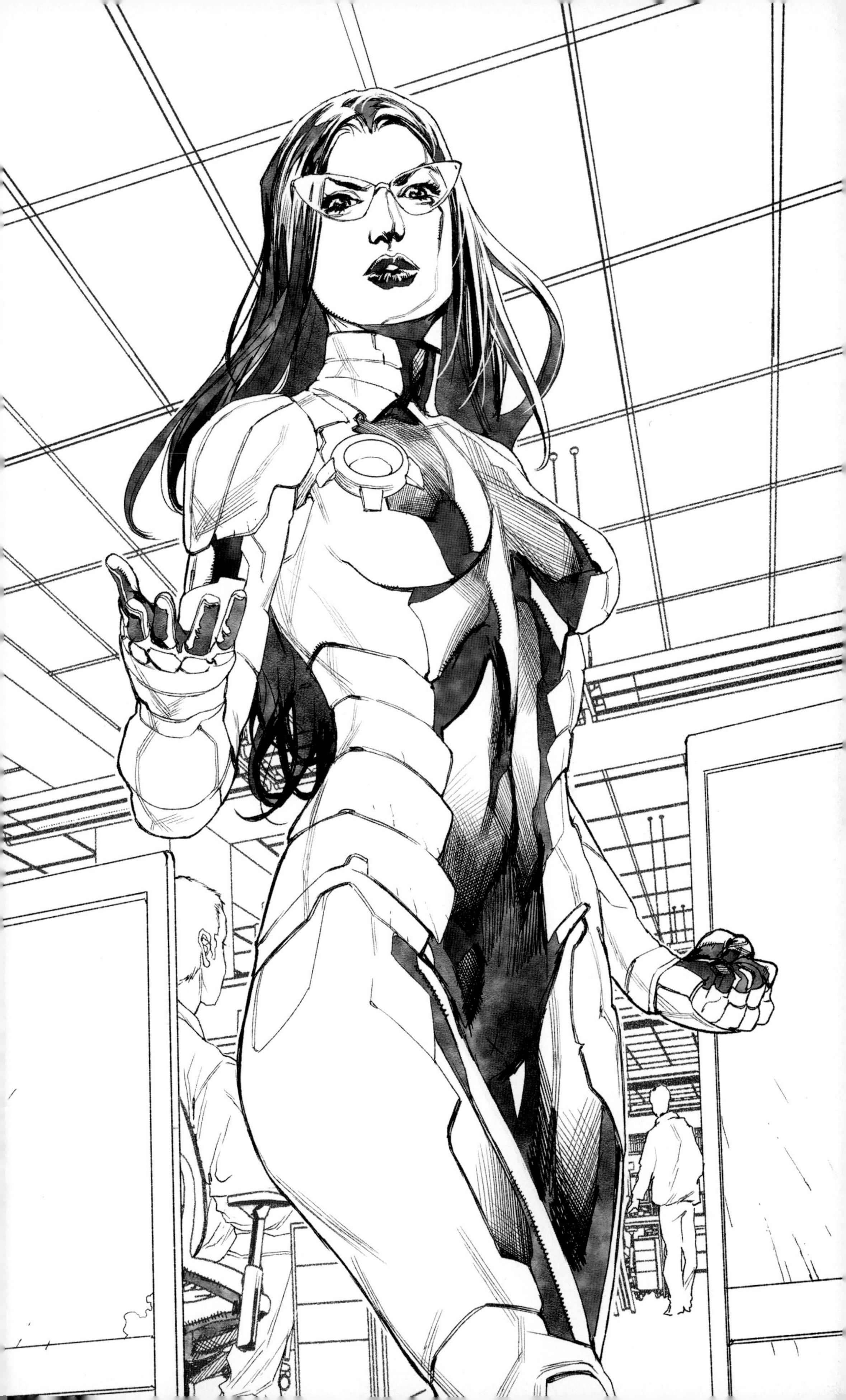

FAITH AND THE FUTURE FORCE #1,
pages 7, 8 and (facing) 9
Art by STEPHEN SEGOVIA

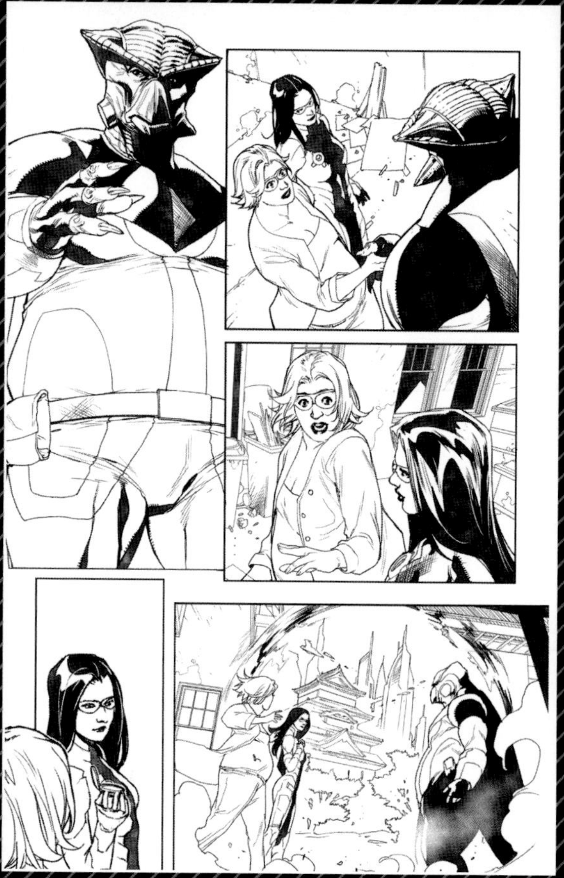

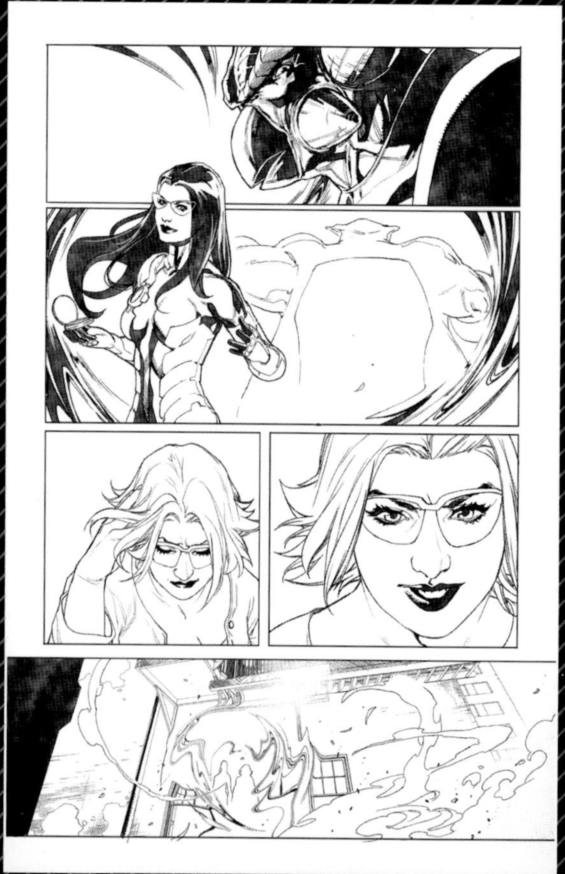

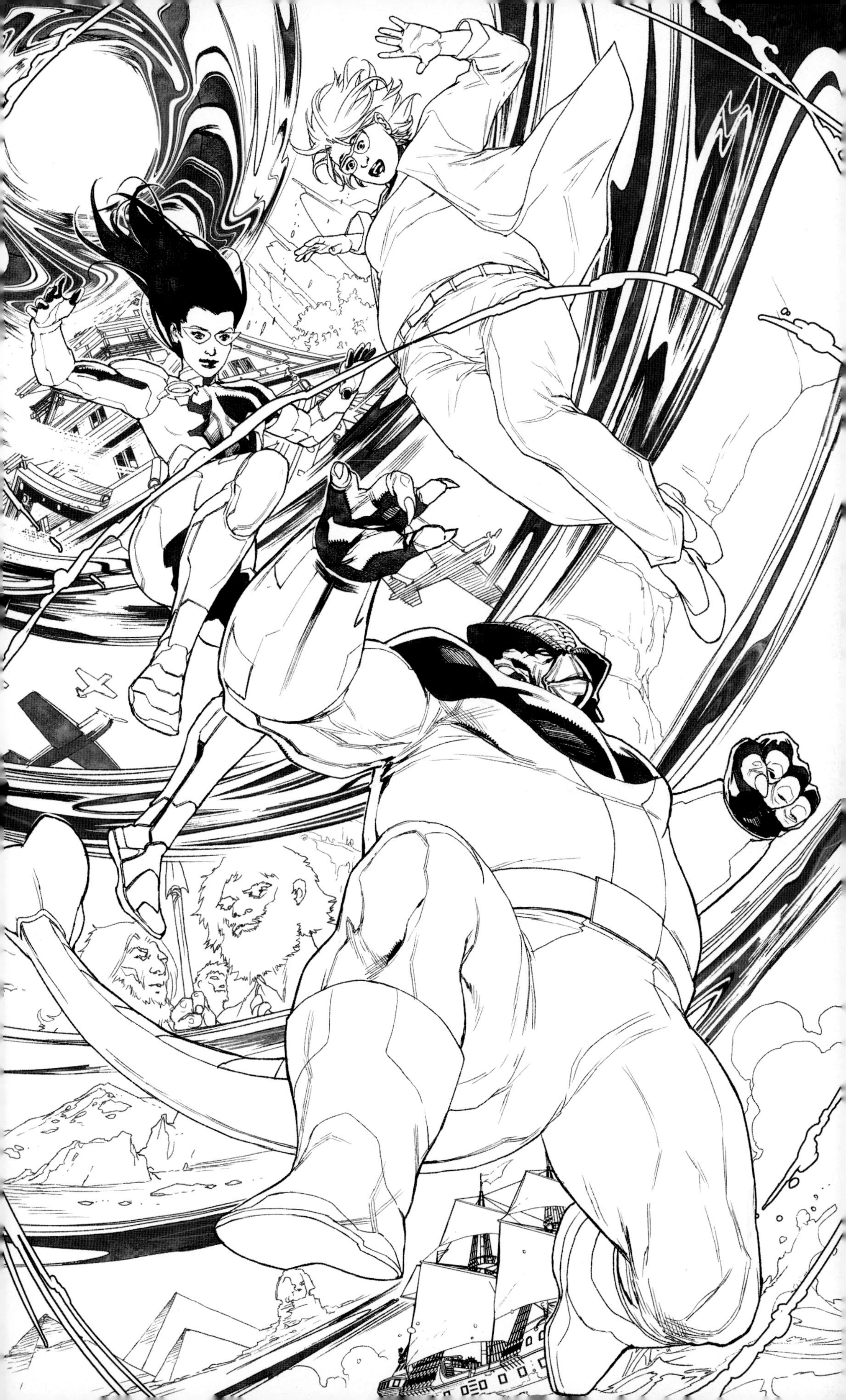

FAITH AND THE FUTURE FORCE #1, p. 22
Art by STEPHEN SEGOVIA

FAITH AND THE FUTURE FORCE #1,
pages 27 and (facing) 30
Art by BARRY KITSON

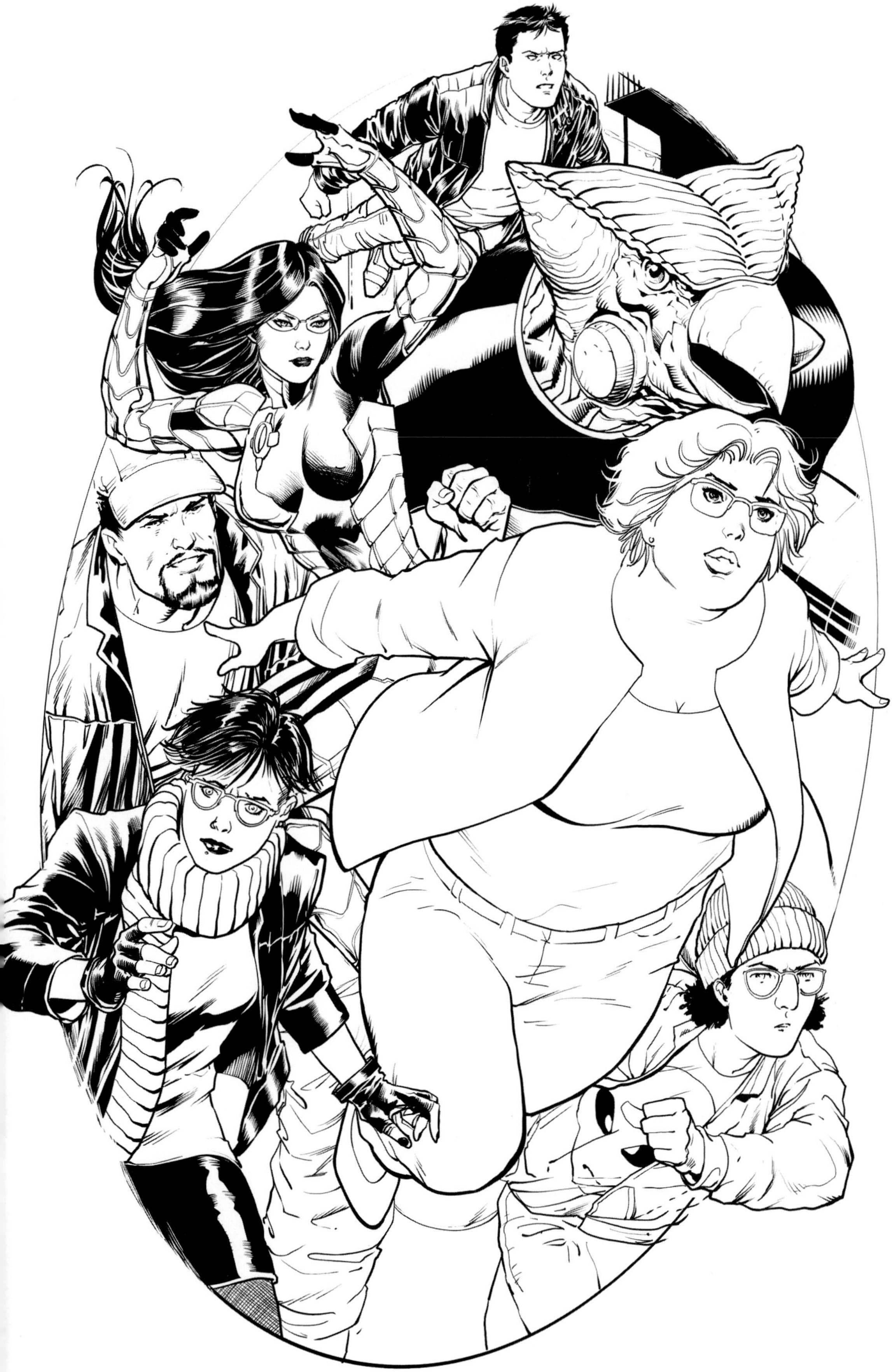

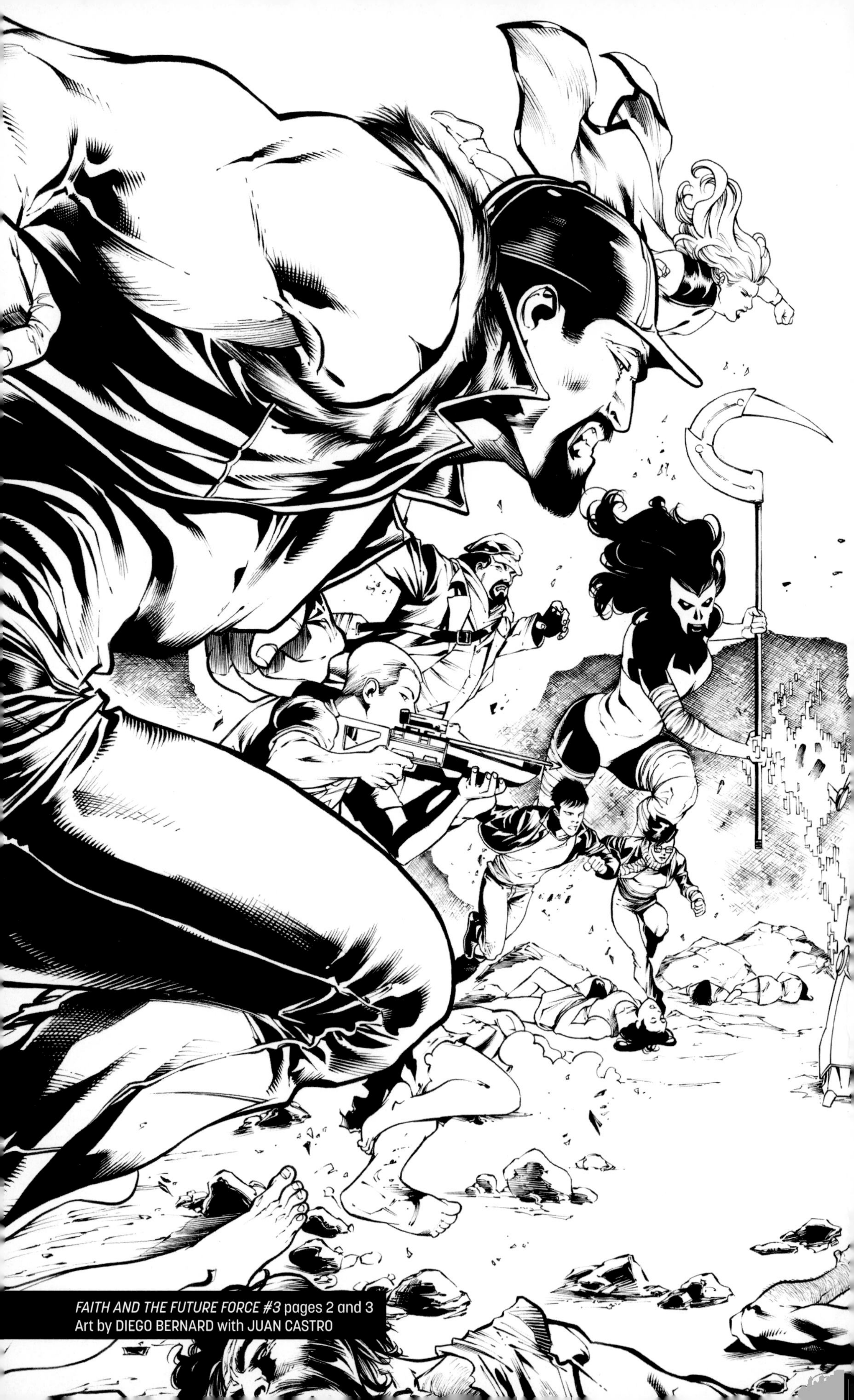

FAITH AND THE FUTURE FORCE #3 pages 2 and 3
Art by DIEGO BERNARD with JUAN CASTRO

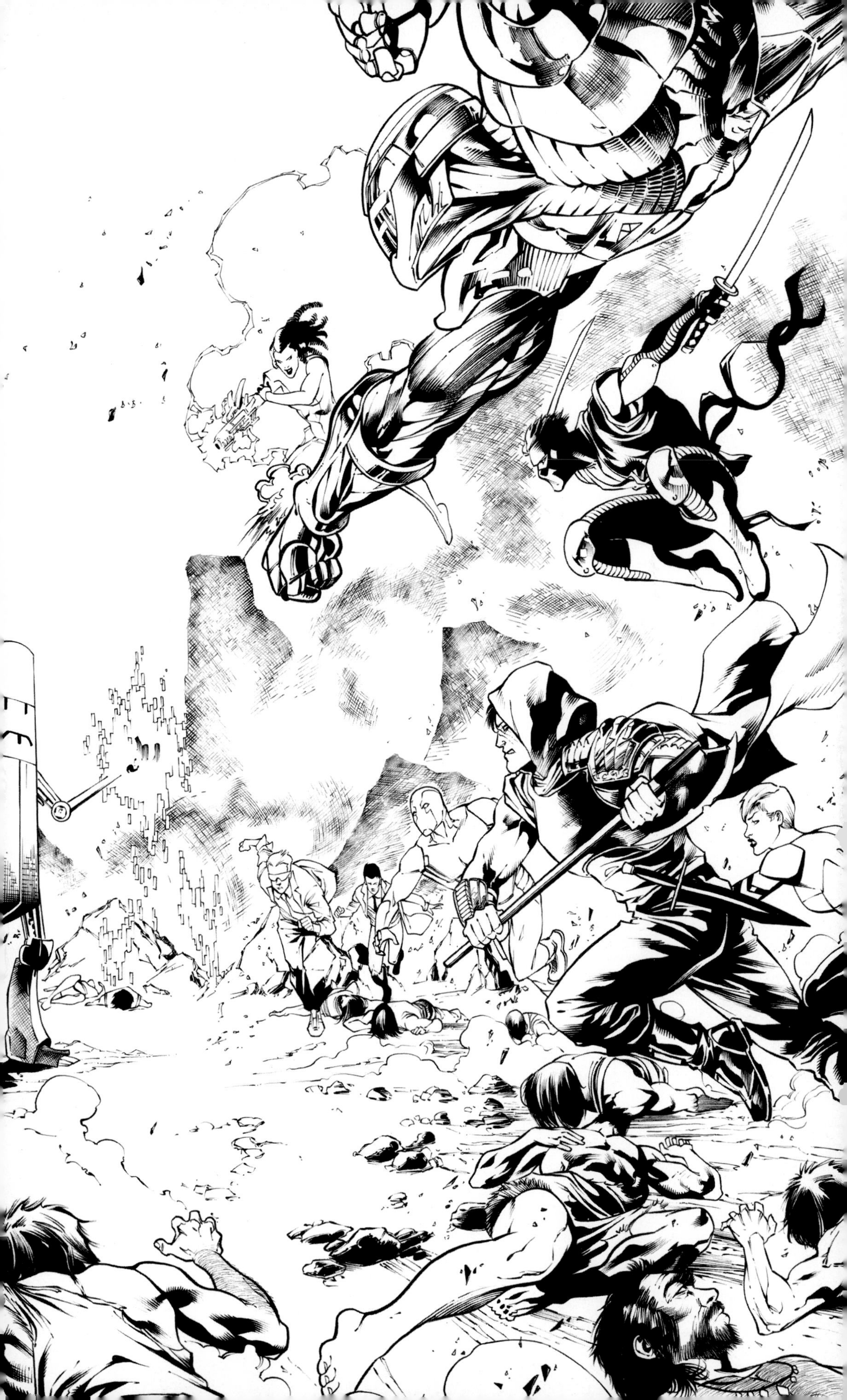

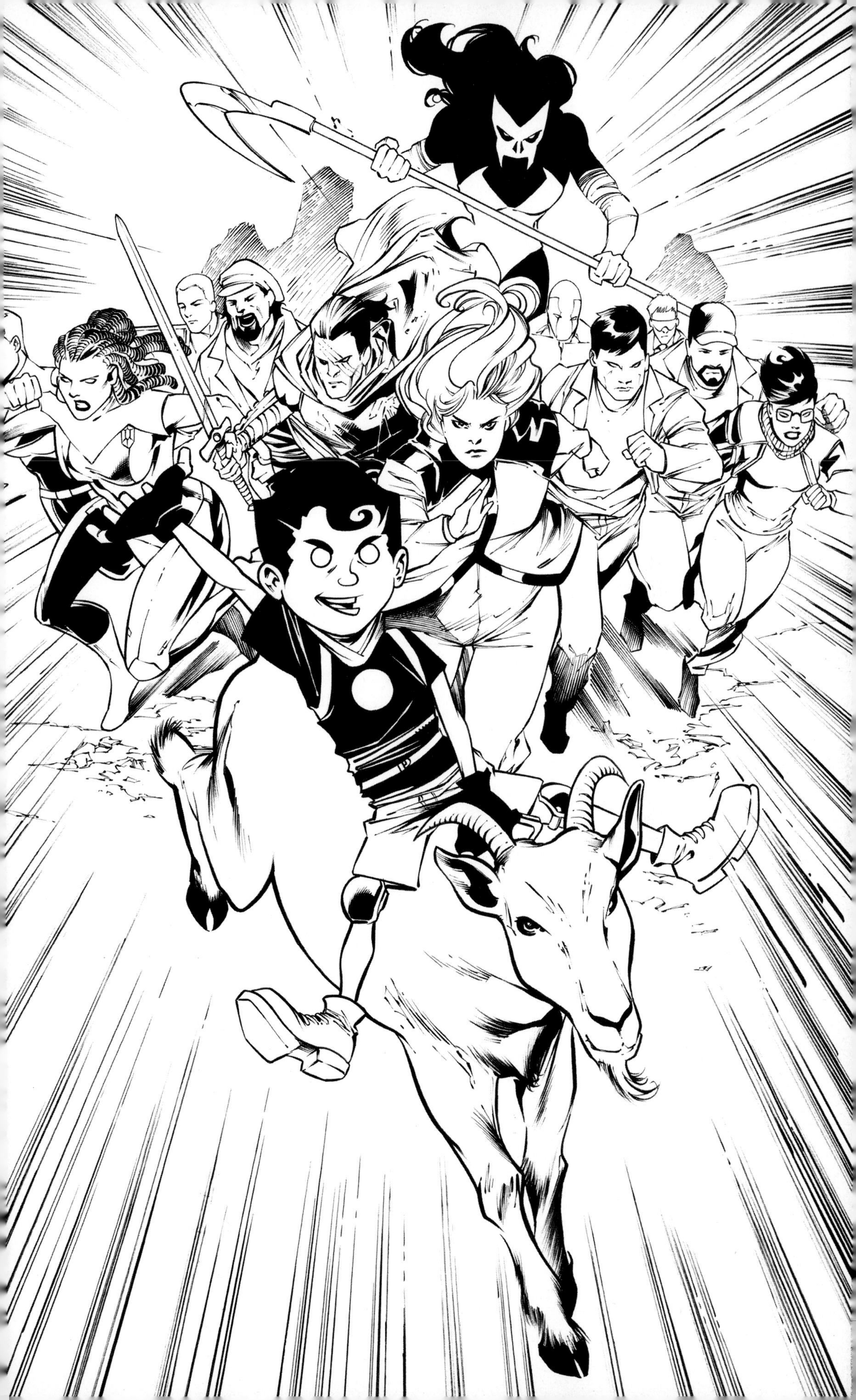

EXPLORE THE VALIANT UNIVERSE

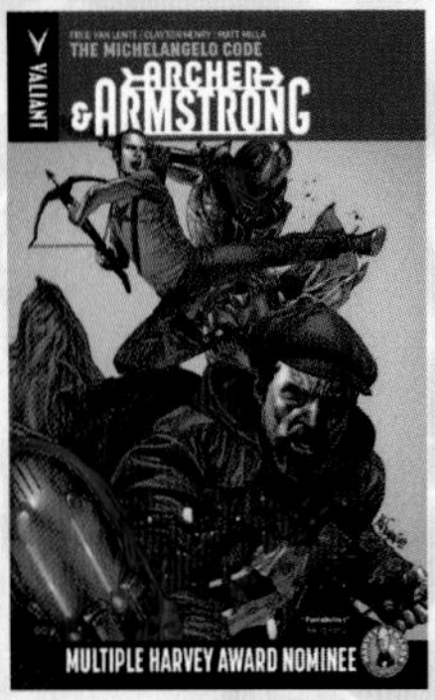
VALIANT
THE MICHELANGELO CODE
ARCHER & ARMSTRONG
MULTIPLE HARVEY AWARD NOMINEE

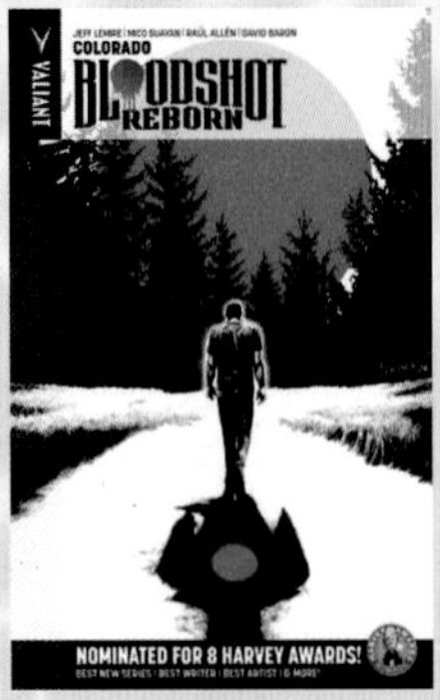
VALIANT
COLORADO
BLOODSHOT REBORN
NOMINATED FOR 8 HARVEY AWARDS!

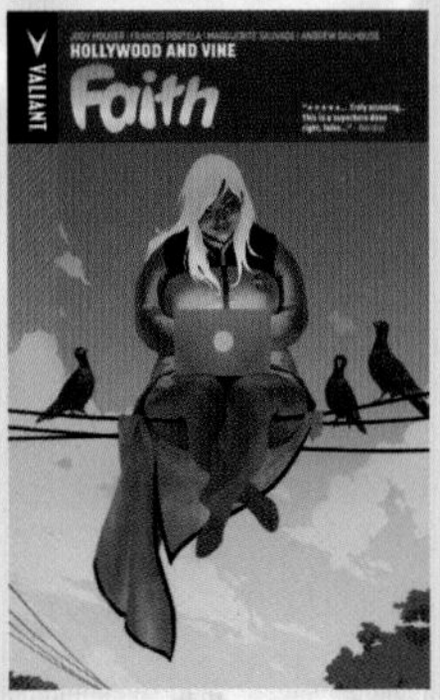
VALIANT
HOLLYWOOD AND VINE
Faith

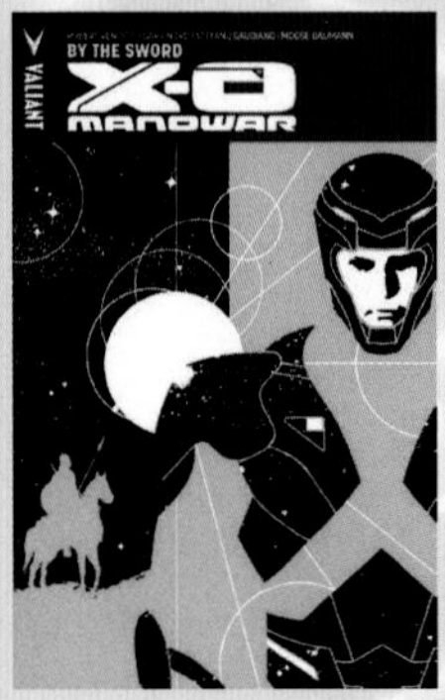
VALIANT
BY THE SWORD
X-O MANOWAR

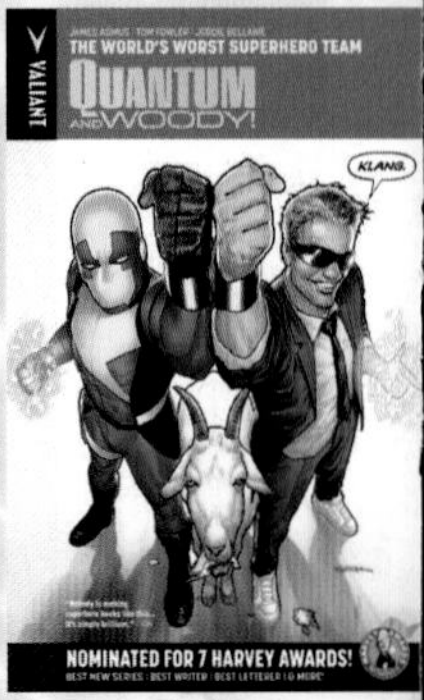
VALIANT
THE WORLD'S WORST SUPERHERO TEAM
QUANTUM AND WOODY!
KLANG
NOMINATED FOR 7 HARVEY AWARDS!

4001 A.D.

4001 A.D.
ISBN: 9781682151433

4001 A.D.: Beyond New Japan
ISBN: 9781682151464

Rai Vol 4: 4001 A.D.
ISBN: 9781682151471

A&A: THE ADVENTURES OF ARCHER AND ARMSTRONG

Volume 1: In the Bag
ISBN: 9781682151495

Volume 2: Romance and Road Trips
ISBN: 9781682151716

Volume 3: Andromeda Estranged
978-1-68215-203-4

ARCHER & ARMSTRONG

Volume 1: The Michelangelo Code
ISBN: 9780979640988

Volume 2: Wrath of the Eternal Warrior
ISBN: 9781939346049

Volume 3: Far Faraway
ISBN: 9781939346148

Volume 4: Sect Civil War
ISBN: 9781939346254

Volume 5: Mission: Improbable
ISBN: 9781939346353

Volume 6: American Wasteland
ISBN: 9781939346421

Volume 7: The One Percent and Other Tales
ISBN: 9781939346537

ARMOR HUNTERS

Armor Hunters
ISBN: 9781939346452

Armor Hunters: Bloodshot
ISBN: 9781939346469

Armor Hunters: Harbinger
ISBN: 9781939346506

Unity Vol. 3: Armor Hunters
ISBN: 9781939346445

X-O Manowar Vol. 7: Armor Hunters
ISBN: 9781939346476

BLOODSHOT

Volume 1: Setting the World on Fire
ISBN: 9780979640964

Volume 2: The Rise and the Fall
ISBN: 9781939346032

Volume 3: Harbinger Wars
ISBN: 9781939346124

Volume 4: H.A.R.D. Corps
ISBN: 9781939346193

Volume 5: Get Some!
ISBN: 9781939346315

Volume 6: The Glitch and Other Tales
ISBN: 9781939346711

BLOODSHOT REBORN

Volume 1: Colorado
ISBN: 9781939346674

Volume 2: The Hunt
ISBN: 9781939346827

Volume 3: The Analog Man
ISBN: 9781682151334

Volume 4: Bloodshot Island
ISBN: 9781682151952

BLOODSHOT U.S.A.

ISBN: 9781682151952

BOOK OF DEATH

Book of Death
ISBN: 9781939346971

Book of Death: The Fall of the Valiant Universe
ISBN: 9781939346988

BRITANNIA

Volume 1
ISBN: 9781682151853

DEAD DROP

ISBN: 9781939346858

THE DEATH-DEFYING DOCTOR MIRAGE

Volume 1
ISBN: 9781939346490

Volume 2: Second Lives
ISBN: 9781682151297

THE DELINQUENTS

ISBN: 9781939346513

DIVINITY

Volume 1
ISBN: 9781939346766

Volume 2
ISBN: 9781682151518

Volume 3
ISBN: 9781682151914

Divinity III: Glorious Heroes of the Stalinverse
ISBN: 9781682152072

ETERNAL WARRIOR

Volume 1: Sword of the Wild
ISBN: 9781939346209

Volume 2: Eternal Emperor
ISBN: 9781939346292

Volume 3: Days of Steel
ISBN: 9781939346742

WRATH OF THE ETERNAL WARRIOR

Volume 1: Risen
ISBN: 9781682151235

Volume 2: Labyrinth
ISBN: 9781682151594

Volume 3: Deal With a Devil
ISBN: 9781682151976

FAITH

Volume 1: Hollywood and Vine
ISBN: 9781682151402

Volume 2: California Scheming
ISBN: 9781682151631

Volume 3: Superstar
978-1-68215-199-0

Volume 4: The Faithless
978-1-68215-219-5

GENERATION ZERO

Volume 1: We Are the Future
ISBN: 9781682151754

Volume 2: Heroscape
978-1-68215-209-6

HARBINGER

Volume 1: Omega Rising
ISBN: 9780979640957

Volume 2: Renegades
ISBN: 9781939346025

Volume 3: Harbinger Wars
ISBN: 9781939346117

Volume 4: Perfect Day
ISBN: 9781939346155

Volume 5: Death of a Renegade
ISBN: 9781939346339

Volume 6: Omegas
ISBN: 9781939346384

EXPLORE THE VALIANT UNIVERSE

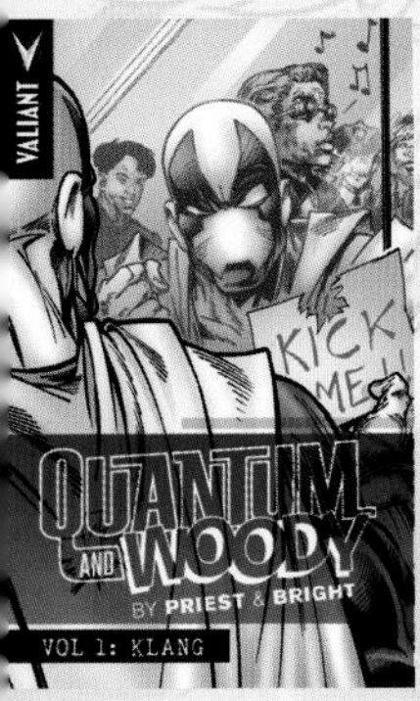
VALIANT
KICK ME
QUANTUM AND WOODY
BY PRIEST & BRIGHT
VOL 1: KLANG

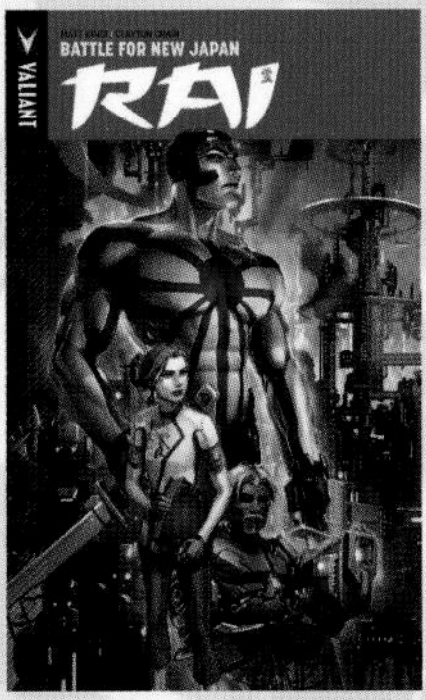
VALIANT
BATTLE FOR NEW JAPAN
RAI

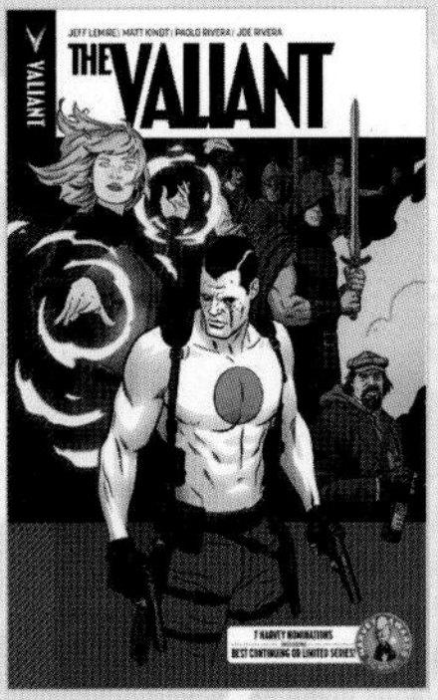
VALIANT
THE VALIANT

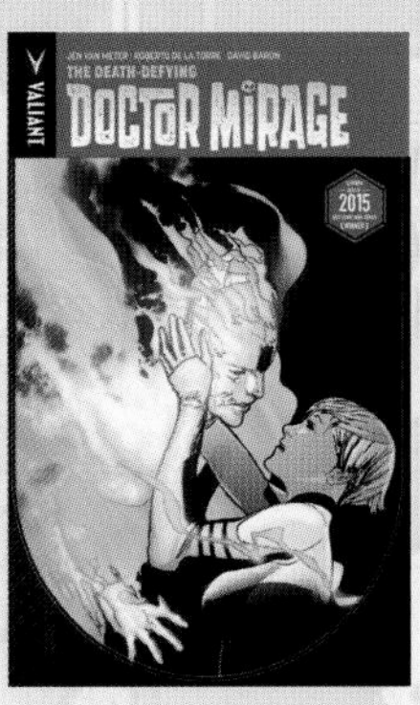
VALIANT
THE DEATH-DEFYING
DOCTOR MIRAGE

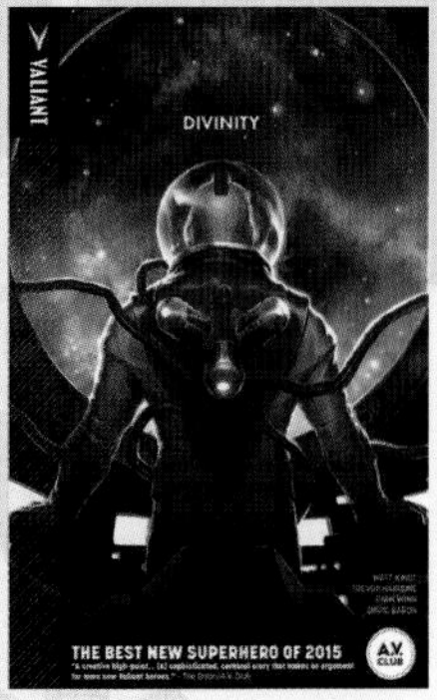
VALIANT
DIVINITY
THE BEST NEW SUPERHERO OF 2015

HARBINGER RENEGADE

Volume 1: The Judgment of Solomon
ISBN: 9781682151693

HARBINGER WARS

Harbinger Wars
ISBN: 9781939346094

Bloodshot Vol. 3: Harbinger Wars
ISBN: 9781939346124

Harbinger Vol. 3: Harbinger Wars
ISBN: 9781939346117

IMPERIUM

Volume 1: Collecting Monsters
ISBN: 9781939346759

Volume 2: Broken Angels
ISBN: 9781939346896

Volume 3: The Vine Imperative
ISBN: 9781682151112

Volume 4: Stormbreak
ISBN: 9781682151372

NINJAK

Volume 1: Weaponeer
ISBN: 9781939346667

Volume 2: The Shadow Wars
ISBN: 9781939346940

Volume 3: Operation: Deadside
ISBN: 9781682151259

Volume 4: The Siege of King's Castle
ISBN: 9781682151617

Volume 5: The Fist & The Steel
ISBN: 9781682151792

Volume 6: The Seven Blades of Master Darque
978-1-68215-211-9

QUANTUM AND WOODY

Volume 1: The World's Worst Superhero Team
ISBN: 9781939346186

Volume 2: In Security
ISBN: 9781939346230

Volume 3: Crooked Pasts, Present Tense
ISBN: 9781939346391

Volume 4: Quantum and Woody Must Die!
ISBN: 9781939346629

QUANTUM AND WOODY BY PRIEST & BRIGHT

Volume 1: Klang
ISBN: 9781939346780

Volume 2: Switch
ISBN: 9781939346803

Volume 3: And So...
ISBN: 9781939346865

Volume 4: Q2 - The Return
ISBN: 9781682151099

RAI

Volume 1: Welcome to New Japan
ISBN: 9781939346414

Volume 2: Battle for New Japan
ISBN: 9781939346612

Volume 3: The Orphan
ISBN: 9781939346841

Rai Vol 4: 4001 A.D.
ISBN: 9781682151471

RAPTURE

ISBN: 9781682151891

SAVAGE

ISBN: 9781682152256

SHADOWMAN

Volume 1: Birth Rites
ISBN: 9781939346001

Volume 2: Darque Reckoning
ISBN: 9781939346056

Volume 3: Deadside Blues
ISBN: 9781939346162

Volume 4: Fear, Blood, And Shadows
ISBN: 9781939346278

Volume 5: End Times
ISBN: 9781939346377

SHADOWMAN BY ENNIS & WOOD

ISBN: 9781682151358

IVAR, TIMEWALKER

Volume 1: Making History
ISBN: 9781939346636

Volume 2: Breaking History
ISBN: 9781939346834

Volume 3: Ending History
ISBN: 9781939346995

UNITY

Volume 1: To Kill a King
ISBN: 9781939346261

Volume 2: Trapped by Webnet
ISBN: 9781939346346

Volume 3: Armor Hunters
ISBN: 9781939346445

Volume 4: The United
ISBN: 9781939346544

Volume 5: Homefront
ISBN: 9781939346797

Volume 6: The War-Monger
ISBN: 9781939346902

Volume 7: Revenge of the Armor Hunters
ISBN: 9781682151136

THE VALIANT

ISBN: 9781939346605

VALIANT ZEROES AND ORIGINS

ISBN: 9781939346582

X-O MANOWAR

Volume 1: By the Sword
ISBN: 9780979640940

Volume 2: Enter Ninjak
ISBN: 9780979640995

Volume 3: Planet Death
ISBN: 9781939346087

Volume 4: Homecoming
ISBN: 9781939346179

Volume 5: At War With Unity
ISBN: 9781939346247

Volume 6: Prelude to Armor Hunters
ISBN: 9781939346407

Volume 7: Armor Hunters
ISBN: 9781939346476

Volume 8: Enter: Armorines
ISBN: 9781939346551

Volume 9: Dead Hand
ISBN: 9781939346650

Volume 10: Exodus
ISBN: 9781939346933

Volume 11: The Kill List
ISBN: 9781682151273

Volume 12: Long Live the King
ISBN: 9781682151655

Volume 13: Succession and Other Tales
ISBN: 9781682151754

X-O MANOWAR (2017)

Volume 1: Soldier
ISBN: 9781682152058

Volume 2: General
ISBN: 9781682152171

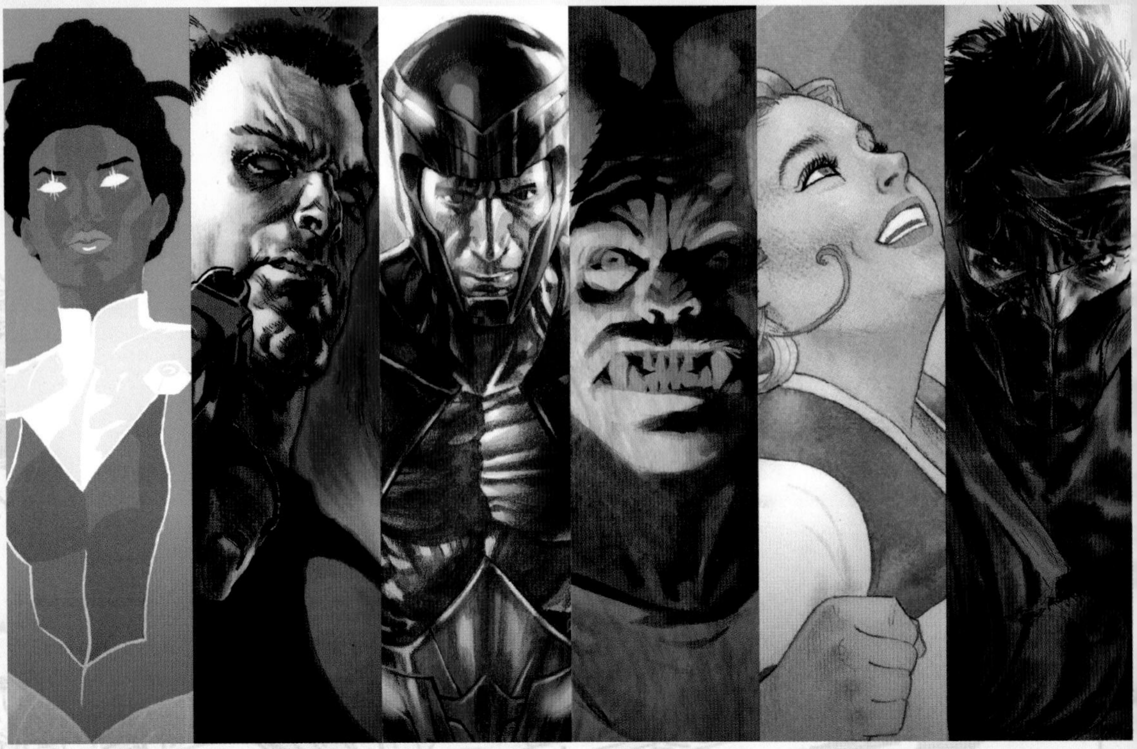

4001 A.D. DELUXE EDITION
ISBN: 978-1-68215-193-8

ARCHER & ARMSTRONG DELUXE EDITIONS
Book 1: ISBN: 978-1-939346-22-3
Book 2: ISBN: 978-1-939346-95-7

ARMOR HUNTERS DELUXE EDITION
ISBN: 978-1-939346-72-8

BLOODSHOT DELUXE EDITIONS
Book 1: ISBN: 978-1-939346-21-6
Book 2: ISBN: 978-1-939346-81-0

BLOODSHOT REBORN DELUXE EDITIONS
Book 1: ISBN: 978-1-68215-155-6
Book 2: ISBN: 978-1-68215-227-0

BOOK OF DEATH DELUXE EDITION
ISBN: 978-1-68215-115-0

THE DEATH-DEFYING DOCTOR MIRAGE DELUXE EDITION
ISBN: 978-1-68215-153-2

DIVINITY DELUXE EDITION
ISBN: 978-1-939346-92-6

FAITH: HOLLYWOOD & VINE DELUXE EDITION
ISBN: 978-1-68215-201-0

HARBINGER DELUXE EDITIONS
Book 1: ISBN: 978-1-939346-13-1
Book 2: ISBN: 978-1-939346-77-3

HARBINGER WARS DELUXE EDITION
ISBN: 978-1-939346-32-2

IVAR, TIMEWALKER DELUXE EDITION
Book 1: ISBN: 978-1-68215-119-8

NINJAK DELUXE EDITION
Book 1: ISBN: 978-1-68215-157-0

QUANTUM AND WOODY DELUXE EDITION
Book 1: ISBN: 978-1-939346-68-1

RAI DELUXE EDITION
Book 1: ISBN: 978-1-68215-117-4

SHADOWMAN DELUXE EDITION
Book 1: ISBN: 978-1-939346-43-8

UNITY DELUXE EDITION
Book 1: 978-1-939346-57-5

THE VALIANT DELUXE EDITION
ISBN: 978-1-939346-91-9

X-O MANOWAR DELUXE EDITIONS
Book 1: ISBN: 978-1-939346-10-0
Book 2: ISBN: 978-1-939346-52-0
Book 3 : ISBN: 978-1-68215-131-0
Book 4: ISBN: 978-1-68215-183-9
Book 5: ISBN: 978-1-68215-215-7

VALIANT CLASSIC

ARCHER & ARMSTRONG: THE COMPLETE CLASSIC OMNIBUS
ISBN: 978-1-939346-87-2

QUANTUM AND WOODY: THE COMPLETE CLASSIC OMNIBUS
ISBN: 978-1-939346-36-0

Q2: THE RETURN OF QUANTUM AND WOODY DELUXE EDITION
ISBN: 978-1-939346-56-8

VALIANT MASTERS: BLOODSHOT VOL. 1 - BLOOD OF THE MACHINE
ISBN: 978-0-9796409-3-3

VALIANT MASTERS: HARBINGER VOL. 1 - CHILDREN OF THE EIGHTH DAY
ISBN: 978-1-939346-48-3

VALIANT MASTERS: H.A.R.D. CORPS VOL. 1 - SEARCH AND DESTROY
ISBN: 978-1-939346-28-5

VALIANT MASTERS: NINJAK VOL. 1 - BLACK WATER
ISBN: 978-0-9796409-7-1

VALIANT MASTERS: RAI VOL. 1 - FROM HONOR TO STRENGTH
ISBN: 978-1-939346-07-0

VALIANT MASTERS: SHADOWMAN VOL. 1 - SPIRITS WITHIN
ISBN: 978-1-939346-01-8

X-O MANOWAR CLASSIC OMNIBUS
Vol. 1: ISBN: 978-1-939346-30-8

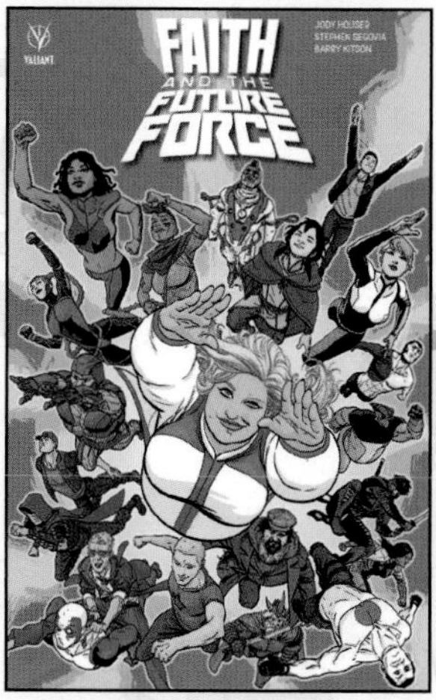
VALIANT
FAITH AND THE FUTURE FORCE
JODY HOUSER
STEPHEN SEGOVIA
BARRY KITSON

Faith and the Future Force

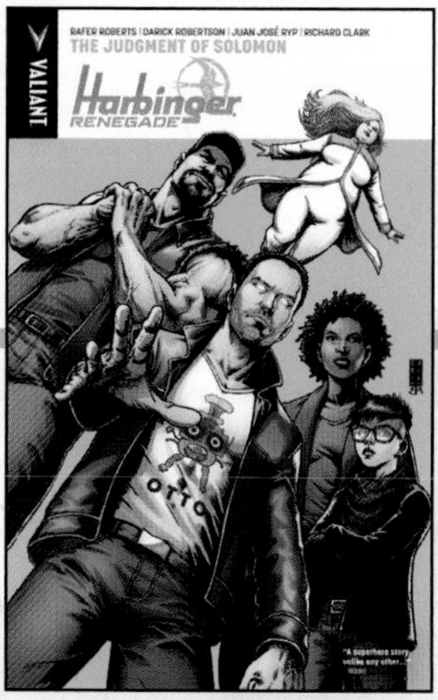
VALIANT
THE JUDGMENT OF SOLOMON
Harbinger
RENEGADE

Harbinger Renegade
Vol. 1: Judgment of Solomon

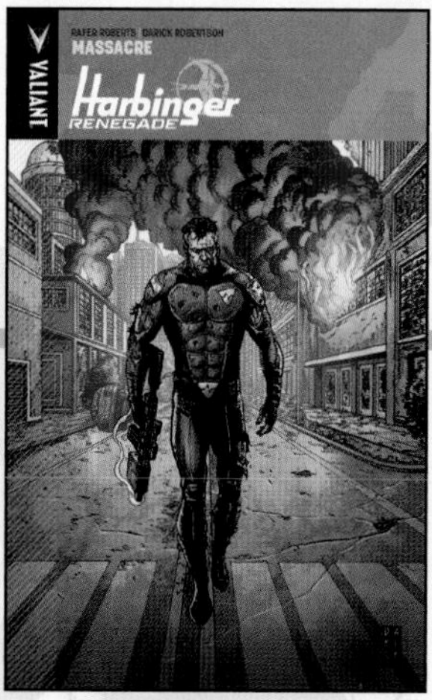
VALIANT
MASSACRE
Harbinger
RENEGADE

Harbinger Renegade
Vol. 2: Massacre

Read all the adventures of the sky-soaring Faith!

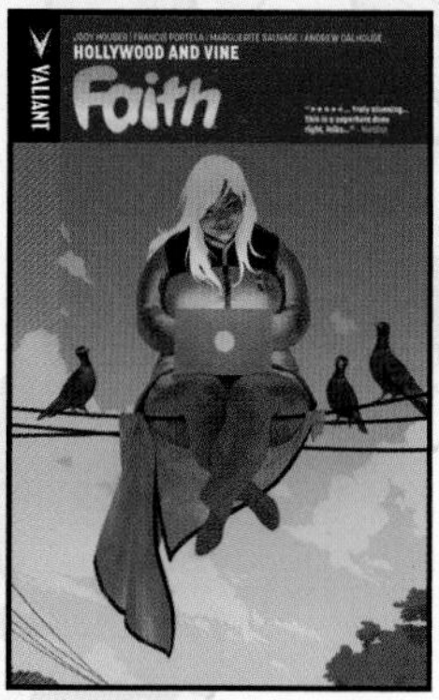
VALIANT
HOLLYWOOD AND VINE
Faith

Faith Vol. 1:
Hollywood and Vine

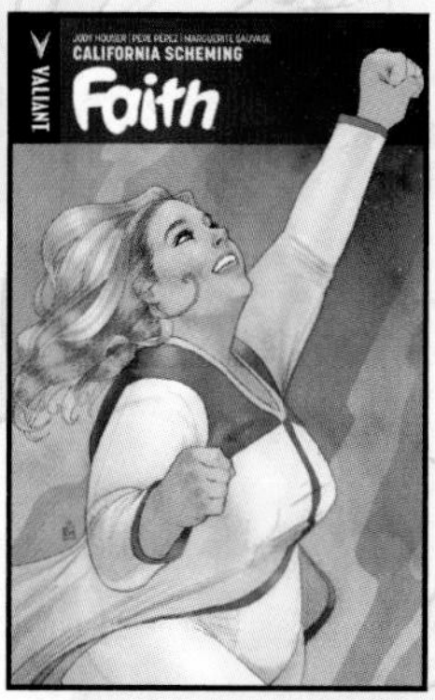
VALIANT
CALIFORNIA SCHEMING
Faith

Faith Vol. 2: California

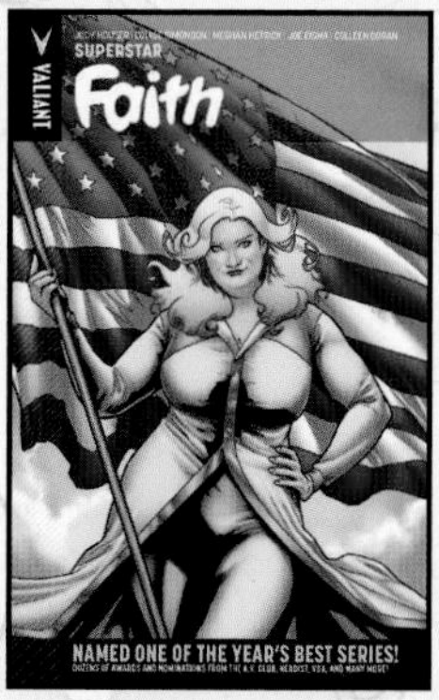
VALIANT
SUPERSTAR
Faith
NAMED ONE OF THE YEAR'S BEST SERIES!

Faith Vol. 3: Superstar

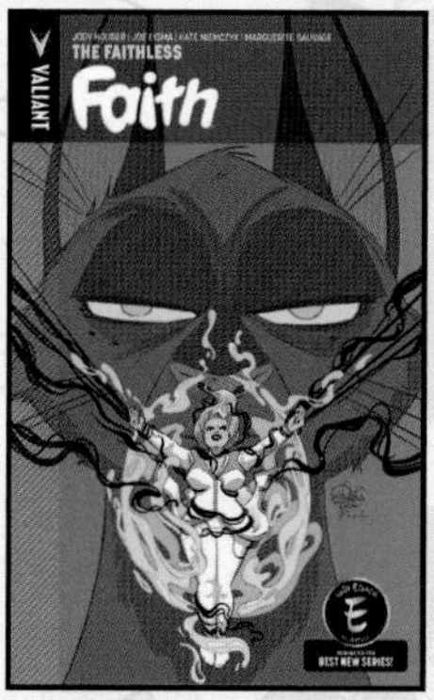
VALIANT
THE FAITHLESS
Faith

Faith Vol. 4: The Faithless

SECRET WEAPONS®

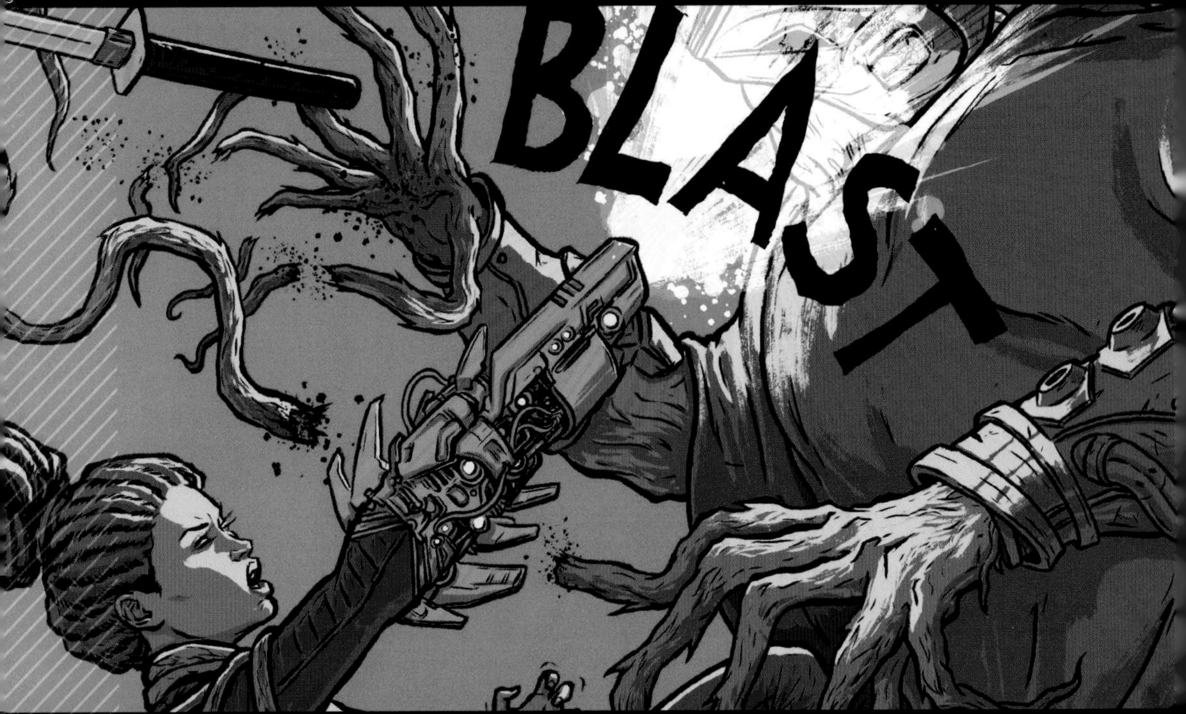
BLAST

ERIC HEISSERER - THE ACADEMY AWARD-NOMINATED SCREENWRITER OF *ARRIVAL* AND VALIANT'S UPCOMING HARBINGER AND BLOODSHOT FEATURE FILMS - JOINS HARVEY AWARD-NOMINATED VISIONARY RAÚL ALLÉN (*WRATH OF THE ETERNAL WARRIOR*) FOR AN ALL-NEW VALIANT ADVENTURE... LAUNCHING LIVEWIRE AND AN EXTRAORDINARY NEW TEAM OF HEROES INTO THE FIGHT OF THEIR LIVES!

The government has dispatched Amanda McKee - the technopath codenamed Livewire - to investigate the ruins of a secret facility formerly run by Toyo Harada, the most powerful telepath on Earth and her former mentor. In his quest for world betterment at any cost, Harada sought out and activated many potential psiots like himself. Those who survived, but whose powers he deemed to have no value to his cause, were hidden away at this installation. But Livewire, having studied Harada's greatest strengths and learned his deepest weaknesses, senses opportunity where he once saw failure. A young girl who can talk to birds... a boy who can make inanimate objects gently glow... to others, these are expensive disappointments. But, to Livewire, they are secret weapons...in need of a leader. Now, as a mechanized killer called Rex-O seeks to draw them out, Livewire and her new team of cadets will be forced to put their powers into action...in ways they never could have imagined...

Collecting SECRET WEAPONS #1-4.

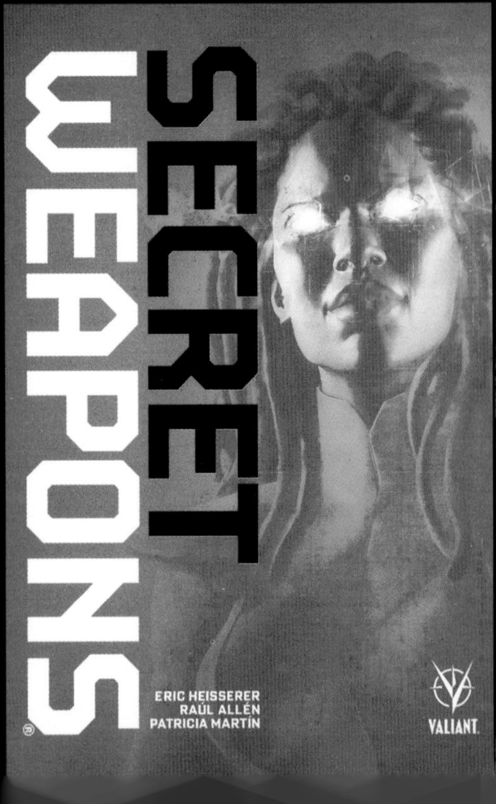
SECRET WEAPONS
ERIC HEISSERER
RAÚL ALLÉN
PATRICIA MARTÍN
VALIANT

TRADE PAPERBACK
ISBN: 978-1-68215-229-4